Imperial Zions

IMPERIAL ZIONS

Religion, Race, and Family in the American West and the Pacific

AMANDA HENDRIX-KOMOTO

UNIVERSITY OF NEBRASKA PRESS | LINCOLN

Portions of this book previously appeared
in a different form as: "'A Rough Stone
from Nature's Quarry': The Problem
of Agency in the Nineteenth-Century
Pacific," in *Women and the LDS Church*,
ed. Matthew Bowman and Kate Holbrook
(Salt Lake City: University of Utah Press,
2016), 149–64; "'Playing the Whore': The
Domestic and Sexual Politics of Mormon
Missionary Work on Tahiti Nui and in
the Tuamotus," *Journal of Mormon History*
41, no. 3 (July 2015): 58–97; and "To
Forsake Thy Father and Mother: Mary
Fielding Smith and the Familial Politics
of Conversion," *Dialogue: A Journal of
Mormon Thought* 45, no. 3 (2012): 26–37.

The University of Nebraska Press is part
of a land-grant institution with campuses
and programs on the past, present, and
future homelands of the Pawnee, Ponca,
Otoe-Missouria, Omaha, Dakota, Lakota,
Kaw, Cheyenne, and Arapaho Peoples,
as well as those of the relocated Ho-
Chunk, Sac and Fox, and Iowa Peoples.

∞

Library of Congress Cataloging-
in-Publication Data
Names: Hendrix-Komoto,
Amanda, author.
Title: Imperial Zions: religion, race, and
family in the American West and the
Pacific / Amanda Hendrix-Komoto.
Other titles: Studies in Pacific worlds.
Description: Lincoln: University
of Nebraska Press, [2022] | Series:
Studies in Pacific worlds | Includes
bibliographical references and index.
Identifiers: LCCN 2022005486
ISBN 9781496214607 (hardback)
ISBN 9781496233462 (paperback)
ISBN 9781496233790 (epub)
ISBN 9781496233806 (pdf)
Subjects: LCSH: Church of Jesus Christ of
Latter-day Saints—Doctrines. | Families—
Religious aspects—Church of Jesus Christ
of Latter-day Saints. | Race—Religious
aspects—Church of Jesus Christ of
Latter-day Saints. | Polygamy—Religious
aspects—Church of Jesus Christ of
Latter-day Saints. | Families—Religious
aspects—Mormon Church. | Race—
Religious aspects—Mormon Church. |
Polygamy—Religious aspects—Mormon
Church. | Mormon Church—Doctrines. |
BISAC: HISTORY / United States /
19th Century | RELIGION / History
Classification: LCC BX8643.F3 H445 2022 |
DDC 248.4/89332—dc23/eng/20220224
LC record available at https://
lccn.loc.gov/2022005486

Set and designed in New Baskerville
by Mikala R. Kolander.

To the web of women who gave me courage and intellect,
and to the daughters who we nurture now.

CONTENTS

ILLUSTRATIONS

ACKNOWLEDGMENTS

I began writing this book while a graduate student at the University of Michigan. The structures of graduate school—sponsored lectures, graduate seminars, and the proximity created by a cohort of fellow scholars—generated a sense of community that I have come to miss as an assistant professor finishing her book during a pandemic. Kathleen King and Lorna Altstetter were able department administers who always welcomed students into the History Department's office. They ensured we finished our exams on time, helped us apply for funding, and listened to any difficulties we were having. They were an important part of the community at the University of Michigan, and the university is poorer for their retirement. My fellow graduate students Graham Claytor, Jonathan McLaughlin, Ronit Stahl, Benjamin Hicklin, Jonathan Farr, and Aston Gonzalez helped to create a welcoming environment that challenged me intellectually while supporting me whenever I struggled. Kara French, Sara Lampert, Benjamin Cronin, Patrick Parker, Trevor Kilgore, Elspeth Martini, and Allison Abra were senior to me in the program, but were always willing to mentor younger graduate students. Jacqueline Antonovich was often the only other western historian in lectures and discussion groups and offered a much-appreciated perspective. She, together, with Melissa Johnson and Marie Stango, reminded me that it was okay to be working class and a first-generation college student. Susan Juster, Mary Kelley, Kali Israel, Terryl Givens, and Damon Salesa were ideal dissertation committee members—offering comments on chapters, pointing out areas where I needed to refine my argument, and offering their intellectual support without qualification. Susan and Damon have become a model for the type of PhD advisor I want to be—endlessly supportive but also offering clear guidance on how to excel.

The First United Methodist Church in Ann Arbor supported me academically and socially. Robert Roth, Doug Patterson, and Nancy Lynn encouraged parishioners to ask questions about colonialism and sexuality. When I had my first child, the women of the church organized a meal train and babysat for me when I had to have a surgical biopsy of a lump in my breast. I still miss the friendship that Mike and Becky Wong and the Austerberries offered. Daniel Ramirez was a fellow parishioner and an unexpected representative from the History Department at the baptism of my oldest child. He has served as a constant reminder about the grace we all experience.

Non-Mormon scholars have frequently asked me about the reception that I have received among the Latter-day Saints as a non-Mormon. Although people often assume that the church will be hostile to critical work, I have found the opposite to be true among those dedicated to the church's history, including those who work for the Church History Library and official institutions. The staff at the Church History Library was infallibly willing to accommodate my requests as a researcher. Brittany Chapman Nash and Bill Slaughter offered intellectual as well as research assistance, challenging my views when necessary and freely giving the knowledge they had gained over years working in the archives. Max Mueller and Connell Donovan were amiable co-researchers who made my days in the archives invaluable.

I also benefited from the community of Latter-day Saint scholars that has formed around the Mormon History Association. W. Paul Reeve, Quincy Newell, Laurel Thatcher Ulrich, Andrea Radke-Moss, Spencer Fluhman, Farina King, John Turner, Patrick Mason, Laurie Maffly-Kipp, Mees Tielens, Jonathan Stapley, Natalie Rose, Blair Hodges, Rachel Cope,

Lisa Olsen Tait, Susanna Morrill, Jenny Reeder, Tona Hangen, and Kris Wright were more than generous with their time and enthusiasm. This book would not be what it was without them. The *Juvenile Instructor* blog was an early supporter of my work and provided me with the space to learn how to write for an academic audience. Its members—Joseph Stuart, Benjamin Park, Christopher Jones, Jared Tamez, and Robin Scott Jensen—formed an early cohort of Mormon historians who read each other's work and listened to the difficulties we were having in the field. Charlotte Hansen Terry and Sasha Coles have been wonderful friends and have mentored me as much as I have mentored them. Elise Boxer, Farina King, Stan Thayne, and Sujey Vega have been advocates for the inclusion of indigenous and Latinx histories and shaped my own work beyond what I could enumerate. Matt Bowman has been an important mentor throughout my time as a Mormon historian. Without him, it is unlikely that this book would have been finished. Likewise, Joseph Stuart has calmed my fears and offered reassurance more times than I count.

Several people have offered feedback on this manuscript—some more than once. Members of the *Juvenile Instructor* offered early feedback and read chapter drafts. W. Paul Reeve, Quincy Newell, and Angela Pulley Hudson were generous in their critiques and willing to offer their keen insights to improve the book. They have also become mentors—promoting my work and scholarship more than anyone deserves. Jana Riess helped edit the manuscript and served as a sounding board. Her hard work has made this book better than it deserves. The writing group that she formed—Patrick Mason, Melissa Inouye, David Howlett, Laurie Maffly-Kipp, Matthew Bowman, and herself—has read multiple chapters and each time has contributed immensely to making this a better work.

Finally, I have benefited from the intellectual community at Montana State University. Mary Murphy has been a wonderful example of what it means to be a female scholar, while Mark Fiege and Janet Ore have been constant cheerleaders of my work. They confided to me once that they believe that they are at their best when they are in service to others, and I have benefited from their ethos. Robert Rydell was a welcome presence in the department—offering advice and wisdom garnered over years of service to the university. Tim LeCain has been unfailingly understanding of what it means to have small children and be a faculty member. I have appreciated his constant good cheer and advice. Susan Cohen, Brett Walker, Catherine Dunlop, Molly Todd, Jim Meyer, Pete Schweppe, and Michael Reidy have been wonderful colleagues, and Maggie Greene has constantly offered a sympathetic ear. I especially appreciate Michael and Susan's attempts as department chairs to create a sense of community in a time when we are all physically isolated from one another. The Ivan Doig Center for the Study of the Lands & Peoples of the North American West offered financial support at key moments, as did money from a Scholarship and Creativity Grant. Susan Kollin and Alex Harmon have been wonderful interlocuters outside of the History Department. I have also appreciated the caliber of the graduate students with whom I have worked: Anthony Wood, Jennifer Dunn, Micah Chang, Amanda Hardin, Steve Peterson, Kirke Elsass, and Casey Pallister have all contributed to this text through their willingness to share their insights. Anthony Wood's enthusiasm for the history of the American West was infectious. He has been very supportive of my work, and I look forward to watching him become a colleague.

Beyond Montana State, I have been blessed to have developed a wide-ranging academic community. Steve Maughan began as my undergraduate advisor and became a friend. The Coalition for Western Women's History helped me make the transition from being a graduate student to an assistant professor. It also provided me with the sense that I was part of a cohort of young scholars. I look forward to watching the careers of Brianna Theobald, Katie Philips, Lindsey Passenger-Wieck, and Katrina Jagodinsky unfold. Cathleen Cahill has been instrumental in creating this community and has been an understanding presence within the coalition. Molly Rozum has been a mentor to me within the coalition. Kittie Bowen has been an amazing guide through the anxieties of being a female academic and has more than earned her fee as a therapist.

Finally, a thank you goes to my family. Like many women, I grew up in a matriarchy. My mother and sisters, Deloris and Anita, formed an early example of the importance of relationships between women. My grandmother Naomi nurtured my interests, and I regret that this book was not completed before her death. My husband, Jordan, has sacrificed just as much as I have to bring this book to fruition. My daughters, Eleanor and Rosie, don't quite understand what I do, but I have appreciated their pride when they tell others that I am a teacher and their willingness to read or watch Netflix while I edit my book.

I am sure that there are people who I am forgetting. Writing a book is a humbling experience. No one is ever quite equal to the task, and the inevitable errors in this book are all too obviously my own.

NOTE ON TERMINOLOGY

During this book's round of revisions, the Church of Jesus Christ of Latter-day Saints announced that it no longer considers the term "Mormon" to be an appropriate abbreviated name for the church. It also asked that scholars refrain from using abbreviations like LDS. I have tried to use the style guide that the church released in conjunction with this announcement. Although some of its preferred terms contain theological claims or conflict with the way other churches describe themselves, whenever possible I have tried to respect the desires of Latter-day Saints to be called by the full name of their church. As one of my colleagues has said, the ultimate question is whether Latter-day Saints get to decide what they will be called. As a result, I use the terms like "the church" and "the restored gospel," even though many readers do not assent to the religious claims contained within those words.

I want to note, however, that there are a few exceptions to my general avoidance of the term "Mormon": the term is used when describing the image of Latter-day Saints in the nineteenth century. The image of the "Mormon" was an important part of cultural understandings of the church and the term helps convey the derision that the restored gospel initially met. I have also retained the term "non-Mormon," which is important to capture how nonmembers in Idaho and Utah self-identify.

The oppositional politics of "non-Mormon" is not captured by other alternatives, and it is the term that most people belonging to that group would prefer.

Another difficulty comes from this book's emphasis on families. Historians are accustomed to using last names when referring to individuals. At times, however, the sheer number of family members bearing the same last name required me to rethink how I referred to them. At times it was necessary to add a middle initial to differentiate between people. I finally decided to use first names to avoid confusion when necessary. I do, however, maintain the custom of using last names when possible. I am hoping my efforts help readers navigate the multitude of Smiths that populate these pages.

Imperial Zions

INTRODUCTION

The last week of January 1863 was frigid in the Intermountain West. Trout had likely long abandoned the upper layers of ice-clogged rivers for warmer water, and deer may have already begun stripping the bark from nearby willow trees out of hunger.[1] The Northwestern Band of the Shoshone Nation had camped on the banks of the icy Bear River, in present-day Idaho, to celebrate the Warm Dance.[2] As the Northwestern Shoshones danced and sang prayers, Colonel Patrick Edward Connor was planning to attack the band and arrest their leaders.[3]

Connor attacked on January 29. Unfortunately, it is impossible to know what happened next. Few soldiers wrote about their experiences, and newspapers published conflicting accounts. According to Shoshone oral traditions, American soldiers shot women and children indiscriminately. People spoke frequently afterward about a fifteen-year-old boy who "lay [down] . . . on the freezing battlefield" with his grandmother in hopes that the soldiers would not find him among the mutilated corpses.[4] In another story, a woman forced to choose between discovery and her child's life let her baby drown in the Bear's icy water.[5] Local Latter-day Saints were not directly involved, but they cheered the massacre. The minutes of the Logan First Ward were chillingly explicit in their approval. "We, the people of Cache Valley," the document read, "looked upon the movement of Colonel Connor as an intervention of the Almighty, as the Indians had been a source of great annoyance to us for a long time."[6] For his part, Connor was promoted to general after the massacre.[7] The community pushed the bodies of their kin into the Bear River.[8]

Uncertain of their future, the tribe signed a treaty with the U.S. government that exchanged their claims to some of their homeland for a small annuity of $5,000, an amount that could never support the entire community. In the years after the treaty, people frequently commented on the poverty of the Northwestern Shoshones. The *Corinne Reporter* contained frequent stories about American Indians begging local white settlers for food. In 1869 the *Deseret News* scoffed that Chief Pocatello's name meant "give-us-another-sack-of-flour-and-two-beeves."[9] Religious visions revealed to the Shoshones that God meant for them to convert to the Church of Jesus Christ of Latter-day Saints. Doing so would relieve their poverty and provide them with a future as settled farmers.

Like many indigenous peoples, the Northwestern Shoshones maintained their history through family stories and oral histories. Historians like Brigham Madsen and Kass Fleisher relied on the willingness of Shoshone women to welcome them into their homes and share the Native community's history. One of these women was Mae Timbimboo Parry, whose grandson Darren remembered her in a 2018 essay as a "quiet and thoughtful" woman who beaded "buckskin moccasins and gloves."[10] She also struggled with her experiences in U.S. boarding schools. According to her grandson, a teacher told her that she would "turn out to be just these other [Indian] children, sitting in the dirt and being useless for the rest of [her] life."[11] She also heard stories about the massacre from elderly Shoshone men and women who had survived the atrocity. Her anger made her an activist. She served on White House committees, worked with other Native communities on the return of ancestral remains, and ensured that indigenous people's stories would be preserved. Some white historians who visited with her struggled with her perception of them. After she spent hours in Timbimboo's home, Fleisher described the elderly woman as "distrustful" of white academics.[12] She felt that they did not represent her people's stories accurately. Her question to

FIG. 1. Mae Timbimboo Parry (1919–2007) was a historian for the North-west Band of the Shoshone Nation. The stories that she told about her family and community history became the basis of the work that several academic historians produced on the Bear River Massacre. Photo courtesy Darren Parry, councilman for the Northwestern Band of the Shoshone Nation.

her grandson and to white historians, however, was similar. Years after her death in 2007, Darren remembered his grandmother constantly asking, "What is your story going to be?"[13]

Darren has brought this question to historians of the Latter-day Saints. He insists on the importance of this history and its connection to the "sacred." In a book that he published on the Bear River Massacre, he explicitly connects the massacre's history to the sacredness of the land and his people's identity.[14] He asks white settlers to confront the histories they have half-forgotten but can also playfully tease those with whom he feels comfortable. At one conference, he laughingly told me that the aim of white historians was to discredit Native Americans. Although Darren was joking, I have taken his injunction to be reflective about the stories we tell seriously. As a child in southeastern Idaho, I had heard stories about the violence Native communities endured—but only through folklore and family legends. My stepfather told me a story when I was in high school about Native women who had drowned their children during a massacre or famine. Local folklore suggested that children haunted local rivers, crying softly for the mothers who had killed them. The story was likely not about the Bear River Massacre, but it contained a whispered reminder of the poverty and violence Native people experienced. Darren, however, asked people to tell the story of the Bear River Massacre and what his people had endured not as a ghost story or a bit of local lore but as a fully realized part of American history. He asked that his people's story be included in history textbooks and be remembered in carefully rendered monuments.

I had already written my dissertation and become interested in Native Mormon history when I first met Darren, but his insistence on the importance of Native history has influenced my work and how I see myself as a scholar. Like many people who grew up in southeastern Idaho, my family's history is entwined with Native and settler histories. My father's ancestors had converted to the Church of Jesus Christ of Latter-day Saints in upstate New York in the 1830s. They followed Brigham Young to the Great Basin, where they helped to settle Springville, Utah, before moving to Idaho. My mother's family, however, had a more diverse background. Her grandmother worked at an Episcopalian day school on the Fort Hall Indian Reservation and married a Native man who had attended the school. They later divorced, and my great grandmother subsequently had children with my great grandfather, a light-skinned man who had fled Mexico after its revolution.

I ultimately decided I wanted to tell a story that placed the development of restoration theology in conversation with their missionary work. Joseph Smith believed that the Book of Mormon was a history of Native Americans and other indigenous peoples. According to the text, Native Americans a were descended from a group of Israelites who fled the destruction of Jerusalem around 600 BCE and founded an impressive civilization in the Americas. Jealousy, however, caused part of the community to forget their covenants and become a cruel people. God darkened the skin of the wicked to prevent the righteous from desiring their bodies. Eventually, the righteous people of the Americas died out, leaving only the unrepentant. The Book of Mormon then claimed that these people—which it called the Lamanites—would eventually be redeemed and restored to their previous status as God's chosen people. In the last days, they would be called back from the places God had scattered them to their original homelands where they would assist in the building of Zion.

The Book of Mormon allowed Latter-day Saints to explain the degradation of Native peoples while believing it prophesied their redemption. Many people found the Book of Mormon compelling. It created a sacred past for the Americas and promised converts a future in which they would participate in the redemption of God's chosen people. Latter-day Saints won few Native converts, but some Native Americans found this vision persuasive. After the Bear River Massacre in 1863, for example, many Northwestern Shoshones converted to the Church of Jesus Christ of Latter-day Saints. Traditional Shoshone religious practices had emphasized their ability to access the divine.[15] Through dreams and dances, Shoshones became imbued with spiritual power and came to understand the workings of the supernatural. In the 1870s a Shoshone man named Ech-up-way received heavenly visitors who told him "that the

'Mormons' God was the true god, and that he and the Indians' Father were one; that he must go to the 'Mormons,' and they would tell him what to do; that the time was at hand for the Indians to gather, and stop their Indian life, and learn to cultivate the earth and build houses."[16] The tribe's conversion to the Church of Jesus Christ of Latter-day Saints drew on their earlier religious traditions, even as it reoriented their lives away from their seasonal rounds and towards settled agriculture.

The church also experienced successes in the Pacific. By the 1850s many Latter-day Saints believed that Polynesians were descendants of the same Israelite people as Native Americans. In an 1882 memoir the apostle George Q. Cannon remembered the Hawaiian people as being filled with the Holy Spirit. He described them laying hands upon the sick to heal them and, in one case, even raising the dead with their faith.[17] Polynesians and Native Americans possessed unique ways of being, but white Latter-day Saints saw them as being similar and even equivalent to one other. The naming of Native Americans and Polynesians as Lamanites flattened the differences between the two. Moreover, the process of colonization would have similar effects. It reduced to Native Americans and Polynesians to similar positions, leading the United Nations to recognize both groups as "indigenous people" in the twentieth century.[18]

For white Latter-day Saints, the conversion of the Northwestern Shoshones and large numbers of Native Hawaiians provided some evidence of the truth of the Book of Mormon. It was possible to read these conversions as the beginnings of a spiritual awakening that would culminate in the redemption of the Lamanite. There were always tensions within the Church of Jesus Christ of Latter-day Saints, however, over the place of Native peoples within the faith. After Joseph Smith's death in 1844, the church splintered as several men tried to claim his prophetic mantle.[19] The individuals who followed Brigham Young to the valleys and deserts of what was then Mexico became the main body of the church. As the community moved across the Great Plains, they encountered more Native Americans than they had before.

The symbol of the Lamanite contrasted sharply with the brutal realities of colonialization. Native Americans typically did not respond to the gospel with mass conversion. Instead, they fought for their way of life—stealing Latter-day Saint cattle and demanding gifts of bacon, flour, and bread when Saints destroyed their traditional foodways. The ensuing violence caused some Saints to question whether Native Americans were really the children of God. Latter-day Saint leaders tried to respond to the queries of their followers in their sermons and counsel but were never fully able to resolve the tension between the Book of Mormon's image of Native Americans and the Native communities they encountered in the Great Basin.[20]

Understanding the tensions in restoration theology surrounding Native Americans brings Latter-day Saints into conversation with the major themes of the nineteenth century. That century, which began with the dislocations of industrialization and the increasing racialization of the franchise before climaxing with the violence of the Civil War and Reconstruction, was defined by questions about race and the family. White Americans came to identify the family as the center of the nation's democracy. Nineteenth-century Protestants believed in the importance of transforming Native American domestic practices. They encouraged Native converts to abandon the kinship networks that had structured their societies for centuries and to adopt the nuclear family as the focal point of their community. Although Latter-day Saints accepted many Protestant assumptions about Native Americans, they did not agree that the nuclear family was the best way to order society. Instead, they adopted an expansive understanding of the family in which ritual adoptions bound Latter-day Saints to new kin in the eternities.[21] Polygamy expanded on Joseph Smith's original revelations creating complex kinship networks that went far beyond what most Americans were comfortable with.

The Saints' adoption of new ideas about the family raised questions about the role that the family should play in national life. The creation of a straight, white, monogamous family was key to American ideas about citizenship and the nation in the nineteenth century. The exploration of Latin America, the Pacific, and Africa in the early modern period brought Europeans into contact with people who had very different understandings of sexuality. Europeans racialized the sexual practices of people of color. The historian Jennifer Morgan famously found passages in European travelogues describing African women who could "suckle" their children by flinging their breast "over their shoulder."[22] She argues that these travelogues portrayed African women as grotesque as part of a larger project to solidify racial differences.

In the nineteenth century, middle-class people used racialized language to describe the sexual practices of the poor. The founder of the Salvation Army famously referred to the impoverished people in his own country as "Darkest England."[23] The organization also published pamphlets describing working-class men and women as "low-browed" and "fierce . . . with such faces as scarcely seem to belong to their sex, dirty public houses, as full as they could be, old, grey-haired men tottering both with age and drink."[24] Middle-class philanthropists believed that disordered working-class and poor households contributed to moral decay. Journalists like James Greenwood built their careers on descriptions of the sordidness of working-class lives.[25]

These images were not limited to Great Britain. Clare Lyons has argued that the rise of the middle class in nineteenth-century Philadelphia pathologized working-class sexuality. The working class's "moral code," which had "allowed for serial nonmarital monogamy, self-divorce, add comma and boisterous, bawdy, and public heterosocial sex play," became a form of "social deviance."[26] Middle-class people also pathologized the sexuality of African Americans, making it easy for them to apply racialized descriptions of sex to the white working classes.

White Americans eventually applied similar racial images to Latter-day Saints. In 1855 *Putnam's Monthly* published Francis Lieber's treatise on the restoration. The German-American political theorist argued that monogamy was "written in the heart" of the white race and was as fundamental to European society as the idea of property.[27] He told his readers that "monogamy does not only go with the western Caucasian race, the Europeans and their descendants, beyond Christianity, it goes beyond Common Law. It is one of the primordial elements out of which all law proceeds, or which the law steps in to recognize and to protect. . . .

It is one of the elementary distinctions—historical and actual—between European and Asiatic humanity."[28] To abandon monogamy as the Latter-day Saints had done, then, was to abandon whiteness. In *Reynolds v. United States* (1878), the Supreme Court rejected the claim of Latter-day Saints that the constitution protected their right to practice polygamy. The court's decision cited Lieber. "Polygamy," it argued, "leads to the patriarchal principle, and which, when applied to large communities, fetters the people in stationary despotism." It warned that polygamy could not "long exist in connection with monogamy."[29] The Reynolds decision reinscribed the association between monogamy and whiteness that had long existed in European literature and philosophy and used it proscribe the practice of polygamy among Latter-day Saints.

The racialization of Latter-day Saints encouraged white Americans to see the Saints as a people apart and to treat them as they would later Puerto Ricans and other subject peoples. Amy Kaplan has argued that the Supreme Court case of *Downes v. Bidwell*, 182 U.S. 244 (1901) established Puerto Rico as an intermediate place that was both a part of the United States and foreign to it. The United States claimed the authority over Puerto Rico's domestic and foreign policies but did not recognize its people as citizens.[30] In his opinion on the case, Justice Edward Douglass White described the people of Puerto Rico as "alien and hostile." His colleague Henry Billings Brown worried that any territory that Americans acquired in "distant" places would be "inhabited by alien races, differing from us in religion, customs, laws, methods of taxation, and modes of thought."[31] Drawing on these statements, Kaplan argues that the justices who ruled in *Downes* created a legal status for Puerto Rico that allowed the United States to extract the territory's resources without completely facing the racial and cultural threat of annexation.[32] Other territories such as Hawai'i, Guam, and American Samoa assumed a similar place in the American imagination. A study of the history, however, remind us that distant islands were not the only places to occupy this liminal state. In the second half of the nineteenth century, the United States assumed formal control over Utah and used its power to try to reform the Saints' domestic practices. Men who practiced polygamy were frequently jailed or forced to live as refugees from the law. Utah became a liminal state. It was neither completely a part of the United States nor apart from it.

I am not the only historian to focus on the racialization of Latter-day Saints or the role that indigenous people played in restoration theology. In 2002 Sarah Barringer Gordon published an impeccably argued exploration of the role Mormonism played in constitutional debates about religious freedom in the nineteenth century. She argues that white Americans cast Mormons as nonwhite to justify their exclusion from the American body politic.[33] W. Paul Reeve's *Religion of a Different Color* investigates the role that polygamy and interracial marriage played in the racialization of the Saints.[34] Placing the uncertainty of Mormon whiteness against their missionary work, however, raises questions for the field of Mormon studies. How did the racialization of Latter-day Saints affect their interactions with Native people? In what ways did Latter-day Saint sexuality shape their missionary work and the colonization of the Great Basin? How did restoration theology change in response to the difficulties of settling Zion?

It has been almost two decades since Jan Shipps used a "doughnut metaphor" to describe the place of the Church of Jesus Christ of Latter-day Saints in the history of the American West, but most historians of the American West still "[circle] all around the Great Basin," assiduously side-stepping Mormon history.[35] In the nineteenth century, however, people saw the church as being just as menacing as slavery. Newspapers frequently portrayed it as an octopus whose tentacles threatened to "strangle" those around it.[36] These fears partially reflected a belief that Latter-day Saints threatened American settlement. White Americans feared that church members were actively inciting Native Americans against non-Mormons. As early as the 1830s, one of Joseph Smith's counselors urged the Saints conceal their belief that the redeemed Lamanites would one day help build a godly Zion. Doing so, he warned, would "stir up the people to anger."[37] The rumors did not stop after the Latter-day Saints were expelled from Missouri. Mid-nineteenth-century newspapers in Arkansas, Kentucky, and Ohio pointed to the 1857 Mountain Meadows

Massacre as evidence that church members had colluded with American Indians to prevent white settlement.[38] Two decades later, newspapers as far away as Vermont reported that Native Saints were threatening to destroy a non-Mormon community in Utah.[39]

Examining the racialization of Latter-day Saints reminds us that whiteness was about more than skin color; it was about domesticity, religious belief, and authority. The Saints transgressed white, middle-class ideas about how the family should be ordered. They also accepted the reality of prophecy and the idea that God had a physical body. As a result, many white Protestants doubted the whiteness of the Saints and worried that the church was colluding with Native Americans. Challenges to the Saints' whiteness affected their missionary work. Like other white Americans, Latter-day Saints sought to transform indigenous lives. Orson Pratt used their ability to do so as evidence of their superiority as settlers. In 1859, Pratt gave a speech in the tabernacle in which he described what the Great Basin would have looked like without the Saints' inspired settlement. Without the effort of Latter-day Saints, he argued, Utah would have been a land of "dreary wastes"—"vast solitudes . . . interrupted only by the howling of wild beasts."[40] The Book of Mormon, however, had inspired the Saints to tame the deserts and had caused "the sterile regions" to "rejoice and blossom as the rose."[41]

Native Saints were divided in how they responded to the text. White Latter-day Saints read the scripture as an explanation of the degradation of Native Americans and other indigenous people. Some Native Saints, however, saw the restored gospel as a spiritual alternative to white Christianity that empowered Native people. In the nineteenth century American imperialism ripped apart Native families and severed their ties to the land. In imagining Zion, the restored gospel resacralized the landscape and named it as the inheritance of the descendants of the Lamanites. Latter-day Saints believed that Native people would work with their white brethren to build the Kingdom of God. The Northwest Band of the Shoshone Nation traveled to Logan, Utah, in the 1880s to help build a Latter-day Saint temple. For white Latter-day Saints, the temple represented a claiming of the land and a symbol that the faith they had envisioned was coming to fruition. For some Northwestern Shoshones, however, the temple was an extension of their previous faith. They had long recognized the ground on which the Logan temple had been built as a "sacred place" where "miraculous healings" had taken place.[42] They constructed a spiritual narrative in which God had always cared for their people and had anointed them as a chosen race. Some white Latter-day Saints saw this reading of the Book of Mormon as an extension of the spiritual practices of the first generations of Mormonism. Others, however, rejected it as a "whiff of nonsense."[43]

Not all Native Saints agreed with this interpretation of the gospel. After the Bear River Massacre, Pocatello converted to the Church of Jesus Christ of Latter-day Saints, which the historian Brigham Madsen described as an "impulsive" act designed to provide his people with a future.[44] Pocatello believed that the Latter-day Saints would provide his people with knowledge about how to farm and material aid to do so. While in Salt Lake, he asked that church leaders baptize him and several of his people. He soon became disenchanted with the unwillingness of the church to protect his people and to claim them fully as Latter-day Saints. Although they were willing to baptize him and his people, he felt that they had not treated his people as equals or stood with them against non-Mormons. According to Madsen, Pocatello was not alone in his disillusionment. Many Native converts "became apostates from their faith" because of the failures of the white church.[45]

This book examines the contradictions within restoration theology surrounding race, sexuality, and the body. It argues that the emphasis within the early church on the physicality of God raised questions about what God looked like. Nineteenth-century assumptions about the nature of the divine encouraged Latter-day Saints to see God as white and male. If God was a god of reason, he could not embrace female irrationality or the savagery of Native Americans. Most white Protestants rejected the idea that God was a physical being with parts. For them, the idea that God had literal hands and feet seemed to belittle the divine. They saw the restored gospel as being akin to the "idolatry" of the Roman Catholics or Hindus.

The racialization of the church in the nineteenth century rested partially on the physicality of their religion. In addition to accepting an embodied God, Latter-day Saints believed in the reality of miracles. They described a world in which God was active in the world and in which miracles were possible. The development of Latter-day Saint polygamy in the 1840s only deepened Protestant suspicions about the restored gospel. The straight, white, monogamous family was at the center of American ideas about belonging. In rejecting monogamy, Latter-day Saints seemed to reject whiteness. Although many Latter-day Saints claimed to have been descended from the Puritans and identified as Americans, the community had also explicitly left the boundaries of the United States in settling Utah. They were not completely a part of the United States nor separate from it.

This is not a book, however, that focuses exclusively on white Latter-day Saints. It argues for the importance of understanding the experiences of Native Saints. Early restoration theology created the possibility for an alternative Christianity that empowered Native peoples. For Native peoples, I suggest, the restored gospel offered a way forward. The colonization of the Great Basin devastated the foodways that had sustained Native peoples for generations. Native Saints adopted white methods of agriculture to sustain their families and feed their children. Native Americans participated in Latter-day Saint pageantry celebrating the Latter-day Saint settlement of the Utah territory. In one particularly memorable parade that I discuss in a later chapter, Native men held signs proclaiming that they would become "white and delightsome," referring to a controversial phrase in the Book of Mormon that seemed to associate the redemption of the Lamanites with physical changes to their skin. There is evidence, however, that they did not see themselves as acquiescing to white culture in using these terms Adopting certain aspects of Latter-day Saint culture was not a concession that their way of life was less valuable than that of white Latter-day Saints; it was a way to preserve their identity.

The evangelizing mission of Latter-day Saints made it seem threatening. The British Library contains a record of the surveillance that the

East India Office undertook of Mormon missionaries in the 1880s. It describes their arrival in what is now Myanmar and the conversion of a few South Asian people, including an elderly woman and her son. It also includes articles from the *Rangoon Times* and letters from various government officials reporting on the whereabouts of the Latter-day Saint missionaries. The file is slim, but its very existence serves as an example of the suspicions Saints encountered in foreign spaces.[46] Understanding the racialization of Latter-day Saints and the experiences of Native Saints means reaching beyond the boundaries of the United States to understand how the church and the restored gospel changed as it moved through different imperial spaces. This book follows Latter-day Saint missionaries as they moved from the American West to the Pacific and back again. The result is a story that spans multiple continents and generations as families negotiated what it meant to be a Saint.

To help readers orient themselves, the book begins by outlining the major themes of restoration theology in the nineteenth century. The first chapter explores how the Latter-day Saints' ideas of about embodiment influenced their racial and gendered ideologies. I argue that the faith's emphasis on the body raised questions about the organization of the family in the afterlife. Unlike many Christians, Latter-day Saints believed that the passions that individuals felt in this life would extend into the next. Rather than being extinguished at death, sexual desire, hunger, and other human wants would continue; individual bodies would become perfected and brought into accordance with the divine will until they became exalted. The family was to be the mechanism through which this perfecting occurred since individuals could not attain the highest blessings of the restored gospel without marriage. The Saints' emphasis on embodiment also raised questions about the nature of race. For much of the nineteenth century, Latter-day Saints emphasized the impermanence of some racial identities. They believed that indigenous people would be physically whitened in the millennium as they remembered their Israelite identity. The Saints' missionary work was an attempt to redeem the descendants of the Book of Mormon and remove the darkness that had marked their skin for thousands of years.

Chapter 2 focuses on challenge that Latter-day Saint missionary work offered to developing ideas about the family. The command that Latter-day Saints travel to the nations of the earth and the islands of the sea to spread the gospel meant that women were frequently asked to care for their families in their husbands' absences. Latter-day Saint women created alternative kinship networks to provide for themselves and their children. When Joseph Fielding left to serve a mission in Great Britain in 1837, he left behind two sisters, Mary and Mercy. The two women developed a deeply affectionate relationship with each other. Although contemporary understandings of marriage demanded that relationships between husbands and wives take priority over those between women, Mary and Mercy continued to rely on each other after their marriages to an extent that troubled their husbands' families. Polygamy further complicated these relationships. Latter-day Saint elites initially denied that Smith had received a revelation reviving polygamy. Rumors circulated inside and outside of the Latter-day Saint community about sexual indiscretions. The attempts of the Relief Society, a Latter-day Saint women's organization, to determine which rumors were true brought women's lives under increased scrutiny.

Chapter 3 shifts its focus to early Latter-day Saint missionary work among Native Americans and Polynesians. Although early Saints sometimes imitated Native Americans in their spiritual practices, they found few converts among American Indians. A Cherokee woman named Peninah Shropshire Cotton was likely one of the first Native women to participate in Latter-day Saint polygamy. Her son believed that she had been a "Godsend" to the Latter-day Saints, "just as Sacagawea the Indian maid had been to the Lewis and Clark expedition."[47] Before the Utah exodus, there were no more than a dozen Native American converts.[48]

White Latter-day Saints, however, interpreted their presence in Nauvoo as the inbreaking of the Kingdom of God. They believed these conversions were the first of many and that they would soon see thousands of Lamanites coming together to build the kingdom and inaugurate the end of days. Their vision was global. Early Latter-day Saints came to believe that the descendants of the peoples of the Book of Mormon would sail from the Pacific to the city of Zion. This chapter examines the logics of Latter-day Saint missionary work; it also asks what conversion meant for local communities. Ultimately, I argue that Native Americans and Polynesians who converted to the restored gospel saw it as a source of political and spiritual power. The restoration placed them at the center of its sacred texts and offered them the opportunity to prophesy and heal the sick. The religion became a way for some Native people to resist colonialism even as white Latter-day Saints saw it as a civilizing force. Although the restored gospel required them to reorient their lives towards the temple and remade some of their spiritual practices, it allowed them to maintain their culture and placed them at the center of God's redemptive plan. It also, however, recognizes that all Native people were not drawn to the restored gospel. For some, the message of the restoration was alienating. It required that they forsake the religious texts and practices that previously organized their lives. In Tahiti, for example, Native as well as white Protestants opposed the spread of the church in the region.

Joseph Smith's death in 1844 changed conversations about Native Americans and their place within restoration theology. The man who had reopened the heavens and discovered a previously hidden sacred text had died—leaving Latter-day Saints temporarily without purpose or meaning. As they sought new meaning, the Saints turned to the conversion of Native Americans as a possible way forward. The Council of Fifty served as a temporary government for the church after his death. In one meeting, the Council called upon Lewis Dana, an Oneida man who had joined the church, to travel west to "[sow] the seeds of the gospel" among the Lamanites.[49] Their hope was that the conversion of Native Americans might fulfill God's promises in a way that Joseph Smith's death seemed to render impossible. As Latter-day Saints moved across the Great Plains, however, they came into more substantial contact with Native Americans than they had before. Over time, Latter-day Saints became uncertain whether the Lamanites were redeemable. Church leaders in nineteenth-century Utah would sometimes call for the extermination of Native Americans who refused to be cowed.

Chapter 4 focuses on the resulting shifts in the Latter-day Saints' understandings of the family. I argue that Mormons established the practice of polygamy while they were serving missions among Native Americans and attempting to transform their cultural and familial practices. In addition to creating model farms throughout Utah for Native Americans, they came to believe in the power of Latter-day Saint families to change individual Native Americans. White Latter-day Saints incorporated American Indians into their families through plural marriage and the adoption of Indian children. They hoped that doing so would create Native Saints who could then serve as missionaries to their people. Latter-day Saints also created an argument that their form of polygamy was more virtuous than that practiced by Native communities or white fur traders. Contrary to accusations that polygamy was just another form of licentiousness, Latter-day Saints were deeply invested in developing a form of polygamy that was just as a "virtuous" and "respectable" as monogamy. They discovered, however, that it was difficult to reconcile their ideas about a sacred Lamanite past with the experiences of settling the American West. Native Americans did not convert to the church in large numbers, as the Council had predicted. Although some Native people adopted the restored gospel to preserve their communities, others refused and openly opposed Latter-day Saint settlement.[50]

The final two chapters focus on the tensions that arose between the symbol of the Lamanite and the realities of colonization during the second half of the nineteenth century. Chapter 5 examines a probate case concerning John T. Garr, a white Latter-day Saint who was called to settle the Cache Valley in the 1850s. Garr fathered a mixed-race child, who he called Johnny, with a Shoshone woman and then raised him within his household. As an adult, Johnny married a white woman named Elizabeth. Together they had five children. After Johnny died in a wagon accident, Garr brought his grandchildren and daughter-in-law into his home. The probate case focused on whether Garr's grandchildren should inherit his estate. Garr's sister Eliza denied that he had ever claimed Johnny as his own and argued that the boy was the illegitimate son of a Welshman named Jones. The case exposed tensions within the community over Latter-day Saint relationships with Indian children. The physical and cultural dislocations Native Americans experienced in nineteenth-century Utah created turmoil within their communities. Ute men raided less powerful Indian communities and then sold their captives to white Latter-day Saints. Poverty also led some families to offer their children to white families for purchase. The Saints brought these children into their homes in hopes that it would speed the eventual redemption of the Lamanites. The trauma that accompanied their entrance into the white Latter-day Saint community, however, made it difficult for Indian adoptees to fully assimilate into white society. Not only had violence and poverty forced them from their natal homes but they also lived in a community that did not value their culture or bodies. When Johnny was a young child, for example, white soldiers massacred over 250 Shoshones in what is now called the Bear River Massacre. Johnny's white Latter-day Saint community celebrated these deaths.

The Garr case highlights the conflict between the Saints' elevation of indigenous people as Israelites and the racism present in Mormon culture. The final chapter explores how Native Mormons created meaning out of their faith despite white Mormon racism. It examines the establishment of Washakie, Iosepa, and Lā'ie as Native Latter-day Saint towns in the late nineteenth century. I argue that these towns allowed Native Saints to reestablish communities torn apart by colonialism. For Native Hawaiians, Iosepa became a sacred place representing their attachment to Utah and their importance to the Latter-day Saint faith. The Northwestern Shoshones who helped build Washakie likewise saw the town as an opportunity to create their own community. They held dances and gathered to worship and pray.[51] These communities, of course, faced the same racism that Johnny had. White Mormons saw the towns as a testament to the truth of the restored gospel and as evidence that Native Saints had abandoned their savagery and accepted the superiority of whiteness. For Native Saints, these towns had a different meaning, one focused on the maintenance rather than the destruction of cultural traditions.

As a white woman, I cannot fully capture the Native Latter-day Saint experience. I hope, however, that I have done justice to the complexity of the nineteenth-century church and its relationship to indigenous people in the American West and the Pacific. Darren Parry, whose memories of his grandmother opened this book, consistently emphasizes one thing when speaking about her role in preserving Shoshone history: his people's history was just "as important as any pioneer story." My own connections to the story are to white settlers. Some of the people who appear in the text, such as Aidah and Albert Clements and Mary Ann Barzee Boice, I first encountered not in academic texts but in xeroxed records in family histories. Although several of my great aunts and uncles are Shoshone, none of them are Latter-day Saints or belong to the Northwest Band. My relationship to my great grandfather, however, taught me that race and power have become so entwined that they are inseparable. I also learned the importance of telling empathetic stories that honor the people within them, lest those histories be erased. I recognize that the stories I tell here are personal as well as academic. The stories within this book have meanings beyond what I have given them. I hope, however, that their subjects would recognize some truth within the book's arguments and that the story I have told is a step toward a history of the restored gospel and the Intermountain West that recognizes how power structures have shaped the experiences of its inhabitants.

CHAPTER 1

THE RACE AND SEX OF GOD

In May 1840 an Oneida man named Lewis Dana brought his family to Commerce, Illinois, to be baptized into the Church of Jesus Christ of Latter-day Saints. Town resident Phebe Carter Woodruff excitedly wrote a letter to her husband proclaiming that Dana had walked "hundreds of miles to become acquainted" with the restored gospel. She was particularly jubilant about the possibilities the family's conversion offered for the restoration's future. Although she did not name the family's tribal affiliation—and perhaps didn't care enough to find out—she was excited the husband was "an enterpreter [*sic*] to six tribes" and had significant authority within Native communities. She likely hoped his influence would inaugurate the mass conversion of Native Americans and, with it, the establishment of God's kingdom on earth.[1]

Phebe was not the only Latter-day Saint to exult in the possibilities of Native American conversion. For white Saints, the baptism of Native Americans represented the inbreaking of a prophetic future in which thousands of Native Americans would flock to the Latter-day Saint community to build Zion. Latter-day Saint worship practices often embodied this hope in the 1830s. The Latter-day Saint missionary Parley P. Pratt visited a community of Saints in Ohio where the members pretended to be Native Americans. They mimed scalping before descending to the floor, where they would "slide or scoot. . . . with the rapidity of a serpent." According to a contemporary, they called this activity "sailing in the boat to the Lamanites."[2] Other Latter-day Saints claimed to see visions of American Indians "on the banks" of western rivers "waiting to be baptized."[3] Others believed that they had received the ability to preach in Indian tongues and spoke before unseen audiences with their newfound ability.

These "strange spiritual operations" horrified Pratt, who saw them as symptoms of excess.[4] The people who participated in them, however, saw them as legitimate spiritual experiences that allowed them to begin the reopening of the heavens that Joseph Smith's prophecies had announced. For many early Latter-day Saints, Smith's visions were not a singular event. Instead, they had ushered in an age in which women, children, and men would prophesy, spreading the good news and warning the wicked to repent. They believed that God was calling the world to reform one last time before establishing his heavenly Zion. As part of these last days, God would reclaim Native Americans as His people. They would be recognized as the children of Israel and would receive the Book of Mormon as their history. As a result, their bodies would physically transform as they shed their Indian features and became "white and delightsome."[5] The focus of the Book of Mormon on indigenous people eventually compelled Latter-day Saints to send missionaries not only to Native Americans but also to the Pacific Islands.

The emphasis of the Latter-day Saints on the redemption of the Lamanites demonstrates how deeply embedded the movement's theology was in nineteenth-century racial politics. By 1843 white Latter-day Saints imagined the afterlife in material terms. They emphasized the resurrected body's solid nature and described a God of flesh and blood. While they believed in a resurrected white body, they explicitly christened Native Americans a chosen people and argued that the Second Coming could not occur until they had been redeemed. This belief compelled Latter-day Saints to seek out the people that they saw as descendants of the Lamanites.

Gender was equally important to the restored gospel. By the 1840s Latter-day Saints envisioned an eternity patterned after the households that individuals established in this world. Men and women would continue to procreate and relish bodily joys such as eating and drinking. The families they established during their mortal lifetimes would become the "seeds" of the kingdoms they would enjoy in the next life. The glory that children attained added to that of their parents, ensuring that righteous individuals would experience ever greater degrees of exaltation. This vision required both men and women. Although people would eventually be exalted regardless of their gender, women's bodies would bear children throughout the eternities and allow links to be formed between men.

Joseph Smith's revelations created an expansive system in which knowledge would be accumulated until humanity reached perfection. Although Smith initially accepted the propriety of the nuclear family, he eventually adopted an understanding of the family that was as expansive as their vision of the eternities. Early Latter-day Saints began to think of the family as a community of faith as well as a biological unit. By the time that polygamy was officially introduced in the early 1840s, they imagined an eternity in which all of humanity would be knit together through temple rituals that sealed individuals together.[6] Polygamy allowed male Latter-day Saints to multiply the connections between families.

Latter-day Saint theology compelled Saints to travel to the Pacific and the American West to try to redeem the indigenous peoples they found there. Like other Christian missionaries, they sought to transform indigenous family structures and sexual practices. The marital practices that Latter-day Saints adopted, however, placed them at the margins of Christian society. As a result, other missionaries viewed their work with suspicion. Latter-day Saints were constantly pulled between justifying their own sexual practices and transforming those of indigenous people. They also found that the expansiveness of Joseph Smith's revelations created a space for other people to claim their own prophetic power. Latter-day Saint leaders responded by emphasizing the orderliness of revelation and the importance of submitting to the priesthood's authority. Latter-day Saints found themselves in an unstable position in the nineteenth century. They inhabited a boisterous religious landscape where Protestant ministers traveled from town to town proclaiming the gospel and encouraging Americans to turn away from sin.

Latter-day Saints saw the disorder of the religious world they inhabited as a problem. They believed that Joseph Smith's visions provided them with an answer to the divisions they saw within modern Christianity. Smith proclaimed that he had restored the true gospel and that no other church held its "fullness." Protestants, however, derided those who followed Smith as "Mormonites" and considered them to be less than white.[7] Latter-day Saint ideas about embodiment and gender seemed laughable to white Protestants who saw God as a being beyond matter and space. Violence forced the Saints to move from New York to Ohio, Missouri, Illinois, and finally, Utah. The figure of the "Mormon" became important within nineteenth-century American thought. Latter-day Saints saw their faith as bringing order to a fundamentally disordered world. The mission field became a place where they could claim the order and respectability that had been denied them.

This chapter introduces restoration theology. Smith's revelations created a deeply embodied faith that encouraged individuals to seek their own knowledge about God. His revelations, however, also introduced disciplinary mechanisms that marginalized certain members of the faith. The tension between individual revelation and institutional power defined the Latter-day Saint experience in the nineteenth century. It also defined their missionary work. Latter-day Saints believed that it was their responsibility to call Native Americans and other indigenous people back to God and help them reclaim their Israelite heritage. They also used their ability to transform the lives of indigenous people in the American West and the Pacific as an argument for their own respectability. God had commanded them to redeem the Lamanite, but their ability to do so was also a part of their political argument for their acceptability as Americans. In the popular imagination, the "Mormon" was a figure of derision. Latter-day Saints sought to reclaim their image through mission and transform the image of the Mormon into an upright, respectable pioneer. They denied, of course, the effects that colonization had on the very indigenous people they sought to reclaim.

Embodiment and Restoration Theology

The theology of the restoration did not arise out of a vacuum. The religious landscape of nineteenth-century America was a raucous, disorderly place. White Baptists challenged southern hierarchies by evangelizing slave quarters and naming Black men and women their "brothers and sisters."[8] The movement of white families into Indian territory undid the familial and religious structures of American society, leaving them outside of patriarchal and church control.[9] And, finally, members of dissident religious movements such as the Shakers retreated from mainstream society to small enclaves where they radically reimagined the family.[10] Individual religious experience mirrored the disorder of public religious life in the United States. In camp meetings throughout the nineteenth century, individuals barked like dogs and jerked in bizarre dance movements.[11] The physical bodies of white women and the enslaved mingled with those of white men, and the former were just as likely to feel the power of God as the latter. For many Christians in the nineteenth century, these spiritual practices represented a fundamental disordering of the kingdom of God. The mingling of peoples of different races, genders, and classes collapsed categories that many people saw as essential to social and religious order.

Joseph Smith's visions were a part of this religious ferment. His later descriptions of the visions he received at age fourteen emphasized the "confusion" he had felt as a child over the array of churches in the early republic. Writing to his followers, he explained that when he encountered conflicting interpretations of biblical texts he lost "all confidence" that he could answer a "question by an appeal to the Bible."[12] He saw his visions as providing order to the religious landscape and rejected the abstract theology that he believed had led Christianity astray in favor of embodied knowledge. In one revelation God urged Joseph Smith to grasp the hands of the angelic beings who visited him to ensure that they were not the devil in disguise.[13] If they were divine, God told him, he would be able to feel the hardness of their flesh.

Smith eventually came to believe that God also had a body. In the last years of his ministry, Smith developed a theology that rejected the

Christian trinity and argued that humans were consubstantial with God. In this understanding of the world, God had once been a human being and had only attained his divinity after enduring a mortal probation. After his death he was exalted and became the ruler of their universe. Even in his divine state, however, he was a physical being. He had hands, arms, feet, and even genitals.[14] Contained within this vision of the divine was the promise that Latter-day Saints would go through the same progression. The Latter-day Saint community came to imagine an eternity in which individuals would progress throughout the ages, becoming perfected until they eventually became gods themselves. The restoration's imagining of God as a being with human passions and parts led to questions about what sexuality, family structures, and gender would look like in the heavens.[15]

As restoration theologians tried to answer these questions, they came to imagine a deeply embodied afterlife. In *Key to the Science of Theology*, for example, Parley Pratt described this world in rich, sumptuous terms. The godly, he wrote, would be "clothed in the finest robes of linen, pure and white, adorned with precious stones and gold."[16] They would "eat, drink, think, converse, associate, assemble, disperse, go, come, possess, improve, love and enjoy."[17] Pratt emphasized the materiality of celestial worlds. Along with other early Saints, he envisioned a heavenly world made of the same substance as the earthly one. He believed that individuals would still hunger, thirst, and experience desire after they became gods. Although people would be perfected and deified in the resurrection, they would still feel the same passions that they had on earth.[18] The Latter-day Saint idea of God was one in which the deity lived in an earthly paradise and felt human emotions.

In many ways this emphasis on God's physicality collapsed the distance between humans and the divine.[19] Early Latter-day Saints embraced the idea that they would eventually become deified and rule over worlds in the same manner as their Heavenly Father. This concept had its origins in Smith's early revelations. As Smith was retranslating the Bible, he received a vision in which he saw multiple heavens, the highest of which was filled with men who were "Gods, even the sons of God."[20] By the 1840s he interpreted this vision as meaning that individual humans could be exalted and become gods themselves. He made these connections explicit in an 1844 funeral sermon, where he told those who had assembled, "God himself was once as we are now." If they could see through the veil that separated heaven and earth, he added, they would see God as "a man . . . like yourselves in all the person, image, and very form as a man." He then told his audience that they would eventually be glorified and would progress as God had done.[21]

Smith's understanding of the divine placed him at odds with many other early American religious groups. For many early modern Christians, the presence of disorder within manifestations of the divine reflected the radical distance they placed between earthly flesh and God. As the historian Benjamin Park points out, many medieval and early modern theologians saw "the body as a temporary prison" from which the soul would be freed at death.[22]

This understanding of the body affected the way that individuals experienced the divine during the eighteenth and nineteenth centuries. Many people described mystical experiences as painful. Founding Shaker Ann Lee, for example, called her suffering during her religious experiences "so great, that my flesh consumed upon my bones."[23] Her exertions emphasized the sinfulness of the body and the importance of transcending her degraded flesh to lose herself in something greater and more powerful. Contemporary reports of visions and spiritual gifts echoed the intense agony in which Lee found herself. In 1799 a Connecticut man published an account of his vision of heaven. Before passing through the veil, he was "disturbed with a pain in [his] breast, which darted at times across [his] bowls [sic]."[24] Eventually, it racked his entire body until he expected to feel the "pangs of death." As soon as his soul was "freed from the cage which had confined it, all things around [him] wore a delightful complexion."[25]

Nineteenth-century Latter-day Saint spiritual practices were no less embodied. Individual Saints spoke in tongues, laid hands upon each other during prayer, and healed the sick. White Americans sometimes made connections between the religious practices of Latter-day Saints and those of people color. In 1833, for example, the *York Gazette* told readers that the moral condition of the Latter-day Saints degraded every year "until they have now nearly reached the low condition of the black population." The article later described the religious practices of the Saints—implicitly connecting their belief they could "converse with God and his angels" to their moral degradation.[26] According to historian W. Paul Reeve, newspapers also reported on the charismatic religious practices of the few Black members of the church. He cites the *Albany Journal,* which claimed that "a man of color, a chief man, who is sometimes seized with strange vagaries and odd conceits" lived among the Latter-day Saints.[27] In another newspaper, Reeve points out, the same Black convert pretends to "fly."[28] The portrayal of Latter-day Saints as nonwhite intensified after their adoption of polygamy.[29] Even in the 1830s, however, descriptions of their spiritual practices questioned their respectability and whiteness.

Joseph Smith's revelations had opened the heavens, and the prophecies, visions, and angelic tongues that flowed forth thrilled Latter-day Saints. The Saints also discovered, however, that it could be difficult to contain the religious experiences of their coreligionists. Latter-day Saint leaders believed it was their responsibility to bring order to the enthusiastic religious practices of their followers. Joseph Smith encouraged his followers to only accept religious experiences that imparted knowledge. In 1842 he published an editorial in *Times and Seasons* explaining how individuals could judge whether spiritual manifestations were the result of demonic powers or the indwelling of the Holy Spirit. After detailing the ease with which "false spirits" might appear as manifestations of the divine, the article castigated those who would judge spiritual gifts by the "creeds of men" and instead exhorted them to measure the effects and knowledge gained through these experiences against scripture.[30] It argued that Methodists, Presbyterians, and other enthusiasts would often claim to have manifestations of God in which they would faint—their "animation . . . frequently entirely suspended." When they awoke, however, they could say nothing more than "hallelujah, or some incoherent expression."[31] Because God was a god of revelation and knowledge, the author suggested, this "heterogenious [*sic*] mass of confusion" could not be a result of his inspiration. The article was equally scornful of Quaker silence, which did not allow the individual to say anything more about God than he already knew.[32] For early Latter-day Saints, spiritual experience could not be judged by the emotions that individuals felt or the power they believed they were imbued with. Rather, spiritual experiences and revelations had to be judged in relationship to the knowledge they produced.[33]

This understanding of revelation was important because it allowed Latter-day Saints to distance themselves from the suggestion that Latter-day Saints were racially suspect. Throughout his ministry, Smith emphasized the ordered nature of his church. He saw himself as creating a church that answered the period's religious and social tumult.

This emphasis on reason relied on assumptions about gender as well as race. In the eighteenth century, philosophers had adopted a gendered epistemology that portrayed women as unable to use reason to "regulate their actions." Instead, they were overly emotional—governed "by arbitrary inclinations and opinions."[34] Joseph Smith drew on these assumptions about women as he distanced himself from female prophets like Joanna Southcott and Ann Lee. He portrayed himself as a reasoned man who experienced the divine in his body but did so in a way that led him to knowledge rather than confusion. The epistemology of other Latter-day Saint leaders was just as gendered as Smith's. In *Key to the Science of Theology*, Parley Pratt drew upon 1 Corinthians to argue that a righteous man should "be the head of a woman, a father, and a guide of the weaker sex" and indeed was "designed" to be such.[35] Pratt's vision of the eternities—as expansive and breathtaking as it was—was one in which women would be subordinate to their husbands.

By the 1840s the Latter-day Saint idea of God was also explicitly gendered.[36] In 1845 Eliza R. Snow could imagine a "primeval childhood" in which she had known the female God who had given her birth.[37] The Latter-day Saint emphasis on eternal kinship ties, however, tempered the vision's radicalism. Pratt's *Key to the Science of Theology* made clear that God the Father was the revelatory power behind Smith's knowledge of the universe. Heavenly Mother was a nurturing figure and the "Queen of Heaven," but she was not named in the Godhead nor in the restoration scriptures. The church's emphasis on embodiment promised deification for both men and women, but when Latter-day Saint spoke of God they most often spoke of God the Father.

The emphasis on reason allowed Latter-day Saints to discipline each other's spiritual practices. Smith's visions promised individual Saints that they would be able to prophesy and receive divine revelations. At times, however, individuals transgressed the boundaries of what others found acceptable. The ecstatic spiritual experiences at Kirtland, where members imitated Native Americans, were one such instance. For the nascent church, however, the question was how to respond to its members' religious practices. Latter-day Saint understandings of the divine made this question even more intractable. Many charismatic communities checked the wild spiritual practices of their members by emphasizing asceticism. Shaker communities, for example, had strict behavioral codes that required individuals to deny themselves pleasure to physically weaken the flesh and increase the possibility of spiritual enlightenment. Methodists also emphasized the importance of ensuring that individual members lived by the word of God even as they embraced ecstatic movements; to facilitate such accountability, they asked followers to meet frequently in small bands wherein they discussed each other's sins.[38] Thus, the discipline they lived by curbed the disorder that violent shaking and enthusiastic dance introduced in these communities. Glossolalia was acceptable because it provided individuals with information about God; barking like a dog or swooning was not. The result was a gendered understanding of the divine that elevated male reason over other kinds of spiritual experience.

The discomfort that Latter-day Saints felt with some of the disorderly aspects of their faith was shared by people outside of the faith. Concerns about the church only intensified after the death of Joseph Smith and the removal of the church to Utah. Throughout the nineteenth century white Protestants accused Latter-day Saints of having embraced the faith out of delusion. As we will see in the next section, the figure of the

"Mormon" came to represent the possibility that the corruption of religious faith would degrade white Americans—leading them to embrace polygamy and theocracy. Discussions of Latter-day Saints employed nineteenth-century ideas of race and gender to emphasize the ways that "Mormons" failed to live up to the standards of respectability.

The Figure of the "Mormon" in the Nineteenth Century

The idea that indigenous people were at the center of God's redemptive narrative compelled early Latter-day Saint missionaries to travel to the American West, Latin America, and the Pacific in search of the descendants of the people of the Book of Mormon. Early Latter-day Saint missionary efforts, however, were not uncontested. Their multiplication of spiritual gifts, insistence upon God's physicality, and marital innovations challenged nineteenth-century Protestant theology. For American Protestants, restoration theology undermined God's transcendence, transforming him from an exalted figure who had "laid the earth's foundation" and "shut up the sea" into a degraded personage of flesh and blood.[39] The reactions of American Protestants to the restored gospel focused on what they saw as its audacity. For them, the Church of Jesus Christ of Latter-day Saints was a radical affront to traditional conceptions of God.

The impudence of "Mormonism" in the nineteenth century, however, was just as much about its marital practices and ideas about indigenous people as it was about theology. Protestant pastors, U.S. senators, and respected journalists cast the church as an "Oriental" religion that accepted sexual practices unbecoming of white men. The Civil War catapulted discussions about domesticity and marriage to greater prominence, transforming what may have been a small discussion about Latter-day Saint marriage patterns into a much larger debate about relationship of marriage to the recently solidified American nation.[40] The Latter-day Saints became part of a national discussion of how marriage and sexuality should be defined.

The literary scholar Terryl Givens locates the church's challenge to traditional Christianity in its willingness to collapse "the sacred and the profane."[41] As Givens points out, Christian theology rests upon the willingness of God to enter human history. It is God's physicality in the figure of Christ that leads to the atonement. By the mid-nineteenth century, however, this foundational event had been mythologized by the centuries that passed since its occurrence. According to Givens, the restoration was a "re-historicizing [and de-mythologizing] of Christianity."[42] Early Latter-day Saints saw themselves as reenacting biblical history. Just as Joseph Smith became a modern reincarnation of the Old Testament prophets, the expulsion of the Saints from Missouri became a "recapitulation" of the Hebrew exodus from Egypt.[43] The idea that Latter-day Saints were reenacting biblical history drew ridicule from non-Mormons who criticized Smith's boldness in claiming to have found a record of God's dealings with the indigenous peoples of the Americas. Ironically, Puritan leaders had claimed centuries earlier to have reconciled the discovery of the Americas with biblical history.[44] The Latter-day Saints' claim that the Book of Mormon was an ancient American record materialized this belief in a way that other Americans found ridiculous.[45] They lampooned the Book of Mormon as a "golden Bible" and denigrated Smith as a latter-day "Mahomet."[46]

Early critics of the Latter-day Saints mocked the men and women who accepted Smith's prophetic claims, calling them "deluded fanatics."[47] In his history of the church, Eber D. Howe claimed that Mormonism was a "more recent, more absurd, and, perhaps more extensive delusion" than "Jemima Wilkinson, the Barkers, Jumpers and Mutterers," all of whom he saw as "folly."[48] Charles Dickens's weekly magazine *Household Words* likewise called the church a "homely, wild, vulgar fanaticism" filled with individuals who admitted to "singing hymns to nigger tunes, and seeing visions in the age of railways."[49] "Mormonism" served as an example of the possible folly of religion throughout the nineteenth century. Authors pointed to it as evidence that false prophets could easily dupe the masses into believing their assertions of spiritual power. Although nineteenth-century Christians believed the miracles contained within the Bible, they had distanced themselves from the miraculous. One of the central tenets of the Reformation was that the "age of miracles" had ceased. Many American religious leaders began to view the miraculous with suspicion. They saw them not as evidence of the transformative power of the divine but of the gullibility of the masses. The idea that Latter-day Saints were credulous helped to define what "Mormonism" meant in the public imagination for much of the nineteenth century. The restoration was seen as a religion that offered its followers a pagan god who appealed to minds too gross and untutored to understand serious theology.

Although reactions to the restoration initially focused on its theology, the formal announcement of polygamy fundamentally changed the way that non-Mormons portrayed the church. Rumors had long circulated about sexual irregularities in the community of Latter-day Saints in Illinois. It was not until 1852, after the Latter-day Saints had migrated to Utah, that the Church of Jesus Christ of Latter-day Saints announced it had adopted the practice of polygamy.[50] In a speech confirming the practice, the apostle Orson Pratt created a grandiose vision of polygamy in which the multiplication of marital ties would increase the rate at which preexistent spirits—considered the very "sons and daughters of God"—were born into mortal bodies. The "seed" of nineteenth-century Saints would like Abraham's, "numberless as the stars."[51]

Despite the expansive beauty of early descriptions of polygamy, a cacophony of dissent, ridicule, and disbelief greeted Pratt's announcement outside of Utah. Mark Twain famously remarked that Latter-day Saint women were so deformed and hideous that any man who married one had actually "done an act of Christian charity which entitles him to the kindly applause of mankind, not their harsh censure." He felt that "the man that marries sixty of them [had] done a deed of open-handed generosity so sublime that the nations should stand uncovered in presence."[52] Likewise, the humorist Artemus Ward wrote that it took Brigham Young "six weeks to kiss his wives" and described the old man's consternation when, upon falling in love with a girl, he was forced to marry her "three sisters" and her two grandmothers.[53] In his analysis of Twain and Ward, Richard Cracroft points out that one of the grandmothers was toothless.[54]

Although the jibes that Twain and Ward made against the church were intended to be humorous, the attacks that appeared in novels and newspapers in the nineteenth century often failed to find humor in the new faith. Appearing before the U.S. Congress, a representative from Nevada called the restored gospel an "unbridled indulgence" and expressed embarrassment that "the barbarous social practices of the Asiatic" could now be found "among a Saxon people in this noon of the nineteenth century."[55] A book published in 1884 called it "the seraglio of the Republic," "the brothel of the nation," and "hell enthroned."[56] The descriptions often portrayed Latter-day Saints as foreign or "exotic." J. C. Bennett's 1842 exposé of the church, for example, claimed that Joseph Smith had performed "blackest deeds of felony" and called him "the Mormon Mahomet."[57]

In identifying the Saints as racially different, such writings sought to reinforce the eroding separation between white and nonwhite sexualities. Anti-Mormon pamphlets even suggested that polygamy had fundamentally changed the bodies of Latter-day Saints. Two scientists at the 1861 New Orleans Academy of Sciences described the differences between pink-cheeked women and men who participated in proper Christian marriages and those who had forsaken such marriages for "Mormonism." Their report drew on the writings of Robert Bartholow, a surgeon who had speculated that "the yellow, sunken, cadaverous visage," "thick, protuberant lips," and "low forehead" of Latter-day Saints may have been the result of "the premature development of [their] passions, or to [their] isolation."[58]

These terms were often used to describe the bodies of people of color. Two years after the academy's meeting, an article in the *Atlantic Monthly* portrayed Asian women as having "thick, protuberant lips, copper skins, and lanky, black hair."[59] James Nicol's *Introductory Book of the Sciences* defined the races of the world using their facial features. He saw the African race as having "their head narrow and compressed, their forehead low and convex, and the mouth and lower part of the face projecting."[60] The language that Bartholow chose to describe Latter-day Saints explicitly racialized them. He believed that the shape of their foreheads and lips marked them as nonwhite despite their protests otherwise.

The identification of Latter-day Saints as racially or physically other, however, was never entirely stable. Even as non-Mormons sought to etch difference on the bodies of the Saints, they were often forced to admit that Latter-day Saint men and women were no different from their Christian counterparts. White, middle-class readers took pleasure in the descriptions of Latter-day Saints as exotic and sensual; exposés of the church sold well in the nineteenth century. When Ann Eliza Young, the erstwhile nineteenth wife of Brigham Young, published a book accusing her former husband and his desert Saints of murdering dissenters, seducing young girls, and sanctioning the slaughter of immigrant wagon trains, the celebrity that resulted catapulted her into a career as a lecturer in Boston, San Francisco, and New York.[61] Images of Latter-day Saints as crazed, brutal people filled nineteenth-century novels, including Sir Arthur Conan Doyle's *A Study in Scarlet*.[62] Depictions of sexual difference as leading to violence and racial degradation extended to the other religious groups. As historian Kara French has pointed out, anti-Catholic novels portrayed convents as places of seduction and brutality. "The Lady Superior," she writes, "was simultaneously depicted as a rake on par with the villain of the most prurient seduction novel and a wicked enchantress out of a fairy story."[63]

Even as such portrayals sought to underscore the exoticism of Latter-day Saints, they raised the possibility of racial mixing. The English author William Hepworth Dixon made the mixing of different races within the bodies of Latter-day Saints explicit in his book *White Conquest*. He claimed that Latter-day Saints had learned polygamy from local Native Americans and that Latter-day Saints were nothing more than "white Indians."[64] For him, the origin of polygamy among the Saints lay in "Shoshone wigwam" rather than the family structures of the Old Testament.[65] The white bodies that inhabited the American West were susceptible to the contagious sexual practices of the Native American tribes that surrounded them. Therefore, it was possible that the men and women who traveled west on foot and in wagons each year would eventually join the Latter-day Saints in becoming white savages.

Works like Dixon's provided readers with an illicit thrill, as they imagined the mingling of bodies that were supposed to be kept separate while enjoying their own safety and distance. The naming of Latter-day Saint as racially and physically "other" was a complex practice. On the one hand, it sought to reinforce the boundaries between white and nonwhite peoples that were so important to American and European understandings of empire in the nineteenth century. On the other hand, in raising the possibility that savagery lurked beneath the white skin of Latter-day Saints, it put the very categories that it tried to guard against into play. The idea that the Saints had betrayed their fundamental whiteness was just as important to their image in the nineteenth century as their marital innovations or acceptance of spiritual gifts. Even those people who supported the Saints portrayed them as being uncomfortably close to Native Americans and other indigenous people. When Elizabeth Kane, who later become a doctor, toured southern Utah with her husband, she described dozens of Indians living in the town, with "the grave and dignified bearing of the Navajoes [sic] contrasting favorably with the slouching walk of the dirty Pi-edes."[66] The individual Latter-day Saints in her descriptions sometimes seemed to become Indians. One of Young's wives, for example, called herself "Bigham [sic] Squaw."[67]

According to Givens, much of the violence that Latter-day Saints experienced in Missouri was related to the impropriety of their relationships with indigenous people. He argues in *The Viper on the Hearth* that white men and women feared that Latter-day Saints would join with American Indians to destroy white communities. In 1848 a former Latter-day Saint named Catherine Lewis claimed that there were "two or three tribes of Indians" who had been ready "to go through, avenge, and destroy the people of Carthage" at the time of the deaths of Joseph and Hyrum Smith.[68] Givens also cites a woman from Nebraska who claimed that the people who lived around the Latter-day Saints were "very much scared" that the Saints would "soon be upon them and slay men, women, and children." She used evidence that Latter-day Saints women were "marrying in with the Indians" and were attempting to join the two communities. The woman ended with the claim that there were "a great many women here that are almost scared to death, they are just ready to run."[69]

The woman's statement, which constructed the Church of Jesus Christ of Latter-day Saints as a threat to the virtue of white women, brought together many of the fears about the church in the nineteenth century. Although Joseph Smith saw his revelations as reopening the heavens, white Americans saw them as debasing Christianity. The marital innovations that Latter-day Saints adopted and their willingness to foreground Native Americans in their theology only deepened outsiders' suspicions. White Protestants in the United States feared that Latter-day Saints were blurring the boundaries between whiteness and people of color. Their emphasis on physical embodiment seemed uncomfortably close to Native American ideas about the divine. The church's attempt to redefine race and gender placed it in conversation with some of the major themes of nineteenth-century American history. The restoration sought to redefine the nature of the Christian family at a time when white Protestants believed that properly managed households were essential to good government. White Protestants saw the church as a transgressive force that threatened to undo the bonds that held American society together.

It is no surprise that Latter-day Saints objected to the image that white Protestants painted of their church. They saw the restoration as a movement that promoted order and good governance. Far from rejecting Protestant ideas about respectability, they embraced them and argued that the restored gospel was a better way to civilize the American continent than Protestantism. Latter-day Saints launched missions to indigenous people in the Americas and the Pacific throughout the nineteenth century. The Book of Mormon shaped the consciousness of Latter-day Saints and the missionary work that they undertook. Janiece Johnson has used memoirs, correspondence, and annotated versions of the Book of Mormon to demonstrate that the first generation of Saints used the newly discovered scripture "to narrate their lives."[70] Latter-day Saint newspapers frequently reprinted sections of scripture to give access to people who otherwise might not have been able to obtain a copy. Latter-day Saints saw their missionary work through the Book of Mormon. Scripture was not, however, the only thing that shaped their missionary work. Like other nineteenth-century Christians, Latter-day

Saints were invested in proving their respectability and their fitness as citizens. Their missionary work among Native Americans became part of their argument for their whiteness and place within American society.

Native Americans, Family, and the Book of Mormon

Although the Book of Mormon would eventually encompass the history of multiple generations and would purport to be a history of the Americas, it began as a family story. According to the text, a man named Lehi received a vision telling him to flee the destruction of Jerusalem. He also learned that two of his children would fall away from God, and in so doing, curse their descendants with dark skin. Lehi begged his children "to hearken to his words" and "keep the commandments of the Lord."[71] His sons, however, refused to do so. Instead, they turned away from God. The Book of Mormon describes their progeny as "a blood-thirsty people" who have become convinced of their own righteousness and victimhood.[72] Rather than recognizing their kinship with Lehi's other descendants, they "have an eternal hatred towards [them]" and try to murder them.[73] The story of this family became influential among the Latter-day Saints and affected how members understood Native Americans.

Although early Latter-day Saints saw the Book of Mormon as a Native American history, the text foregrounded white, middle class understandings of the family.[74] Native Americans frequently embraced understandings of kinship that extended beyond the nuclear family. In Speaking of Indians, for example, the Dakota scholar Ella Deloria describes a complicated understanding of kinship within her community in which no one is "unattached" to the other people. "The most solitary member," she writes, "was sure to have at least one blood relative, no matter how distant, through whose marriage connections he was automatically the relative of a host of people."[75] Latter-day Saints eventually embraced this more encompassing vision of the family through temple rituals and the development of polygamy. In the early 1830s, however, restoration theology focused on the nuclear family. This is particularly true in the Book of Mormon. Although the scripture follows the descendants of Lehi through multiple generations, it refuses to adopt a more inclusive vision of the family. The terms cousin, uncle, and aunt rarely, if ever, appear in the text. The text also highlights the relationship between fathers and sons. The Book of Mormon, for example, is named after a father who commands his son to complete the record of God's dealings with the descendants of Lehi.

At one point the Book of Mormon chastises the righteous descendants of Lehi—which it calls the Nephites after one of his sons—for adopting polygamy without an explicit command from God. He condemns David and Solomon for having "many wives and concubines" before telling the people that "whoredoms are an abomination."[76]

The Book of Mormon gave Latter-day Saints the language to justify the removal and "civilizing" of Native Americans. They assumed that Native American family practices were part of their degradation and believed that their redemption would fundamentally transform their culture. White Latter-day Saints also believed that Native Americans needed to accept white methods of agriculture and live as small land-holders. As a result, they celebrated Andrew Jackson's Indian removal policies for helping to bring about "the happy time when Jacob shall go up into the house of Lord, to worship him in spirit and in truth, [and] to live in holiness."[77] In one pamphlet Parley P. Pratt admonished Native Americans that it was time to "lay down your weapons of war [and] cease to oppose the Gentiles in the gathering of your various tribes." He then told his imagined Indian readers that U.S. Indian policy had been "foretold by your forefathers, ten thousand moons ago . . . the hand of your great God is in all this."[78] Pratt believed that Indian removal was divinely ordained. He was unable—or unwilling—to see the cultural loss, physical suffering, and political instability that Indian communities experienced because of Jackson's policies.[79] His autobiography described a group of Native Americans coming to accept the Book of Mormon and the changes that it would create in their lives. The chief tells Pratt and the other Latter-day Saint missionaries traveling with him that Native Americans would "cease to fight" and would "become one people" who could "cultivate the earth in peace" if they accepted the Book of Mormon as a history of their ancestors.[80] The vision that the chief outlines is like the agrarian vision that Latter-day Saints promoted to Native families.

The belief that Native Americans needed to be redeemed led Latter-day Saints to launch Indian missions. In 1830 Joseph Smith sent several missionaries to visit the Shawnee and Delaware people in what would become the states of Missouri and Kansas. The mission failed. The missionaries could not spend much time with the Indian communities and made little, if any, headway in convincing Native Americans to adopt the Book of Mormon as a sacred text. Latter-day Saint leaders, however, remained interested in the conversion of Native Americans. After the Oneida convert Lewis Dana arrived in Commerce in 1840, he traveled to Indian Territory where he preached to other Native American communities. Like the white missionaries, he had little success converting indigenous people. Throughout the 1840s, however, he symbolized the promise of their sacred scriptures concerning the descendants of Lehi for white Latter-day Saints. If an Oneida man had converted to the restored gospel, surely other Native people would be interested as well. The Northwestern Shoshone fulfilled the same role later in the nineteenth century, suggesting that the scriptures would be fulfilled despite the setbacks the Latter-day Saints had incurred.

There is some suggestion that white Latter-day Saints were to do more than serve as heralds to Native communities; they were also to marry Indian women. According to some sources, Joseph Smith received a revelation in July 1831 commanding Latter-day Saints "to take unto [them] wives of the Lamanites and Nephites, that their posterity might become white delightsome and just."[81] Unfortunately, there is scant documentation of this revelation. Most of the details come from an 1861 reminiscence of W. W. Phelps. Written thirty years after the fact, the document is heavily influenced by the intervening history of the Saints, which included marriages between white Latter-day Saints and Native Americans. There is little contemporary evidence to support this claim. In 1831, however, an Ohio newspaper printed a letter claiming that Smith had received a revelation telling Latter-day Saints missionaries to make a "matrimonial alliance" with American

Indians.[82] Together, these documents suggest that early Latter-day Saint missionaries would marry indigenous women. While it is possible they believed that these marriages would civilize the women that they married, the evidence is thin.

White Latter-day Saints were ambivalent about the marriages that occurred between white male Saints and indigenous women. Benjamin F. Grouard, an American shipwright who had traveled to the Tuamotus Islands in the southern Pacific Ocean, married an indigenous woman named Tearo after his first wife failed to answer his letters. Their marriage was short-lived, as she died soon after giving birth to a daughter.[83] He remarried a Native woman named Nahina and brought her to the United States in the 1850s. Her life there was difficult. Many of the white women among the San Bernardino Saints considered her unkempt and savage. Eventually, Nahina decided to return to the Pacific. Other Latter-day Saints missionaries who married indigenous women had similar difficulties, even if they did not ultimately choose to separate their wives from their children.

Much of the discomfort white Latter-day Saints felt toward these marriages related to wider discourses within American culture about interracial marriage. The historian Ann McGrath has called marriages between Native Americans and white settlers "illicit love." She argues that these marriages transgressed community and familial norms even when they were not explicitly illegal. Because the state formally recognized these relationships, they raised questions about inheritance, legitimacy, and national identity that "casual sex" did not.[84] The discomfort white Americans felt about interracial marriage extended to the Pacific. White men who abandoned whaling ships to live among indigenous communities in the nineteenth century were viewed as suspect, if slightly exotic, figures when they returned to the United States and Europe. Women had a difficult time reintegrating into white society. Their very presence in the Pacific seemed to name them as prostitutes and loose women.[85]

The Book of Mormon enshrined many of these tensions. In 2 Nephi 5: 21–25, God curses the Lamanites with dark skin for their transgressions. The text contains a suggestion that dark skin is repugnant. According to

Nephi, God gave the Lamanites dark skin so that the Nephites would not find them sexually "enticing." God tells Nephi and his people that the Lamanites will be "loathsome unto thy people" until "they shall repent of their iniquities." He castigates anyone who would have children with the Lamanites, telling Nephi that any "seed" that joined with theirs would be "cursed even with the same cursing." At times, however, the Book of Mormon seems to empathize with Lamanite women. Mosiah condemns the priests of King Noah for kidnapping twenty-four Lamanite women as they sang and danced.[86] Jacob 3: 7–8 condemned the Nephites for failing to treat their wives with as much care and love as the Lamanites demonstrated with theirs. "Behold," the text begins, "their husbands love their wives, and their wives love their husbands; and their husbands and their wives love their children." It then shames the Nephites with a rhetorical question: "Wherefore, how much better are you than they, in the sight of your great Creator? Oh my brethren, I fear, that unless ye shall repent of your sins that their skins will be whiter than yours, when ye shall be brought with them before the throne of God."

The continued indifference of Native Americans to proselytizing led white Saints to become cynical about the possibility that they would be redeemed from what white Latter-day Saints saw as "savagery." Many Native Americans also found Latter-day Saint beliefs bewildering. The claim that the history of their ancestors had been recorded in a language they could not read (reformed Egyptian) likely alienated many Native American communities. They had their own origin stories that had nourished their communities for generations. Some who did convert to the restored gospel in the nineteenth century probably saw their conversion as a method of allying themselves with the Church of Jesus Christ of Latter-day Saints. They hoped that doing so would provide them with a measure of protection against the encroachment of white settlers.[87] They may have also interpreted Latter-day Saint promises of whiteness in a way removed from ideas of skin color. As I discuss in chapter 6, Latter-day Saints staged a parade at Fort Supply in 1856 in which a group of Native American men carried a banner saying, "We shall yet become a white and delightsome people." The speeches that some of the Native participants gave immediately afterward suggest that they saw whiteness as being as much about agriculture and access to food as skin color.[88] In Hawai'i, the position of the church outside of official Protestant Christianity allowed Latter-day Saints missionaries to stand against colonialism in a way that other American missionaries could not. The restored gospel became a way for Polynesian converts to reassert an indigenous identity and critique the excesses of state-sponsored Protestantism.[89]

Although some American Indians did come to believe in the restoration, many white Latter-day Saints came to see them as antagonists. Conversion also rarely provided Native communities with protection against white encroachment on their lands. White Latter-day Saints frequently formed new communities on Native land, inciting violent encounters that only deepened the uncertainties white Saints had about the role of American Indians within their faith. In the sermons that he delivered from the 1850s, Brigham Young continued to identify Native Americans as Lamanites. At times he suggested that Latter-day Saints should adopt a different course than other white Americans had in their relationships with American Indians. In one sermon, he told the congregation that if they had treated the Native communities that surrounded them with benevolence, "There never would have been a single difficulty."[90] At other times, however, he bristled with hostility, lamenting that they were "fallen in every respect, in habits, custom, flesh, spirit, blood, desire." In response to news that the militia that the Latter-day Saints had formed had executed several Ute men, he expressed approval. In a message to a Saint living nearby, he wrote a solemn warning for Native peoples: *"Let it be peace with them or extermination."*[91]

Ironically, Young's statement used similar language as former Missouri governor Lilburn Boggs in his "Extermination Order," which expelled Latter-day Saints from the state. In September 1857 Young had given a speech in the Salt Lake City bowery condemning non-Mormons for their treatment of Latter-day Saints:

I have been driven from place to place; my brethren have been driven, my sisters have been driven; we have been scattered and peeled, and every time without any provocation upon our part, only that we were united, obedient to the laws of the land, and striving to worship God. Mobs repeatedly gathered against this people, but they never had any power to prevail until Governors issued their orders and called out a force under the letter of the law, but breaking the spirit, to hold the "Mormons" while infernal scamps cut their throats. I have had all that before me through the night past, and it makes me too angry to preach . . . they are organizing their forces to come here, and protect infernal scamps who are anxious to come and kill whom they please, destroy whom they please, and finally exterminate the "Mormons."[92]

The speech came in the middle of a horrific war between white Latter-day Saints and their Ute neighbors. The violence that he was willing to unleash with the word "extermination," however, is notable. Young and other Latter-day Saint leaders knew what it was like to be on the receiving end of an extermination order. They had watched as mobs had attacked their leaders and had raped their wives. Faced with the Native American resistance, however, Latter-day Saints came to see them as a people who needed to assimilate or be removed violently.[93]

The Book of Mormon provided Latter-day Saints with a justification for doing so. The scripture told the story of the Gadianton robbers, a secret organization that attacked Nephite settlements. It described them as "infest[ing] the land" and portrayed their destruction as a righteous deed.[94] In 1851 Young explicitly compared Native Americans to this group and told the people of Parowan, Utah, that they needed "to have sufficient men there to be secure from the children of the Gadianton robbers who had infested the mountains for more than a thousand years and had lived by plundering all the time."[95] In the 1830s and '40s, the Book of Mormon had provided Latter-day Saints with texts that they could use to argue for the centrality of Native Americans to God's story. By the 1850s, however, the Saints sometimes drew upon its language to understand what they saw as the degradation of Native people and their refusal to convert to the gospel. The Book of Mormon could be used to name Native Americans "a chosen people." Yet it could also be used to justify their extermination.[96]

Latter-day Saints struggled to reconcile the tensions within their faith throughout the nineteenth century. The revelations that Joseph Smith received encouraged them to see God as a figure that was active within history. They believed that God gave individuals revelation. They also, however, believed in the importance of and valued religious experience that imparted knowledge. This emphasis on reason allowed the Saints to distance themselves from the figure of the "Mormon." It also, however, marginalized women and people of color. Although the Book of Mormon foregrounded the history of Native Americans, it contained passages that allowed white Latter-day Saints to label indigenous people as savages. Latter-day Saints would at once name American Indians as God's chosen people and belittle their culture, beliefs, and heritage. The ability to transform the way that Native Americans lived became a part of the Latter-day Saints' argument for respectability.

The history of Latter-day Saint missionary work is integral to understanding their relationships with other Americans. It also allows us to see how Latter-day Saints engaged contemporary discussions about the relationship between the family and respectability. Latter-day Saints distanced themselves from accusations that they had embraced the faith out of delusion. They saw the priesthood as a method for disciplining the faith and ensuring that the community they were constructing corresponded to the dictates of God. They also believed that it was their job to educate Native people about their relationship to the restoration. Far from accepting that Native Americans might have their own understanding of God, they encouraged them to turn away from their previous traditions and embrace the gospel. They saw the traditions of Native Americans as degraded remnants of a great past, not as things that were valuable in their own right. Nineteenth-century Latter-day Saints saw themselves as being on the vanguard of Christianity. Far from rejecting Protestant ideas of redemption, race, and respectability, they saw their faith as fulfilling them. This chapter has offered readers a general introduction to the theology of Latter-day Saints and their position in nineteenth-century American society. The following chapters chart the contradictions, lacunae, and tensions that developed as the Latter-day Saints evolved from a small community on the Mississippi to a "Great Basin Kingdom."[97]

CHAPTER 2

THE BONDS BETWEEN SISTERS

In 1879 Emma Smith died in Nauvoo, Illinois, at the age of seventy-four. According to archaeological evidence, her children clothed her body in a "brown silk dress" and buried her near the unmarked grave of her first husband.[1] It is impossible to read about Emma's life and death and not feel sympathy for her. Her husband's calling as a prophet forced her to live as a kind of perpetual refugee. As Latter-day Saints fled homes in Ohio, Missouri, and Illinois, Emma constantly feared the violence that local militias and law enforcement officials might wreak upon her family. The resulting poverty may have affected her ability to bear living children. Emma lost child after child to stillbirth or illness throughout her life. In 1828 she bore a son with severe physical disabilities. She named the child after her husband's brother, connecting him to the Smith's family legacy and to the emerging church. Despite her attempt to bind him to her family, she could not save his life. A little less than three years later, she gave birth to twins who only lived a few hours. In 1832 an adopted son died when a crowd assaulted her sleeping husband and forced Emma to flee with the child and his sister. The child, already sick with measles, likely died from exposure.[2] Two more of her sons died before they were a year old. As she mourned her children, her husband bound additional women to himself as wives. Emma vacillated between embracing the expansive theological vision the church offered and demanding that her husband forsake polygamy. For her, the restored gospel was as full of pain as it was possibility.

Historians of the Latter-day Saints have often emphasized the vast potential that the restoration's early theology held for women. Female Latter-day Saints would progress eternally with their husbands in the afterlife, gaining "knowledge upon knowledge," "precept upon precept," and thrilling as new worlds opened to them.[3] The instability of the early church, however, meant that women were often subjected to gendered violence and poverty. In 1843 Addison Pratt left his wife Louisa to serve as a missionary in the Pacific Islands. Just a few years earlier a militia had attacked a community of Saints in Caldwell County, Missouri. Several men retreated to a blacksmith's shop, where they hoped to defend their community, while their wives and children hid in the nearby woods.[4] Addison's decision to travel throughout the Pacific Islands as a missionary, proclaiming the gospel to the "islands of the sea" and "foreign lands," meant that Louisa had to deal with the violence that beset the Latter-day Saints on her own.[5] She lived as though she were a "widow," subsisting on whatever money she could obtain or earn.[6]

When the time came for Addison to depart, Louisa accompanied him to the steamboat with their children. She described the scene in her memoir, commenting that one of their daughters was "inconsolable." She lamented that her attempts to calm her child were unsuccessful and indeed only made her cries "more piteous." The girl believed that "her father would never return."[7] His call to the Pacific must have seemed like a call to the grave. Like many families of Latter-day Saint missionaries, they received few letters and those that did arrive were spaced by months or years. The length of Addison's mission was also uncertain. He might labor for a few years or decades. Addison's family feared that his assignment would mean burial in a shroud weighted with rocks at sea or an unmarked grave on an unknown island.

Other female Latter-day Saints shared her difficulties. Mary Fielding was forced to rely on others for food and kindness when her brother decided to travel to Great Britain as a missionary. Beyond missionary work,

Latter-day Saint women endured poverty and were asked to share their husbands. Nancy Lampson Holbrook traveled with her husband with two small daughters to Ohio and then Missouri. According to Andrea Radke-Moss, she was forced to wash their clothes in a river and boil them to try to remove the dirt. She later developed cholera.[8] Emma Smith was famously asked to share her husband with other women, discovering after multiple stillbirths that several of her friends had secretly married her husband.

Latter-day Saint theology emphasized the importance of the family. By the 1840s it promised believers that their families could be bound together in the eternities. The relationships that individuals formed with members of their immediate family also gave them access to the priesthood. Latter-day Saints also used the proprieties of their families to defend themselves against accusations of immorality and to promote the gospel. White Protestants had heard rumors about the sexual practices of Latter-day Saints by the mid-nineteenth century. The respectability of individual families allowed Latter-day Saints to point to these individuals as evidence that the restored gospel promoted virtue rather than licentiousness. Although Latter-day Saint missionaries originally traveled without their families, their families also provided evidence of their moral turpitude. Latter-day Saint families became examples of the truthfulness of the gospel both inside and outside of the United States.

The realities of everyday life, however, frequently threatened to undo family bonds. While the restoration offered women an opportunity to ensure that familial relationships extended beyond death, conversion disrupted the lives of individual families. As individuals gathered with the Latter-day Saints, they left behind their mothers, fathers, siblings, and sometimes even spouses to do so. Missionary work meant that even those whose families had joined the Latter-day Saint community experienced periods of separation.

The instability of Latter-day Saint families encouraged women to form alternative kinship networks. Women often found that they needed to rely on their female family members and friends for support. The secrecy surrounding the practice of polygamy, however, undermined their ability to do so. Although polygamy eventually became an important aspect of Latter-day Saint identity in the nineteenth century, the practice was not public in Nauvoo. Individual women who married Latter-day Saint leaders were expected to keep their marital status secret. Instead of publicly claiming their husbands, they frequently continued to live with their parents. Female Latter-day Saints often did not know the names of all the women their husbands had married. The resulting climate of distrust made women vulnerable to sexual slander while they struggled to support themselves in the absence of husbands and fathers.

The restoration at once created and foreclosed opportunities for women. Deprived of the economic support that their husbands would have offered them, female Latter-day Saints created societies for each other's relief, nursed each other's children, and cared for each other's bodies. The intimacy that resulted sustained them in difficult times. However, the religion also limited women's ability to form close relationship with each other. Studying the theological prescriptions for the emotional lives of families and the reactions that female Latter-day Saints recorded to their husbands' absences in their diaries, personal correspondence, and public speech allows us to imagine how the Saints grappled with the instability of the family. Emphasizing the complex experiences of Latter-day Saint women in this period also recasts our understanding of the church's missionary work. Latter-day Saints like Addison Pratt and Joseph Fielding were only able to preach throughout the world because their female relatives endured poverty in their absence.

The Family in the Restored Gospel

The Latter-day Saint investment in the family was part of a wider change in American culture in the nineteenth century. Although descriptions of good wives in the seventeenth and eighteenth centuries had portrayed them as affectionate, understandings of marriage among white, middle-class Protestants in the early nineteenth century emphasized the importance of love in forming suitable matches.[9] Although it is easy to caricature the Victorian family as a sexless institution, contemporary understandings of marriage centered on romantic love. The historian Karen Lystra has analyzed correspondence between lovers in the nineteenth century to understand their expectations of each other and marriage. In a letter to his beloved, a man named Eldred Simkins wrote that he could not think of a better way to spend his Sunday evening than "speaking to her whom I love more than all the world."[10] In another letter, a woman tells her boyfriend that "my heart craves the sound of your voice tonight and will not be satisfied." A final man writes after reading a letter from his lover that if he "could . . . have taken a delicious kiss from your lips I should have been almost too happy."[11] Lystra's analysis suggests that these letters were not unique. People frequently wrote of the physical and emotional passions that they felt in the decades surrounding the Civil War.

This marked emphasis on emotional relationships threatened to cause American couples to turn inward and focus their emotional energy on each other rather than the wider community. American understandings of romantic love, however, emphasized its transformative quality. Lystra demonstrates that people believed the emotions they experienced in their relationships drew them closer to God. Simkins told his lover that thoughts of her had made his mind "finer and brighter." It had also turned him toward the divine as he became "happy and grateful to the Great Creator for his many, but most undeserved blessings."[12] Instead of causing him to become more self-centered, Simkins believed that the love he experienced had enlarged his sense of charity.

Restoration theology drew upon this image of marriage in wider American culture as inherently elevated. In his descriptions of the material afterlife, the Latter-day Saint intellectual Parley P. Pratt emphasized the role that the family would play in creating new worlds. He published a work in 1855 in which he imagined that an individual would be "radiant with the effulgence of light" after their exaltation and their "bosom [would be] glowing with all the confidence of conscious innocence." He implied that they would then be "prompted by eternal benevolence and charity . . . to fill countless millions of worlds" with "begotten sons and daughters, and . . . bring them through all the gradations of progressive being, to inherit immortal bodies and eternal mansions."[13] This vision of the eternities was based in the unions of men and women, whose eternal bonds provided opportunities for other beings to be born and then exalted.

Latter-day Saints saw the divine within this description of the eternities and adopted its imagery to describe their own marriages. The English convert Sarah Griffith Richards wrote to her husband that their marriage was "the commencement of a love as enduring as the eternities" that would "not tire of its object." Instead, they would "become more sacredly and strongly united as the countless ages of eternal lives [rolled] on in succession."[14] For her, marriage was fundamentally about establishing a relationship that would allow its participants to progress intellectually and become more godlike as they shed their earthly cares. The Saints believed that individuals would not achieve godliness unless it was through the bonds of marriage.

By the early 1840s, Latter-day Saint leaders argued that marriages performed outside of the church would be invalid after the resurrection unless they had been "sealed" together "by the Holy Spirit of Promise."[15] As a result, Latter-day Saints sought to consecrate their marriages in the temple or endowment house. Doing so was the only way to ensure that they would participate in the glories that the Restoration promised them. Civil marriages would be rendered invalid in the afterlife unless a Latter-day Saint leader had sealed husband and wife in a temple ceremony.[16] The requirement that individuals be married to fully participated in the ever-expanding afterlife of the Saints meant that breaking of these unions had eternal consequences.

The restoration's emphasis on the family became a part of its emotional appeal. Female Latter-day Saints saw the family not simply as a reflection of divine love but as a mechanism through which they would be saved and eventually perfected. The theological musings in Richards's letters reflect the deeper emotional weight that female Saints were asked to place on their relationships with their husbands.

However, it is important to remember that Latter-day Saint conceptions of the family did not focus solely on marital bonds. Some historians have argued that the purpose of sealing in the 1840s and 1850s was as much about creating bonds between men as it was on expanding marital relationships. Sealing was a religious ritual that could create new family bonds or solidify existing ones in the here and now, in the eternities, or any combination of the two. After the early 1840s it was possible for individuals whose biological kin had not converted to the church to be ritually adopted into families that had. These adoptions had social as well as eternal consequences. As historian Gordon Irving has pointed out, adopted sons were expected to "give [their] fathers the benefit of their labor while [adopted fathers] offered their children not only some measure of security in the next world but counsel and direction in this world as well."[17] Tensions remained throughout Latter-day Saint history between biological and ritual relationships. According to historian Jonathan Stapley, the Nauvoo temple listed sealings to biological children separately from adoptive sealings. For example, Winslow Farr and Olive Hovey Freeman adopted eight people into their family, while John Taylor and Leonora Cannon adopted twenty-seven.[18]

Although these adoptions expanded the restoration's notions of kinship, they did not completely undo its emphasis on the heterosexual family. If individuals wanted to be joined to a Latter-day Saint kinship network, they could do so only by being bound to a married couple as a child or by becoming a plural wife. Individuals could also create kinship ties by agreeing to have their daughters sealed to a church or community leader. There was no mechanism, however, through which same-sex relationships could be made eternal outside of a parent-child relationship. Men could not be sealed to each other as brothers, nor women as sisters. For relationships to be incorporated into the kingdom of God, they had to be made legible and incorporated into the preexisting hierarchies found within the nuclear family.

The ability of individuals to remake their families through sealing ordinances did not lessen the importance of missionary work. Instead, the emphasis that the Latter-day Saints placed on family bonds compelled individuals to seek out their family members to convince them of the truth of the gospel. Early Latter-day Saints believed that God would soon bring judgment on humanity. Visited by earthquakes, plagues, and wars, nonbelievers would come to regret their decision not to embrace the Lord's messengers and be baptized into his church.[19] Love and duty drove early Latter-day Saints to seek out their families to warn them about coming judgment. They also worried that they would be held accountable for the sins of those they failed to reach out of willfulness.[20] Phebe Peck urged her friend not "to regect annother call[.] You have been called to repent of your sins and obey the gospel."[21]

Latter-day Saints also longed to be reunited with their family members in the eternities and feared eternal separation from those who rejected the gospel. This desire can be seen in the objects they created. As historian Laurel Thatcher Ulrich has pointed out, the diaries of Wilford Woodruff, who would become the fourth president of the church, are elaborately decorated with motifs taken from genealogical registers, commonly used schoolbooks, and even ornamentation he saw on furniture. She argues that these drawings were not unreflective doodling. Instead, they represented his concern over the unrepentant state of many of his family members. On one particularly poignant page, Woodruff recorded the death of his brother Asahel: "O Asahel among strangers thy lot was cast. Among them thou hast fallen & found a grave."[22] Ulrich argues that this verse and the coffin that surrounds Asahel's name is evidence of Woodruff's anxiety over his brother's eternal fate.[23]

As Woodruff aged he became more and more concerned with baptizing the dead, a ritual that Smith had developed in 1840 as a way for believers to redeem family who had not received the gospel during their lifetimes. It is likely that one of the hundreds of people that Woodruff baptized vicariously during his lifetime was his brother Asahel.[24] When his plural wife Emma gave birth to a son in 1863, he named the boy Asahel. Asahel's name marked him as a living connection to the past. Woodruff, however, could not undo the past. His journals reminded him of the people he had lost even as they celebrated the conversion of some of his relatives.

The autograph books that female Latter-day Saints created served a similar purpose. The autograph album of Woodruff's wife Phebe is filled with poems reminding her that "in our world of sin and sorrow . . . the puresest [sic] joys are fleet."[25] The emphasis on the death and the ephemeral nature of life, however, is frequently accompanied by an admonition to look forward to the day individuals would "meet at last . . . On the heavenly Canaan's shore."[26] Historians such as Catherine Allgor and Erica Dunbar have highlighted the role that autograph books played in fashioning a white, middle-class identity in the nineteenth century.[27] They were equally important for marginalized groups who sought to claim respectability for themselves by demonstrating their ability to enact a particular form of womanhood.[28] In reading and writing admonitions to remember the fleeting nature of joy and the importance of looking toward a heavenly reunion Latter-day Saints taught each other how to think about their relationship to God at the same moment that they reminded their friends not to forget absent loved ones. Phebe's autograph book demonstrates how early Latter-day Saints thought about their families in light of their own conversion to the restored gospel. In stressing the future re-creation of the family, Latter-day Saints did not lessen the importance of family bonds in this life. Instead, the church encouraged its members to rejoin and remake families so that the composition of these units would mirror those that would be created at the resurrection. The autograph book created a physical representation of the familial and friendship ties that an individual had forged in this life and hoped to enjoy in the next.

The realities of the early Latter-day Saint community, however, made it difficult for women to enjoy family life. Violence, combined with the church's missionary work, removed men from their households and left women unprotected. Mary Fielding Smith was one such example. Before converting to the restoration, she had emigrated from England to Canada, where she lived with her brother Joseph and her sister Mercy. The deep, affectionate relationship she had with her siblings allowed her to cultivate an intimate domesticity that would have otherwise been denied to her. In 1836 she converted to the Church of Jesus Christ of Latter-day Saints with her siblings. She immigrated to Kirtland, Ohio, a year later. As a woman in her mid-thirties, Mary was well past the age when she would have been expected to marry and establish a household of her own. In living with her brother and sister, she created a family based not on sexual intimacy but on longtime fondness and filial responsibility.[29] She submitted to baptism not as a single woman but as part of the household that she had organized with her siblings.

Mary soon discovered that conversion to the Church of Jesus Christ of Latter-day Saints could tear families apart as easily as it could unite them. In June 1837 her brother Joseph left for a mission to Great Britain. That same year her sister Mercy married a man named Robert Thompson. Although Mary hoped that her brother's mission would bring the rest of her family into the fold and she was likely happy about her sister's marriage, her siblings' new ventures also left her alone. Mercy's husband was soon called as a missionary. He took his wife with him to Canada, leaving Mary to provide for herself as a single woman for the first time. This would have been a difficult task in favorable financial conditions, but in 1837 the Latter-day Saints faced an economic crisis. The growth the community had enjoyed throughout the 1830s was not sustainable. An economic collapse that year led to widespread discontent. As much as a third of the church's leaders became disaffected.[30] Mary struggled to survive in this climate. At one point she agreed to work for a month at a school but soon found herself "at liberty or without imployment."[31] She asked her sister to pray for her, writing: "I have no doubt but you have many trials, but I am inclined to think you have not quite so much to endure as I have."[32] Ultimately, she became a boarder in the house of Mary Dort.

Part of her difficulty lay in her status as a single woman and in the fact that her brother and sister had left her. Unmarried women relied on kinship networks to provide them with access to resources and employment in the nineteenth century.[33] In moving first to Canada and then to Kirtland, Mary and her siblings had severed the relationship that usually would have provided them with support in times of need. The demands that the restored gospel placed upon church members for missionary work further alienated Mary from her family, calling her brother from home to labor in distant lands while she struggled to find work in an already taxed labor market. Mary's plight was like that of other single women in the United States and Great Britain. The creation of a white, middle-class identity in the early nineteenth century relied on the elevation of motherhood as an ideal form of femininity. Women who remained unmarried and childless were marginalized both financially and socially. In the words of historian Eileen Yeo, "Single women were fated to suffer the shriveling of their wombs through disuse and to become masculinized hags."[34] Although Mary found comfort in a gospel that offered her an opportunity to reunite her family and mirrored her understanding of the scriptures, converting to the Church of Jesus Christ of Latter-day Saints had placed her in a precarious financial position.

Other women faced similar difficulties. When her husband Orson was sent on a mission to Europe in 1839, Sarah Miranda Pratt was living in what one historian has called "a fourteen-by-sixteen-foot 'shanty.'"[35] Her daughter Lydia died just days before her husband left her with their surviving child and no viable income.[36] Brigham Young also left his wife Mary Ann in dire circumstances that year. When he departed for his mission in the British Isles in September, he worried that she would find it difficult to pay bills or provide food for their family and was forced to settle their debts. It was unlikely that Mary Ann could perform much labor. She had, after all, just given birth to a little girl they called Alice.[37]

In addition to poverty, female Latter-day Saints were subject to sexual assault. Rumors of rape accompanied the stories of their male counterparts being torn to pieces by non-Mormon mobs. According to Andrea Radke-Moss, women experienced a kind of gendered violence during the Missouri period of Latter-day Saint history.[38] Although some of the stories contained within the petitions that Latter-day Saints later made for redress may have been exaggerated, there are suggestions that women were sometimes sexually brutalized during attacks on the Saints. For example, family histories suggest that a woman named Hannah Kinney Johnstun bore a child out of wedlock shortly after being violently raped in Missouri.[39] It is only possible to reconstruct Johnstun's story through the memories of her family members and their descendants. At one meeting of the Mormon History Association, one of Johnstun's descendants gave an impassioned presentation about her life and the pain that the family had endured because of their silence about her rape and subsequent pregnancy.[40]

Long after Latter-day Saints fled Missouri and Illinois, rumors circulated about the atrocities that some of them had experienced. The Utah artist Alice Merrill Horne remembered sitting with her elderly grandmother and listening to the women who had participated in the heroic events of early church history spoke in "whispered" tones about their experiences.[41] At one of these gatherings she heard about Eliza R. Snow, a plural wife of the prophet Joseph Smith, being gang raped in Missouri. Horne believed that the abuse had left the prophetess and poet infertile.[42]

Some historians have raised doubts about the veracity of the account; others, however, have asked what evidence would be expected of the rape of a middle-class woman over a century after it occurred. For Radke-Moss, the historian who first publicized the account, doubting the shared memories of female Latter-day Saints only compounds the silence they were forced to endure during their lives. She points out that leaders of the Latter-day Saints were willing to speak of the violation of female members as a group, but shame and propriety kept them from naming individual women who had been abused. Though the Saints were more than willing to use rape as a political tool, individual women could never receive restitution or speak openly of their anguish. Consequently, rumors and whispers may be the only remaining evidence.[43]

Many historians emphasize the empowerment that women found in the restored gospel. They point to the evidence that female Latter-day Saints continued to find solace in the Church of Jesus Christ of Latter-day Saints even as they were "called to pass through so many trials and afflictions."[44] A woman named Melissa Dodge, for example, wrote a letter to her brother and sister telling them that her family took "the Spoiling of our goods Joyfully noing thear is a god in heaven" and that God would soon vindicate them.[45] Dodge's descriptions of her life serve as a reminder that female Latter-day Saints did not necessarily see poverty and violence as evidence that the restoration was not the work of God. Instead, they believed that God would ultimately redeem the faithful community from its suffering. It is also important, however, not to pass too lightly over the difficulties that women among the early Latter-day Saints faced. Although the restoration offered women a vision of an eternity in which they would reunite with their husbands and watch as

ever-expanding worlds unfolded, it also required their husbands to temporarily abandon them to spread the gospel throughout the earth. Many
Latter-day Saint women turned to their female relatives to help feed their
families. These alternative kinship networks made the missionary work of
Latter-day Saints possible by providing for the families their husbands left
behind. They also, however, undermined restoration's theology emphasis
on heterosexual coupledom by providing women the opportunity to
forge bonds outside of those the Latter-day Saint hierarchy sanctioned.

Alternative Kinship Relations

In the fall of 1837 Jerusha Smith, the wife of Joseph Smith's brother
Hyrum, called her children to her bedside to "bid them . . . farewell."[46]
She had been pregnant with their fifth child when her husband was
appointed to Missouri. It was likely a difficult birth. Afterward, Jerusha
slipped into an illness from which she never recovered.[47] According
to the official history of the church, her last act was to ask one of her
children to tell their father "that the Lord has taken your mother home
and left you for him to take care of."[48]

Hyrum remarried only a few short months after his wife's death.
Members of the Kirtland community may have been upset at the short
amount of time between the two events; Jerusha's body had only recently
been laid in the Kirtland Mills Burying Ground and her daughter was
less than three months old.[49] According to stories that circulated within
the Smith family, however, the marriage may have been the result of
divine revelation. At the time of Jerusha's death, Hyrum had recently
been called to the First Presidency, the church's highest governing
body. His responsibilities were enormous. Mary Fielding was thirty-six
years old and childless. In marrying her, Hyrum found a mother for his
children. The marriage also offered a home to a woman who otherwise
would have lived alone and outside of the kinship networks that usually
sustained women. No contemporary record of the revelation exists,
however. Whatever the ultimate reason, Mary and Hyrum married on
December 24, 1837.[50]

The union should have brought Mary into the heart of the Latter-day

Saint community. Her marriage to Hyrum made her a part of the family of the prophet. The economic difficulty that Kirtland experienced, however, was only one of the obstacles that she encountered in her marriage. Hyrum's position within the church required him to be frequently absent—including trips to Far West, a Latter-day Saint settlement hundreds of miles away in Missouri. The success of the Saints in Missouri had excited locals who resented the presence of a millenarian, theocratic community in their midst. Local Missouri farmers, politicians, and businessman often hounded the farms and homes of Latter-day Saints, threatening men with physical violence and, as we have seen, endangering women with the threat of sexual assault. On August 6, 1838, members of a Missouri militia attacked the Saints to prevent them from voting, which they feared would transform the state into a theocracy. Other outbreaks of violence occurred. To prevent further bloodshed, Smith surrendered to the Missouri militia. Hyrum agreed to accompany him to prison and would remain in a jail in Liberty, Missouri, for several months.[51]

Hyrum's absences placed a great strain on his fledging relationship with Mary and eventually led to misunderstandings between the two. When he agreed to accompany his brother to jail, Mary was several months pregnant. She gave birth just days after his arrest. As Mary lay in bed, her body racked with fever, her sister Mercy tended to her. Mercy also took Mary's newborn child to her breast, nursing the boy along with her own daughter who was just five months old.[52] Hyrum knew little of his wife's difficulties and began to wonder why she had not written him. Eventually, his despair at not having heard any news turned to anger. In March 1839 he wrote to her that even if she had "no feelings for [him] as a husband" she could have sent "some information concerning the little babe or those little children that [lay] near [his] hart."[53]

The miscommunication between the two denied Mary the solace she could have found among the Latter-day Saints beyond her natal family. His comments made her feel isolated. She wrote in response that she could not "bear the thought of [his] having any such suspision and that he must be "unacquainted with the principles of [her] heart." After all, "reason, religion, and honor and every feeling of [her] heart" prohibited her from entertaining "such a thought" of abandoning her poor husband.[54] A few years later, she discovered that rumors circulating about her abilities as a mother had come from the lips of her husband, who accused her of being too strict with his children. Mary felt that she was far from being "an oppressive Step Mother" and had always acted as she thought best.[55] In letters to her husband, she tried desperately to fix their relationship and reassert her position as wife and mother.

Mary's sister supported her throughout these difficulties. When Mary decided that she wanted to visit Hyrum during his imprisonment in the Liberty jail, Mercy put her on a warm bed in a wagon. She nursed Mary son's Joseph F. as well as her own daughter throughout the journey.[56] The intimacy that developed between the two sisters sometimes made the Smith family uneasy. Don Carlos, Joseph Smith's youngest brother, had helped Mercy place Mary in the wagon. Just a month later he wrote a concerned letter to Joseph and Hyrum. After a few sentences about Mary's health, he wrote that, although he did not want to "disrespect" Mercy, he felt that "the family would do better without her than with her."[57] The phrasing of the sentence left its meaning ambiguous. It was possible to read the female pronouns as referring to either Mercy or Mary.[58] The ambiguity of this phrasing may have caused some misunderstandings between Hyrum and Mary. In a later apology, Don Carlos clarified that he had "no fault to find with Mary." He believed that had she been well and "had her own way, there in all probability [would have] been no call for the observations that I made in my letter to you."[59]

While the sisters' close relationship troubled the Smith family, as Don Carlos's letter suggests, mid-nineteenth-century American culture idealized relationships between women, especially sisters, seeing their willingness to sacrifice for each other as evidence of their character. Girls were encouraged to develop close emotional relationships with each other.[60] As a result, the letters they wrote each other were filled with declarations of their love. Jeannie Field Musgrove, for example, began a letter to her friend Sarah with the appellation: "Dear darling Sarah!" She continued the letter with pronouncements of her eternal affection. "How I love you," she wrote, "& how happy I have been! You are the joy of my life. . . . I cannot tell you how much happiness you gave me, nor how constantly it is all in my thoughts."[61] Another woman told her friend to "imagine [herself] kissed a dozen times." She wanted to put her arms around her and "love" her as "wives do their husbands."[62]

What seems to have bothered the Smith family, however, is that the two women had created an alternative family structure that challenged male authority over the household. The creation of the priesthood and the office of the patriarch had formalized male power within the Church of Jesus Christ of Latter-day Saints. Relations between women were an alternative locus of power outside of the channels that the church formally sanctioned. Mary also lived apart from her stepchildren for at least part of the time that Hyrum was imprisoned. The letter from Don Carlos to Hyrum and Joseph suggests that she did so because of ill health.[63] In one of her letters, Mary explained that she arranged to have a man who had expressed "a fixt determination" to free the captives deliver a note to Hyrum.[64] The man never made it to Hyrum, however. Never having any knowledge of the letter, her husband interpreted her silence as evidence of her lack of affection for him. Nineteenth-century Americans expected women to focus their care on their husbands. In this light, Mercy's wiliness to nurse her sister's son and to help her maintain the family economy may have seemed like an intrusion. After marriage, women were to shift their affections to their husbands. American and British novels often suggested that the intense emotional relationships that women developed with other women helped prepare them for the expectations of marriage. They learned to love through loving sisters and female friends.[65] Mary and Mercy's relationship was undoubtedly closer than most because they were sisters. Latter-day Saint women, however, frequently developed relationships with each other that were supportive and caring in nature. As we shall see in a later chapter, many of these relationships were formed through the church's Relief Society.

Disciplining Women

On March 17, 1842, Joseph Smith met with twenty women on the second floor of the Nauvoo Lodge. The meeting opened with singing: "The

Spirit of God like a fire is burning; The latter-day glory begins to come forth."[66] By the end of the meeting Smith had organized them into a Relief Society that aimed to "provoke the brethren to good works in looking to the wants of the poor" and provide charity to those in need of it.[67] When Ellen Douglas became so ill that she could not tend to her children after her husband's death, a member of the Relief Society went to her and asked what they could do. A woman named Ann came to her door a few days later with "such a present as I never received before."[68] Ellen estimated that the supplies they brought her "were worth as much as 30 shillings."[69] She was not the only woman who received aide from female Saints. Elizabeth Kirby permanently moved to Nauvoo shortly after the death of her husband, Francis, who had opposed her gathering with the Saints. Her husband's death gave Kirby the freedom to seek out a new religious community. In a reminiscence that she wrote later in life, Kirby recalled that she "spent a great part of my time sewing and washing and working for the sick."[70] Margaret Judd complained of the frequency with which her mother made her wash dishes for people who were ill. "I was only a little girl," she wrote, "but I could give a drink of water to the poor things burning with fever, also wash dishes and many other little chores . . . How I did hate it! Wasn't it *bad* enough to wash dishes at home, without going to the neighbors?"[71]

At meetings of the Relief Society, women presented the needs of their sisters and discussed how to meet them. On October 14, 1843, Sarah Smith mentioned to those present at a society meeting that "Sister Langdons family [was] sick and without food." Likewise, she noted, "Many of the sick . . . were getting worse with ague and were destitute . . . of food."[72] The society's members donated food and sewed clothing to serve the poor throughout the year.

The support that female Latter-day Saints offered each other extended beyond the temporal world. Although male Latter-day Saints would later claim the exclusive right to bless the bodies of the sick, women initially blessed each other's bodies for childbirth, healed their sisters of diseases, and laid hands upon their children's heads when they took ill. In Winter Quarters, Persis Young ministered to a woman who had recently given birth to a stillborn child and developed an infection afterward. According to the woman's remembrances, Persis "shook as though palsied" as she "laid her hands" on the woman's head and demanded that "every disease that had been, or was then, afflicting me [to leave], and commanded me to be made whole, pronouncing health and many other blessings upon me."[73]

The spiritual and physical labor that women performed for one another provided extra support when the structures that normally maintained the patriarchal family broke down due to disability or poverty. It also gave women opportunities to spread gossip or challenge overbearing husbands. Catherine Allgor has argued that the home served as an informal space of politics in the nineteenth century, one where women could disperse information about influential men and, through entertaining, could create spaces where business was contracted.[74]

One famous story involving domestic violence and gossip is the account of Emma Smith pushing a pregnant Eliza R. Snow down a flight of stairs. Emma reportedly confronted Eliza after seeing the latter woman kiss Joseph and sent her "tumbling," to use the words of one author.[75] Scholars who have examined the account have often focused on its accuracy (or lack thereof).[76] The story can also tell us, however, about women's gossip networks in Nauvoo. One of the sources for this story is the record of Mary Ann Barzee and John Boice, who married on May 7, 1840. Mary Ann remembered visiting a room that her sister-in-law claimed was where Joseph Smith "met in counsil with those women who he had sealed to him."[77] She also mentioned that Aidah Clements, whose son eventually married her daughter, told her that she had seen Emma push Eliza down the stairs. Aidah also told Mary Ann that Emma had "jirked [Joseph] by the collar and talked to him about going after other women."[78] These stories circulated among the Boice family as lore. Information about Joseph Smith and his relationship with Emma became bits of gossip passed between female kin. Other families likely shared similar stories. At times these pieces of information were innocuous. Depending on the situation, however, they could become political. The discord between the prophet and his wife could be used to discredit him in the eyes of the community.

The practice of polygamy eventually upended the relationships that had developed between female Latter-day Saints. Joseph Smith was reticent to publish his ideas about marriage. As a result, knowledge about polygamy in the 1830s and 1840s circulated as rumor and sexual innuendo. Individual women could not be sure who in the community was participating in plural marriage or if their brothers, sons, and even husbands had taken additional wives.[79] Preserving this secrecy required women to learn to speak of their lives in coded language. Zina Huntington, for example, veiled Joseph Smith in her journal using terms like "The Sanctified."[80] Secrecy and mistrust prevented women from developing the full-throated relationships with each other that characterized polygamy in Utah.

Emma knew of her husband's polygamy by 1842 or 1843, though she likely had suspicions much earlier. She used the Relief Society to suss out Joseph's misdeeds. In some ways her husband had given her the authority to do so. When Smith met with the small cadre of women in the Nauvoo Lodge, he had specifically charged them to help male members of the church by "correcting the morals and strengthening the virtues of the female community" so that the elders would not have to do so.[81] The Nauvoo judicial system eventually played a similar role, hearing cases about sexual immorality and intervening in the family lives of church members. The result was a legal system that brought the sex lives of female Latter-day Saints under increased scrutiny at the same moment that the church's hierarchy was expanding and redefining marriage.

It is unclear when Joseph Smith first received a revelation about polygamy, but he probably married a young woman named Fanny Alger in 1833. Emma had recently given birth to a son they called Joseph Smith III and was also caring for Julia Murdock, a young girl they had adopted a year or two earlier. Fanny lived with the family and may have helped Emma with household chores. It was not uncommon for sixteen- or seventeen-year-old girls to do so at the time. At some point, Joseph convinced Fanny to have sex with him.[82] Rumors circulated about the relationship for years afterward. In 1838 a man named Oliver Cowdery referred to the relationship between the two as a "dirty, nasty, filthy affair."[83] According to historian Richard Bushman, Joseph Smith's response was tepid. He "did not deny his relationship with Alger, but contended that he had never confessed to adultery."[84] Emma endured the rumors and their effect on her marriage. In 1836 Fanny ended her relationship with Joseph Smith and followed her parents to Indiana, where she met and married a non-Mormon man named Solomon Custer. They eventually owned a grocery store.[85] Her decision to sever the relationship did not end the stories that circulated about the liaison. In 1872 William McClellin wrote a letter to one of Emma's sons in telling him that his father had "committed an act with . . . a hired girl" decades earlier.[86] Anyone who has a passing familiarity with online discussions among Latter-day Saints about Joseph Smith's adoption of polygamy can verify that members still debate the nature of Fanny's relationship with Joseph and its meaning for the faith.

Smith did not take additional wives for several years after this relationship ended. By his death, however, he had been sealed to dozens of women. In these instances he tried to be more circumspect. Smith attempted to keep the sealings secret, rarely spending significant time with his plural wives and only telling a few of his closest followers about his revival of Old Testament polygamy. Many men and women in Nauvoo did not know that Smith and other church leaders practiced plural marriage. Despite the efforts of elite Latter-day Saints to conceal the practice, knowledge spread about their sexual practices. After his brother Don Carlos died from malaria in 1841, people whispered that Joseph had secretly wed his brother's wife Agnes.[87] Public protests of innocence did little to quell the gossip. In the meetings of the Relief Society, in parlors throughout the city, and in short, stolen conversations, men and women discussed the possibility that Joseph and other influential Latter-day Saints had taken multiple wives.

The rumors meant that women who did agree to be sealed to leaders had to be circumspect about the nature of their families. In 1841 Mercy's husband Robert died from a lung infection and possibly tuberculosis.[88] After her husband's death she sometimes slept at her sister's home; the two women likely shared the care of their children.[89] She eventually agreed to be sealed to Hyrum in 1843. The ceremony bound her to Hyrum during her lifetime and sealed her to Robert for the eternities.[90] It also tied her to Mary. For the Smith family this may have been an easy, if unconscious, solution to the problem of controlling the relationship between the two women. Hyrum's sealing to Mercy brought the women's relationship under his control due to his status as a member of the priesthood.

Mercy was not the only woman that Hyrum married. Three additional women were eventually sealed to him as wives—Catherine Phillipps, Lydia Dibble Granger, and Louisa Sanger.[91] Mercy's relationship with her sister provided her with a respectable reason for living in a married man's household.[92] Hyrum's other wives found it difficult to maintain their relationships with him. In an affidavit describing their relationship, Catherine wrote that she "lived with [Hyrum] as his wife" but was forced to move to St. Louis with her mother to avoid the animosity of those who opposed polygamy.[93] Although Catherine considered herself Hyrum's wife, she was forced to live apart from him. She moved to Salt Lake City after his death.[94]

Latter-day Saint leaders attempted to quell the growing suspicions among the community by bringing those who made accusations about polygamy to court for slander. After William Law accused Smith of trying to create a theocracy, Law was stripped of his position as a high councilor to Joseph Smith and excommunicated for apostasy.[95] Law's high position within the church did not protect him from prosecution; on the contrary, it may have made other Latter-day Saint leaders feel as though his punishment was inevitable once he made accusations against Smith. Allegations of sexual immorality threatened to undo the bonds that held the community together and expose its leaders as potential frauds. At the time of his excommunication, Law had already lost his faith in Joseph's prophetic ability and believed polygamy was a sin against God. He was not alone in his doubts about the practice. Although some Latter-day Saints saw polygamy as a divine institution, many rejected the idea that men should have more than one wife and considered the practice of polygamy evidence of depravity.

Accusations of sexual immorality intensified the church's efforts to control marriage and portray itself as a respectable institution. The church's missionary work and its claim to respectability rested on its ability to control individual families. Polygamy intensified the scrutiny that the church faced. Latter-day Saints did not respond by curtailing polygamous marriages for leaders. Instead, the Nauvoo judicial system disciplined Latter-day Saints who could not maintain order within their households. Wives who would not submit to their husbands' authority and men who used undue violence to subdue their wives could be disfellowshipped. A year before Law was excommunicated, Aidah Clements was brought before the High Council of the Church of Jesus Christ of Latter Day Saints for refusing "to abide the advice of her husband" in "some of his views in his temporal concerns."[96] In spite of previous court appearances suggesting that her husband Albert was physically abusive, the court counseled her to submit to her husband.[97] She ultimately agreed to submit to the ruling and "be in subjection to her husband according to the Scriptures." The court then gave her husband "instruction relative to his duty towards his wife."[98]

Aidah was not the only woman reprimanded for not submitting to her husband. According to court records, a woman named Mary Cook was charged with adultery after she abandoned her husband and married another man. Court testimony reveals a tempestuous relationship in which Mary told her husband that she would "be governed by no man." According to Cook's former husband, she "shamefully misuse[d] his children" and "threaten[ed] to use violence on him." For his part, he admitted he had "whiped her pretty sevearly" to control her.[99] They eventually decided to settle using the English folk custom of wife selling, in which a man ritually sold his wife to another man who then agreed to act as her husband and care for her.[100] According to the court, Mary "held it as a bargain," as did the man who purchased her. Although the court chastised Cook for whipping his wife, it was judged that he "had acted as well as could be expected under [the] circumstances."[101]

The court also tried to curtail extramarital sex. Elizabeth Rowe was brought before the Nauvoo High Council for her "unchristian-like conduct" which consisted of "having been caught in bed with a man not her husband at two different times." The court "decided that the hand of fellowship be withdrawn."[102] Theodore Turley, on the other hand, was charged with "romping and kissing the females and dancing" while traveling to Nauvoo but was allowed to remain a member of the church because he confessed his sins.[103]

By placing men and women who failed to maintain order within their homes or who had sex outside of marriage on trial, the church attempted to control domesticity and sexuality within Nauvoo. These trials allowed the Nauvoo judicial system to portray an image of respectability and decorum even as rumors about polygamy undermined church leaders' authority. In an environment in which sexuality and domesticity seemed unstable and particularly charged, the relationships between women were unusually important. The Nauvoo judicial system attempted to shore up the boundaries of marriage and ensure that individuals acted appropriately. Women who refused to follow their husband's counsel were brought to court and instructed in their duties. If they refused to submit to their husband's authority, ecclesiastical discipline could threaten their livelihood as well as their social position.

This emphasis on disciplining families created tension among the Latter-day Saints. In addition to finding themselves targets of violence from non-Mormons, women whose husbands left on missions could be subject to overtures from church leaders. When Sarah Marinda Pratt's husband Orson went on a mission, she claimed she was pressured by Joseph Smith to become one of his plural wives.[104] Marinda Johnson Hyde faced similar pressure. When her husband left on a mission to Jerusalem in the fall of 1841, she was forced to live "in a little log house" with "greased paper" for windowpanes. A few months later Smith claimed to have received a revelation commanding him to provide "a better place" for her and asked Ebenezer Robinson to house the small family. Some historians have read the revelation, which included the statement that Marinda should "hearken to the counsel of my servant Joseph in all things whatsoever he shall teach unto her," as including a reference to plural marriage. Whatever the meaning of that statement, she was sealed to Joseph the following spring.[105] Although Latter-day Saint leaders saw polygamy as divinely inspired and rejected the idea that it created disorder, others saw it as a form of sexual coercion.

The secrecy and tension surrounding polygamy undermined the bonds that female Latter-day Saints created during their husbands' absences. In Latter-day Saint theology, polygamy was a way to weld individuals together through the creation of an expansive kinship network. In practice, however, polygamy could destroy as well as create connections.

The overtures of Latter-day Saint leaders also marginalized female Latter-day Saints, who became the object of their desires. As Laurel Thatcher Ulrich has pointed out, the most vulnerable women were those who were "unattached" to husbands or fathers. Single women who no longer lived in their fathers' homes had to navigate the pressure to become a part of polygamous families while enduring intense scrutiny. Women frequently policed each other's behavior and reported on members that they believed had not upheld the community's standards.[106] If women refused leaders' sexual overtures, they risked being sidelined and gossiped about within the community. An Illinois newspaper printed a snippet in 1842 detailing the accusations Bennett was making about Joseph Smith. It mentioned that two men had heard Joseph Smith declare that Sarah was "a———from her mother's breast."[107] Although the joking style of the newspaper makes unlikely that Smith ever uttered the phase, the publication of rumors about Pratt would have made her life in Nauvoo more difficult. Women who decided to participate in polygamy fared no better. Unable to openly claim their husbands, they were forced to lie to their friends about their relationships and constantly feared exposure.

Ultimately, the position of women within the early Latter-day Saint community was uneasy. Female Latter-day Saints believed that the restored gospel promised them a future in which the ties that bound them to their friends and family would be made secure. In the here and now, however, the practice of polygamy and the frequent absences of their husbands made it difficult for them to sustain the family bonds at the heart of their faith.

Eventually, these tensions began to change how female Latter-day

Saints thought about their families. The Latter-day Saint belief that their experiences in the eternities would be constructed through kinship networks meant that women initially invested much of their emotional energy in their relationships with their husbands. The men to whom they bound themselves at the altar were more than worldly protectors; they served as the beginnings of the eternal relationships that would open new worlds to female Latter-day Saints in the hereafter. The frequent absences of male Latter-day Saints from the home, however, eventually caused women to shift their primary allegiances from their husbands to the relationships they created with other women. Leaders within the church also encouraged a certain emotional detachment between husbands and wives. As historian Kathryn Daynes argues, they frequently discouraged followers from becoming too invested in ideas about romantic love.[108] Brigham Young, she points out, told male Latter-day Saints to "never love your wives one hair's breadth further than they adorn the Gospel." He told individual men that they should "never love [their wives] so but that you can leave them at a moment's warning without shedding a tear."[109] In another sermon, Young told women that wives who clung "round a husband's neck" too tightly were "dead weight."[110]

Young was not the only person to instruct spouses not to become too attached to each other. As polygamy became more entrenched among the Saints, female Latter-day Saints encouraged each other not to focus too much on their love for their husbands. An important Latter-day Saint leader named Zina Young explained that the Saints ought to regard romantic love as "a false sentiment" that would only lead to jealousy. Within polygamy, she told readers, a woman "must regard her husband with indifference."[111] She must have known the difficulties that love could bring within polygamy. Zina had only been married to her husband Henry Jacobs a few months when Joseph Smith sent her word that "an angel with a drawn sword" had told him that he must "establish the principle" of plural marriage or lose his life.[112] Although she was pregnant with Henry's child, she consented to being sealed to Smith. Despite the sealing, her first husband continued to proclaim his love for Zina. He told her that his feelings would "continue to grow stronger and stronger to all eternity, worlds without end." He also assured her that "all will be made right."[113] After Smith's death, however, Zina became Brigham Young's wife, not Henry's.

The delegitimizing of love among Latter-day Saints in the nineteenth century overturned Protestant assumptions about marriage. Whereas white, middle-class Americans emphasized the importance of romantic love in creating companionate marriages, Latter-day Saints stressed godliness and respect. It is important to note, however, that the ideas Saints developed about marriage also upended the assumptions that female converts had made about their relationships when they initially accepted the restored gospel. Sarah Griffiths Richards's descriptions of her relationship with her husband, mentioned earlier in this chapter, are infused with love. She describes their marriage as "the commencement of a love as enduring as the eternities."[114] In spite of Zina's admonition, these are not the words of a woman indifferent to her husband. When Emma Smith was dying in 1879, her son Alexander heard her say, "Joseph, Joseph." She then stretched out her hand and said "Joseph" once more. Alexander held her hand and asked, "Mother, what is it?" But she was dead. Alexander later found out that his mother had had a vision right before her death in which Joseph showed her a nursery with one of her children. She "caught the child up in her arms, and wept with joy."[115] In the end, Emma's desire was not for endless worlds or expansive knowledge; it was to be reunited with her children. Her final words were an expression of attachment to a decades-gone husband whose actions had betrayed her.

Emma and Sarah obviously loved their husbands. The distance between the affections they felt for their husbands and the ideal Zina described reflects shifts within Latter-day Saint understandings of the family. The expectations that the first generation of women to join the Latter-day Saints had for their marriages had been created under the "emotional regimes" of Protestantism.[116] Like other American women, they had been encouraged to write emotive letters that expressed their desire for their husbands and to invest deeply in marital tenderness. As the nineteenth century progressed, however, Latter-day Saint leaders encouraged female members to change their understandings of the family. The frequent absences of male Latter-day Saints because of missionary work, imprisonment, and poverty meant that women had to create bonds outside of the nuclear family to support their children. They initially did so by turning to their siblings and members of the Relief Society. These decisions upset Latter-day Saint assumptions about the necessity of containing female relationships within the bounds of the heterosexual family. Women used the language of female friendship to express the emotional connections they developed. As they nursed each other's children, healed each other's bodies, and cared for one another when they were sick, female Latter-day Saints developed close, affective ties that at times threatened to overwhelm their relationships with their husbands. The Latter-day Saints eventually celebrated these relationships, arguing by the late nineteenth century that female Saints' independence from their husbands was evidence of polygamy's superiority as a marital system. Church leaders also encouraged women to express their devotion to their sister wives in their letters, poetry, and public speeches. While female Saints became "Mothers in Israel" and "Relief Society sisters," in Missouri and Nauvoo the community had not yet developed language to describe the affective ties that women had for each other. Instead, they appeared as threats to religious leaders.

Women found great comfort in the promises of the restoration, but they also endured hunger, huddled with toddlers and sat before courts as they were prosecuted for sexual immorality. In Nauvoo the women who would eventually be called "Mothers in Israel" struggled to make sense of a new theological and familial system. It was only on the Great Plains, as Latter-day Saints traveled to their desert Zion, that they began to live openly in polygamy and claim the relationships that they had created in the temple.

CHAPTER 3

REDEEMING THE LAMANITES IN
NATIVE AMERICA AND THE PACIFIC

On May 24, 1843, Addison Pratt donated an odd assortment of items—"the tooth of a whale," the skin of an albatross's foot, and "the Jaw Bone of a porpoise," among other things—to the Church of Jesus Christ of Latter-day Saints.[1] Pratt likely obtained the items during his time on board a whaling ship. His gift represented a wider hope among early Latter-day Saints that they would spread the gospel throughout the nations and that their converts would participate in the reopening of the heavens by gathering at Nauvoo. Pratt may have hoped that the objects would seed the beginning of a museum in Nauvoo that would chronicle the history of the church and its expansion across the globe.

His gifts were far from the only artifacts that early Latter-day Saints encountered. Almost a decade earlier, Joseph Smith had collected bones from Native American burial sites and proclaimed them evidence of the truth of the Book of Mormon.[2] Several men accompanied him. They found a skeleton with an arrow lodged in its ribs at the top of one mound. Smith received a vision telling him that these bones were the remains of a Lamanite warrior named Zelph.[3] In 1835 a traveling exhibit brought four mummies to Kirtland. Smith bought the mummies and a collection of papyri from the exhibition and spent the following months trying to produce an Egyptian grammar. From these he generated the

Book of Abraham, an account that he claimed had been written by the patriarch as he traveled to Canaan and Egypt.[4]

Although most Americans would have interpreted these two sets of artifacts as being separated by both geography and time, early Latter-day Saints connected them through the Book of Mormon. For them, the bones were physical evidence of the veracity of scripture. The first proved the Book of Mormon had been engraved by ancient patriarchs on metal tablets and miraculously preserved. The second confirmed the accuracy of the biblical account and transported it into the present. In the early 1840s John Lloyd Stephens published *Incidents of Travel in Central America, Chiapas and Yucatan*, a book that detailed his discovery of Mayan ruins in Central America. These ruins offered further proof to early Latter-day Saints that the Book of Mormon was an accurate history of the Americas.[5]

The restoration's early theology, however, demanded that its followers do more than assent to the historicity of the Book of Mormon. It was an apocalyptic faith that commanded its followers to spread the gospel throughout the world. Early missionaries for the Latter-day Saints traveled to Canada, Great Britain, Italy, and Switzerland. Interest in the Book of Mormon ensured that Native American communities were a part of this list. In 1830 Joseph Smith called four men to visit the descendants of the Lamanites and tell them about the discovery of a history of their ancestors. On November 12 the men visited the Seneca Nation and left two Books of Mormon.[6] They then visited other Native nations to tell them about the Book of Mormon and the role that indigenous people played in its sacred history. The missionaries reported that they were received favorably but that an Indian agent had expelled them from the area before they could meet with real success.[7]

The restoration's early theology had suggested a grandiose vision in which tens of thousands of Native people would recognize the truth of the Latter-day gospel and gather in Missouri and Illinois to build a new Jerusalem. Throughout the 1830s and '40s, however, Native conversions were few. Lori Taylor has identified eleven or twelve Native Americans who converted to the church in its first decades.[8] The paucity of Native converts meant that the few men and women who did convert became important symbols among the Latter-day Saints. It also increased general interest among Latter-day Saints in the Pacific, where missionary work was far more successful. In 1843 Joseph Smith called Addison Pratt and a few other men to serve as missionaries to the Pacific. They arrived in French Polynesia in a time of political turmoil and established a thriving church on the Tuamotus Islands. By the 1850s Latter-day Saints had come to believe that Polynesians and Native Americans were both peoples of the Book of Mormon.

Latter-day Saints in both regions tried to position themselves against the existing imperial system. The U.S. government's expansionist policies disrupted Native communities in North America, expelling them from their land and destroying their ability to provide for their families. White missionaries in the Pacific, meanwhile, converted large numbers of Pacific Islanders to Christianity. Catholic and Protestant missionaries did not see each other's missions as legitimate and sought to discredit each other. Local politics frequently affected the success of individual missionaries. The Saints saw themselves as offering an alternative to U.S. colonialism in the American West even as they disenfranchised Native people. Conversion to the restored gospel offered communities in the Pacific that had been marginalized by Protestant and Catholic missionary work a way to claim spiritual and political power.

Rumors about the sexual improprieties of the Latter-day Saints in Illinois and Missouri followed missionaries to the Pacific and impaired their work among Native communities in the United States. Protestant missionaries feared that Latter-day Saints would fail to discipline Native families and bring indigenous spiritual practices under the authority of the priesthood. In the United States such fears focused on the enthusiastic religious practices of early Latter-day Saints, which resembled Native revival movements. White Protestant missionaries similarly feared that Latter-day Saints would lead Pacific Islanders to commit depraved acts. Latter-day Saint missionaries were unprepared for the degree to which imperial politics and allegations of sexual impropriety would affect their evangelistic outreach. Pratt may have donated porpoise bones and albatross skin to the church because he believed his missionary work was divinely inspired and would be part of a world-altering movement. The Egyptian mummies and Native American bodies were meant to provide evidence of the Book of Mormon's historicity. They also suggested that the promises the Book of Mormon made to Native Americans would soon unfold. Latter-day Saints anticipated a dramatic future in which God literally remade the world. They instead found themselves embroiled in imperial and religious controversies.

The First Latter-day Saint Missions to the Lamanites

Oliver Cowdery traveled to Ohio and Missouri in the fall of 1830 to spread the gospel to the Lamanites. He had served as a scribe for Joseph Smith as he was translating the Book of Mormon. As a result, Cowdery was intimately familiar with the promises that it made to the Lamanites and their descendants.[9] On November 12 he wrote a letter to his brethren telling them that he had visited the Seneca people.[10] As mentioned earlier, his companion Parley P. Pratt wrote that they spent several hours "instructing" the Senecas "in the knowledge of the record of their forefathers."[11] They then traveled to meet the Delawares.

Despite the missionaries' enthusiasm, there were few converts from the Senecas or from the Native tribes they would visit later in their trip. Many Native nations that Latter-day Saint missionaries visited were experiencing increased pressure from white settlement. The Senecas had a long history of fraught relations with white settlers. They had participated in the Seven Years' War and were instrumental in the British capture of Fort Niagara. In 1797 they signed a treaty relinquishing control of much of their New York homeland. By 1838, less than a decade after Cowdery and Pratt first attempted contact, increasing settlement in western New York would lead the U.S. government to try to move the Senecas to Missouri—a forced relocation that most of the nation would resist.[12]

The history of white interactions with the Delaware people was equally long. During the American Revolution, many Delawares had supported the British out of fear that an American victory would cause them to lose their land. Their concerns were prescient. In 1829 the United States government forced them into an agreement to exchange their land near the White River in Missouri for new territory in Kansas. It was one of many forced relocations. By the mid-nineteenth century they had become "refugees"—forced from their homelands in New York and New Jersey to Ohio and then Missouri.[13] Delaware bands were already leaving Missouri in 1830 for what they hoped would be a new beginning.[14] By the time Latter-day Saint missionaries arrived in 1830, many Delawares had already converted to Christianity. Moravian missionaries had established Native Christian towns and translated their hymns into both Mohegan and Lenape.[15] Baptist missionaries also labored among many Native communities. Isaac McCoy established a mission for the Shawnee and Delaware who had gathered in Missouri and Kansas.[16] Occasionally, Native Americans who converted to Christianity were successful in their attempts to remain in their homelands. Sarah Huntington Smith worked with Mohegan leaders to obtain an exception for the community, which had converted to Christianity, to removal.[17] In general, however, conversion was no guarantee that communities would keep their land. The federal government expelled Cherokee, Nez Perce, and Blackfeet Christians along with their "unredeemed" relatives.

The Latter-day Saint missionaries who traveled to Ohio and Missouri probably had little sense of the dislocations that Native communities had experienced in previous decades. Although they recognized that the federal government was removing Native communities from their ancestral lands, they saw the movement of Indian people as part of God's plan for their redemption. For example, W. W. Phelps lauded Andrew Jackson's Indian removal policies in the *Latter-day Saint Messenger and Advocate*, agreeing with Jackson that it was the "moral duty" of the United States "to protect, and if possible, to preserve and perpetuate, the scattered remnants" of the Native American "race."[18] The Book of Mormon itself suggested that the poverty that many Native American communities experienced was the result of their savagery and degradation, not American colonialism.

The sermons, newspaper articles, and scriptures that Latter-day Saints produced encouraged the faithful to see Native Americans as a people in need of redemption. When Latter-day Saint missionaries traveled to Native American communities they presented themselves as offering a new future for the embattled residents. The restored gospel promised that Native Americans would be restored to their place as God's chosen people and that they would be redeemed from the poverty and hunger that beset them. 2 Nephi 30: 6 promised that the descendants of the Lamanites would eventually "rejoice" as they realized that they were Israelites. They would realize that this knowledge was "a blessing unto them." The future that the text imagined for Native Americans was strikingly like the Book of Revelation. A few lines later, it promised that "the sucking child shall play on the hole of the asp, and the weaned child shall put his hand on the cockatrice's den." White Latter-day Saints, the scripture suggested, would work with redeemed Native Americans and people of all nations to build a paradise. The early Saints believed that this vision was compelling and hoped that Native people would recognize its power. Some did. For many Native Americans, however, what the Latter-day Saints offered was no better than the promises of white Protestantism. The restored gospel required that Native Americans exchange the stories that grounded their history and sense of themselves for a new narrative in which they were the descendants of American Israelites. Although white Latter-day Saints saw themselves as restoring Native American culture and history to its fullness, most Native Americans saw conversion to the restored gospel as a cultural loss.

When Parley P. Pratt and his companions visited the Delaware people encamped on the Missouri River they called on William Anderson Kith-tilhund, an elderly chief who had led his people from Ohio to Missouri and finally Kansas. Anderson initially refused to call a council to hear the Latter-day missionaries speak. Eventually, however, he agreed.[19] Pratt's autobiography described his excitement at the reception of the Book of Mormon among the Delaware. He claimed that many in the community believed in the text's authenticity and began "to tell the news to others, in their own language."[20] They invited the Saints to speak to the community, as they had built houses and planted crops for the following year.[21]

Their excitement was premature. Although many of the Latter-day Saints who served as missionaries had grown up in "frontier" spaces, they knew little about the relationships that the federal government had formed with Native communities. U.S. Indian law required individuals to gain permission from federal agents before proselytizing to Native groups. None of the Latter-day Saints had sought access before embarking on the mission. As a result, the agent for the Shawnee told the Saints that they needed to leave the reservation or risk being arrested and brought to the garrison. The Latter-day Saints immediately wrote to William Clark, then the superintendent of Indian affairs, for permission.[22]

Clark had little reason to grant the request of a group of missionaries known for their zealotry. Several Native American communities had experienced religious revivals in the nineteenth century. In 1831 an American artist named George Catlin had visited a Kickapoo village near Lake Michigan. Living among them was Kannekuk, a Kickapoo man who had prophesied that his people would return to Illinois. Like many other Native religious figures, he also encouraged his followers to forsake alcohol.[23] White Americans often interpreted indigenous revival movements as political and social challenges. These movements often wove together political and religious concerns. They presented an alternative form of religious belonging that rejected the cultural and religious superiority of white Americans and asserted that Native Americans would soon return to the lands and traditions that had birthed their communities. The Saints' promise that Native Americans would be redeemed mirrored this promise. Newspapers also described Latter-day Saints as living like Indians. In April 1831, for example, a Charlotte journal reported that the Latter-day Saints were "liv[ing] together in a sort of Indian encampment, holding all things together."[24] Men like William Clark often saw themselves as working on behalf of Native communities by introducing them to capitalism and white forms of agriculture. They would have had little incentive to allow Latter-day Saints to proselytize among their charges.

It is unclear how Clark responded to the Saints' request, as no record exists of his response.[25] We do, however, know that the Latter-day Saints never received formal permission to serve as missionaries in Kansas and Missouri. Their very presence in the territory seemed to excite anger. Oliver Cowdery described the reactions he encountered. He wrote that "almost the whole country, consisting of Universalists, Atheists, Deists, Presbyterians, Methodists, Baptists, and other professed Christians, priests and people; with all the devils form the infernal pit" had been arrayed to prevent the growth of the Church of Jesus Christ of Latter-day Saints.[26] He assured his readers that his faith remained unshaken even though he "dwell[ed] in the midst of scorpions" and told them about a tribe of Native Americans he had heard lived "three hundred miles west of Santa Fe."[27]

Few Native people converted to the church in its first decades despite missionaries' efforts to proselytize among them. Instead, Latter-day Saints came to see the few men and women who did convert as symbols of God's promises to the Lamanites. Peninah Shropshire Cotton, who is identified in her family's history as a Cherokee woman, resided in Nauvoo as an orphan. Although it is unclear when she first encountered the restored gospel, she was living in Nauvoo in 1846 when she was sealed to Daniel Wood as a plural wife. Her son Joseph compared her to Sacajawea and wrote that she was a "Godsend" to the Latter-day Saints. As the community traveled across the Great Basin, she used her botanical knowledge to choose berries and plants that were safe to eat and sewed moccasins for the people traveling with her.[28]

An Oneida man named Lewis Dana became a Latter-day Saint in 1840 and served several missions for the church. In 1845 a church council sent him on a mission to select a new location for the Latter-day Saint community. The council hoped that the location he selected with his companions would bring the Saints into renewed contact with Native Americans. Dana ultimately traveled with Phineas Young, Jonathan Dunham, Solomon Tindall, and Charles Shumway to Kansas in hopes of converting a large number of Native Americans.[29] His fellow church members seem to have regarded him as an important brother and emissary. At one meeting Orson Spencer pressed him to "call upon the red men to come speedily to the help of the Lord against the mighty."[30]

William Clayton referred to him as "the first Lamanite" to have been "admitted a member of any quorum of this church."[31] In February 1845 Brigham Young told his followers that he believed that Dana was "acquainted with nearly all the tribes" and would be able to serve as a missionary to Native communities living in the American West. He imagined two hundred thousand Flathead Indians converting to the church and learning about the gospel of their ancestors.[32]

Yet Native converts remained rare. For the most part the people who joined the Church of Jesus Christ of Latter-day Saints were white settlers from the eastern United States and Great Britain. White missionaries who traveled to Manchester, Glasgow, and Preston found that their message resonated among a working class experiencing massive shifts in their standards of living and the structure of work. By 1851 there were approximately thirty thousand Latter-day Saints in England and Wales.[33] The failure of the Saints to convert Native Americans to their faith led them to redefine their understanding of who was and was not God's chosen people. Latter-day Saints came to see themselves as God's chosen ones, the Israelites.[34] They did not, however, completely abandon the image of Native Americans as Lamanites or forsake the hope that they would convert large numbers of indigenous people. As the 1840s and '50s progressed, the Pacific Islands increasingly became important to this vision. Latter-day Saint missionaries in the Pacific found success that had eluded them among Native people in the United States. They also learned just how difficult it could be to redeem the Lamanites, even when they were willing to submit to conversion.

Spreading the Gospel to the Pacific

The difficulties that Latter-day Saints encountered in the Pacific were partially related to the fact that they were not the first Christian missionaries in the region. The largely Congregationalist London Missionary Society (LMS) first sent missionaries to Tahiti in 1796. They were enormously successful, converting much of the area's populace to Christianity. They struggled, however, with issues surrounding sexual immorality and domesticity. Its directors had initially imagined that some of the single, white men that they sent to the Pacific as missionaries would marry indigenous women. They hoped that these marriages serve as the beginnings of a mixed-race Protestant Christianity in the Pacific.[35] They emphasized that the white men who married indigenous women would not separate themselves from the community. Instead, they were to "build a little house near their brethren."[36] The indigenous women they married, far from being separated from the white wives of other missionaries, would "live in daily communion and worship under the same roof."[37]

In this vision of missionary work, Christian conversion and marriage to white missionaries would create new domesticated roles and new domestic spaces within which indigenous women would learn proper skills of the home and motherhood and eventually become "civilized." This vision was part of a larger emphasis within the early LMS on the promise of interracial Christianity. According to Elizabeth Elbourne, the society initially had a similar dream for its mission in the Cape of Africa—Black and white church leaders would lead an interracial congregation.[38] The LMS expected its missionaries to enact the scenes found within the New Testament where individuals mingled together in Christian society regardless of their skin color or class position.

It is important to remember, however, that the marriages the LMS condoned were implicitly gendered. Assumptions about the nature of familial relationships meant that the directors of the LMS assumed that indigenous women would adopt the customs and religious beliefs of their husbands, not vice versa. Men in the eighteenth and nineteenth centuries were to serve as the public faces and heads of their families.[39] Latter-day Saints adopted similar ideas about gender and assimilation. The London Missionary Society's beliefs about assimilation meant that it was difficult for members of the LMS to imagine a world in which white women would choose to marry native Tahitians. According to Rosemary Seton, an archivist and historian of the LMS, the society only sent one unmarried woman to serve as a missionary before 1864—Maria Newell, who worked as a teacher in Malacca.[40]

The idealized world that the LMS imagined was one in which mixed-raced marriages would transform society—first on Tahiti Nui and eventually throughout the rest of the Pacific. The LMS hoped that the children that resulted from these marriages would be proficient in indigenous languages and well-equipped to proselytize Pacific Islanders. The LMS hoped that after these children had converted their mothers' kin, they would travel to other islands, convert the people they found, and spread the Christian faith throughout the region. The society, however, soon found itself embroiled in sexual scandal. The single missionaries that the LMS initially sent to the Pacific were reckless. As Tony Ballantyne has pointed out, Francis Oakes and John Cock engaged in sex with prostitutes in New South Wales. They were also among the men who slept with Polynesian women.[41] Similar indiscretions occurred in the Cape Colony.[42]

Ultimately, the LMS came to worry that white male missionaries were degrading themselves rather than elevating indigenous women. The society feared that male sexuality was ungovernable. The white missionary wife, once spurned as unnecessary, seemed to offer an ideal solution.[43] Her body provided an appropriate release for white, male sexual desire and would bind men to the domestic sphere by bearing children. Through this process, white women's bodies became vehicles for disciplining white men's sexuality. This reflected the many ways that the body became a site of cultural work in the Pacific islands. How individuals dressed, the people with whom they had sex, and their willingness to tattoo their bodies became markers of their adherence to cultural norms. The presence of white women and children intended to prevent the sexual indiscretions that had initially plagued the LMS by protecting white men from the Pacific's seductiveness. In 1811 the directors of the London Missionary Society underscored their rejection of the organization's earlier missionary policy through a letter informing its members that "none but married" missionaries should be sent from then on.[44]

Sexual sin continued to afflict the society even after the establishment of the figure of the white missionary wife. Stories about the escapades of the children of the LMS circulated throughout the nineteenth-century Pacific. Missionary daughters were found to have had dalliances with indigenous men, and their brothers sometimes ran away, in the words of one historian, to be "circumcised in the native fashion."[45] The sexual immorality within the mission worried the LMS missionaries. David Darling, for example, threatened to resign if something was not done. He feared that his children would become "ignorant, debauched, [and] ruined"—that his sons would be forced to become "sailors" and his daughters would be "a disgrace to their sex"—if he did not leave.[46] He was not alone in his fear. Missionaries' descriptions of their children emphasized the younger generation's affinity with indigenous people. One letter advised the directors of the LMS not to be too harsh with a missionary's daughter because "she had been brought up from her Infancy with the natives—They were the same to her as her own people."[47] The letter uses her position within Tahitian society to explain her sexual liaison. It portrays her as having white skin but being culturally indigenous. The fluidity of her racial identity is used to explain her sexual misbehavior and her inability to accept white standards of domesticity. The sexual misdeeds of early missionaries and their children led the LMS to emphasize the importance of placing barriers between white and indigenous converts. Rather than living among the people to whom they proselytized, the missionaries began building separate houses and established a separate school where their children could be watched.

Latter-day Saints in the Pacific

Latter-day Saint missionaries entered the Pacific in this context. In 1843 Addison Pratt sailed from New Bedford, Massachusetts, on the church's first mission to the Pacific Islands. Benjamin F. Grouard, Knowlton Hanks, and Noah Rogers accompanied him. When they first arrived in the Pacific, Mormon missionaries rejected these measures, choosing to live among their converts.[48] In 1846 Benjamin F. Grouard married a Paumotuan woman named Tearo. In a world where sexual irregularities could discredit individual missionaries, Grouard's decision to marry an indigenous woman was potentially dangerous. It aligned Mormon missionaries not with white respectability but with the beachcombers and whalers who had lived on the margins of white society. When Grouard's companion Pratt initially heard about his plan to marry an indigenous woman, he told him to do as Judas had done: "What thou doest, do quickly."[49] His reaction is somewhat of a mystery. Pratt had performed marriages between white men and Polynesian women in the past. According to the church records that he compiled while on Tubuai, he married William J. Bowen to Poti on July 14, 1844. That same year, he married Orman Clifford to Vaiho, George McLain to Paahaaho, and George Prescott to Metua.[50] Why, then, did he respond to Grouard's marriage with trepidation?

A possible reason is that their missionary work coincided with a difficult time in Tahitian history. The London Missionary Society (LMS) had originally sent a group of missionaries to Greater Tahiti in 1796.[51] These "godly mechanics," as they became famously known, were enormously successful, converting much of the area's population to Christianity.[52]

By the 1820s, however, indigenous revival movements were threatening the society's position in the islands. In 1821 two influential men named Tehoata and Taataino announced that they no longer wanted to be in fellowship with the Protestants in Tahiti. Five years later a man named Teao began to prophesy that God was going to destroy many of the people of Papeete for their sins. At the same time, he encouraged those who accepted his prophetic claims to reject the teachings of the LMS. He preached at one point during the missionaries' absence to warn the people about the destruction that was to come. The Protestant missionaries claimed that his teachings centered on the idea that the Millennium had started and that men could commit adultery and drink with impunity.[53] Although the government soon declared these prophets illegitimate, their popularity speaks to the growing tensions between indigenous leaders and Western newcomers.

Regional politics also shaped the story, as the nineteenth-century Pacific became a site of imperial conflict. Catholic missionaries arrived in Tahiti in the 1830s. The French would ultimately use Queen Pomare's decision to expel them from her kingdom as an excuse to extend a protectorate over the region. The creation of this protectorate represented the loss of sovereignty for the Tahitian people and the end of their existence as an independent nation. Although France would not officially annex Tahiti until 1880, the French colonial government now determined its laws and policies. The LMS worried that the colonial government would use its influence to undermine the islands' Protestant churches and establish French Catholicism.[54]

Latter-day Saint missionaries discovered that violent resistance to the French colonial government had not yet dissipated when they arrived on Tahiti Nui. Rumors circulated that the native Tahitians would kill every white person on the islands if the hostilities continued.[55] Grouard complained that his sermons were "drowned out amidst the roll of the drum & [the] shrill notes of the fife."[56] Concern about the violence caused Grouard to abandon his missionary work on Tahiti in 1845. He decided to travel to the Tuamotus, a nearby island chain that had long existed on the margins of the Protestant mission in the Pacific. His missionary work there was enormously successful. Within a few months he had baptized over six hundred people into the church.[57] His success was partially the result of the decision of the LMS to focus on their missionary work on Tahiti Nui and larger island chains. Since the presence of white missionaries provided communities with increased opportunities for trade and a degree of social and political power in the nineteenth century, the LMS's neglect had politically and socially marginalized the Tuamotus. For his part, Pratt would spend much of his mission on Tubuai, an island around four hundred miles south of Tahiti. His missionary work there was just as successful as Grouard's in the Tuamotus.

For the people of the Tuamotus, Grouard's decision to live among them promised to improve their position among the surrounding communities. The London Missionary Society, however, viewed his missionary efforts with suspicion. Although they had managed to Christianize much of the Pacific, they worried that their success was superficial, and that the presence of Mormon and Catholic missionaries would uproot their fragile hold on the islands.

Latter-day Saint ideas about missionary domesticity only intensified their concerns. Unlike members of the LMS, early Latter-day Saints believed that the social, spiritual, and physical transformation of indigenous people would only occur after the millennium. The Latter-day Saint rejection of the role that domesticity had played in earlier visions of Christian missionary work played into LMS concerns about the potential seductiveness of the Pacific. The belief among Latter-day Saint missionaries that their missionary work would be temporary led them to momentarily abandon their families in imitation of the New Testament apostles. Instead of bringing their families with them to recreate the white domesticity they had enjoyed at home, early Latter-day Saint missionaries initially lived in the homes of indigenous men and women.[58]

It is possible that his concerns about Grouard's marriage arose from the latter's status as a missionary. As a white missionary for the Latter-day Saints, Grouard was to be an exemplar of the community in ways that the beachcombers and whalers who converted to the new faith were not. As far as I have been able to locate, white Latter-day Saints who traveled to Hawai'i as missionaries in the 1850s did not marry indigenous women, although several of their converts were involved in interracial marriages.[59] In marrying an indigenous woman, Grouard raised the possibility that he would be assimilated into Tuamotuan society rather than teaching his congregation about their destiny as Israelites. His marriage also attracted the interest of the LMS missionaries. Although Grouard's marriage grew out of a specifically Latter-day Saint understanding of the role of indigenous people in the millennium, the LMS placed it within their own worldview, seeing it as part of a much larger history in which white men frequently succumbed to the seductions of the Pacific, committing sexual sin and falling into apostasy. Although Pratt did not marry an indigenous woman, his willingness to live in indigenous communities may have raised questions about his morality and chastity. The LMS, wearied by its inability to contain the sexual desires of single male missionaries, may have worried about the decision of male Latter-day Saints to temporarily abandon their wives and travel unhindered by marital ties. Grouard certainly complained about the "fauls reports" the Society circulated against him, although he did not fully elaborate.[60]

Latter-day Saint missionaries also contributed to the LMS's anxieties by tipping the balance in the ongoing conflicts that British evangelists experienced operating in a French protectorate—particularly when the Tahitian people craved independence from the French. Although the British missionaries remained officially neutral in the conflict, British Protestants at home constantly tried to use their influence to pressure Parliament into interfering with the French protectorate. The University of Birmingham, for example, holds pieces of correspondence concerning petitions from the supporters of the London Missionary Society in Tahiti.[61] Even after the British government refused to intervene, the presence of the British missionaries allowed dissident Tahitians to maintain hope that the British would eventually aid them in their struggle for independence. The British missionaries also openly critiqued the French, suggesting that the protectorate had brought moral dissolution rather than benevolent imperialism. One missionary accused the governor of attending licentious dances where the participants were common prostitutes and concubines.[62] Another wrote that the expulsion of Queen Pomare had also expelled "all restraint & religion" from the islands.[63] Latter-day Saint missionaries offered the French an alternative to the troublesome British Congregationalists. Because they were neither French nor British, the Latter-day Saints occupied a unique liminal space: the French colonial government could favor their ministry and undermine the authority of the British missionaries without appearing to zealously promote Catholicism.

As a result, the Latter-day Saint missionaries initially found themselves welcome in the French governor's office. According to Addison Pratt, when the governor received a copy of the Book of Mormon, he told the British missionaries who gave it to him that if they "lived up to the good morals that book taught, they would be verry good men."[64] The LMS, however, refused to cede its position easily. The establishment of a French protectorate did not end the contest for power between the Congregational and Latter-day Saint missionaries; instead, the 1840s saw the two groups constantly jockeying for power and attempting to discredit each other in the eyes of government officials, especially via accusations of sexual impropriety. It was primarily the intimacy between white Mormon men and their indigenous converts that worried members of the LMS. Although Joseph Smith had already started practicing polygamy by the early 1840s, he attempted to hide this secret from both the outside world and the Latter-day Saints. Rumors circulated in Tahiti about the Latter-day Saints, but Grouard and Pratt saw the restoration as a monogamous faith. They believed that the rumors were lies and did not teach their converts about the practice.[65]

The Congregationalists accused Latter-day Saints of having improper relationships with Native people. In 1845 Grouard recorded that the Congregationalist missionaries had accused the Mormons of being "sedicious [*sic*] persons" who would only be "detrimental" to French interests on Anaa.[66] The charges were accompanied by an attempt to show the licentiousness of the Book of Mormon and the demoralizing influence it had had on the Saints. Although the Congregationalists failed in their initial attempts to discredit Grouard, their use of rumors about sexuality to try to discredit him had a long history in the Pacific. The suggestions that an Anglican missionary in New Zealand had developed sexually intimate relationships with young men led to his discharge from the Church Missionary Society in 1837 and his eventual return to Britain.[67] Likewise, Thomas Kendall's affair with a Maori woman in the 1820s, combined with his unwillingness to stop trading muskets, undermined his position as a missionary with the Church Missionary Society.[68] Rumors about sexuality, even when ungrounded, became a way to weaken a person's position in the islands.

Although early Latter-day Saint missionaries rejected rumors about Joseph Smith as lies sent by Satan to impede the progress of the Saints, they were no less willing to gossip about sexual immorality than Protestants. Addison Pratt scoffed at the pretensions of the British Congregationalist missionaries in his letters to church leaders in the United States. One of their daughters, he wrote, kept a brothel for sailors and had been tattooed "from her shoulders to her heels, missing no intermediate portions."[69] The son of another Congregationalist missionary was "one of the most brutish libertines among the islands."[70] In Pratt's eyes, the missionaries were no better than their children. He accused one of them of using the sacrament as an opportunity to survey the islands' young women and select one to visit his bed.[71]

Rumors continued to circulate for years afterward about Simpson's drunkenness and sexual immorality. Congregationalist missionaries in the early 1840s confronted the suggestion that Alexander Simpson, a member of their society assigned to teach the white missionary children, may have molested the daughters of his fellow missionaries during his tenure as schoolmaster. One girl accused him of climbing into a female student's bed and drawing her back before beginning to "pull her about and . . . feel her bosom." He then "attempted to violate her person."[72] The inquiry that followed was difficult and focused as much on the girls' reputations as on the schoolmaster's. Some of the Congregationalist missionaries believed that the evidence undeniably pointed to Simpson's guilt; yet the directors of the LMS felt that they could not fairly convict him with the hearsay and gossip they had collected.[73] As a result, they allowed him to maintain his position in spite of their sense that the girls' accusations were not warrantless.

Rumors did not just circulate among the Euro-American community; they were part of discussions about sexuality and morality among Tahitians as well. LMS missionaries and their associates recorded stories of exchanging money for sex with Native women and, in one instance, watching a Tahitian woman bathe.[74] These stories sometimes contained an element of sexual coercion. During an 1843 investigation, a servant girl named Medua was reported to have complained, "Mr. Simpson is a very annoying or giddy man, he will not cease pulling me about, my sowing will not be well done."[75] It was not until the 1850s that Simpson was finally dismissed from service—for drunkenness, not sexual immorality. The dismissal took so long in part because the LMS had been largely unwilling to accept the testimony of Native men and women into evidence. The Latter-day Saint missionaries had no such reticence. Pratt's descriptions of the illicit sexual behavior of the LMS explicitly relied on the narratives of native Tahitians. His stories quoted their testimony, which he used to discredit the English missionaries. In portraying the missionaries as immoral, Pratt implicitly questioned the propriety of granting them authority over the lives of indigenous people. On the other hand, Grouard's marriage to an indigenous woman opened Mormons up to accusations that they were also committing acts of sexual impropriety. Grouard seems to have regarded his wife Tearo as a buffer against the possibility of sexual immorality. He may have worried that he would be unable to control his sexual desires without an acceptable outlet for them. He may have also felt that Tearo would provide him with status in the Tuamotuan community because she understood their culture and lifestyle. As a married man, Pratt would not have felt at liberty to entertain a similar solution. His wife lived in Nauvoo, and he felt bound to return to her and to provide for their children.

Pratt left the Pacific in 1847 to recruit additional missionaries and find his family after Joseph Smith's death. His absence marked the end of the initial stage of Latter-day Saint missionary work in the Pacific. He returned to the islands in 1850 with his wife Louisa and their children. His sister-in-law Caroline Barnes Crosby and her husband Jonathan accompanied them. The presence of white women in the Pacific changed the nature of Latter-day Saint missionary work in the Pacific. Louisa tried to recreate as much of her life as a white, middle-class woman as she could. Like her Protestant sisters, she hoped to teach Polynesian converts to live like white Mormons. In one instance, she brought three indigenous children into her home. She believed that they would soon "become domesticated," sitting "at the table" with "a knife and fork" and behaving "quite becoming[ly]."[76] Her inability to speak indigenous languages well and her cultural distance from Polynesian women made it difficult for her to enjoy the same closeness that she had experienced with women in Nauvoo. Although her sister had accompanied her to the Pacific, she sometimes felt lonely. She recalled one time when she had retreated to a garden to pray and meditate on her experiences. After sitting down, she "gazed up into the sky and thought of the bright world where our Saviour dwells . . . I thought of the dear sisters in the valley of the mountains, and longed to commune with them."[77]

Louisa distrusted marriages between white men and Polynesian women. During her stay on the island of Tubuai, she met several white men who had married Native women. When a Latter-day Saint named John Layton brought her a barrel of flour, she wrote in her journal that his wife knew "nothing about housekeeping" and that he had to "be father and mother both, to his children."[78] At another point, she lamented that Grouard would not be able to return to Salt Lake City as he wished because he was "tied up, a vessel on his hands and a native wife."[79] She wrote that the Polynesian wife of a white church member was "a childish girl. "She felt it was "a pity, that sensible men should involve themselves with these poor ignorant women." After all, they could not "bring them to their level." Instead, "they must descend to their level . . . to be comfortable with them."[80] Her descriptions of Polynesian women drew on the distrust that many white women of her era felt toward indigenous people. Even when she was being kind to Grouard's wife or Latter-day Saint converts, she could be condescending.

White Latter-day Saints abandoned the Pacific for decades beginning in 1852. Their relationships with the French colonial government had become increasingly strained during the mission. The French worried about the influence of Latter-day Saint missionaries over their indigenous converts. In 1851 colonial officials imprisoned a Latter-day Saint missionary named James Stephens Brown for "attempting to subvert the laws of the protectorate."[81] These concerns were not unfounded. According to Patrick O'Reilly and Raoul Teissier's biographical encyclopedia of Tahiti, Native Saints on Anaa participated in a small rebellion in the 1850s, killing a French gendarme and raising an American flag. Their action can partially be seen as an attempt to reject the authority of the French colonial government and claim protection from the United States. The French government ultimately decided that the presence of white Latter-day Saint missionaries was too risky and expelled them from the parts of the Pacific.[82]

Tensions within the community of Latter-day Saints in the United States became more intense after Pratt and Grouard returned home. Grouard brought his wife Nahina, whom he had married after Tearo's death, with him. Although the majority of Latter-day Saints settled in

Salt Lake City, the experience of Tahitian Saints centered on San Bernardino, California. Several Mormon men who lived there had married Polynesian women. Charles Hill and J. R. Kipp, for example, were married to Hawaiian women. John Layton's wife Teina also lived in the community.[83] The women discovered that their fellow Saints treated them with contempt. A woman named Hakuole Dennis, in an interview with French travelers, claimed that her fellow Saints treated her "as if she were a negress."[84] Several of the women decided to return to the Pacific and abandoned the idea of living among white Latter-day Saints. Nahina was forced to abandon one of her children who was raised by a white family. John Layton and his wife decided to return together, while Thomas Whitaker agreed to let his wife visit Tahiti on the assumption that she would return. As the historian Edward Leo Lyman has pointed out, she never did.[85]

The Polynesian women who traveled to the United States had a deep faith in the restoration. Like white Latter-day Saints who colonized the Salt Lake Valley, they had been willing to abandon their families and follow God to the United States. They would never, however, encounter the Zion they had been promised. For members of the restoration, Zion is a community as well as a place. For Polynesian Saints in the nineteenth century, the community of Saints would never be a welcoming place. They could live in Zion, but they would never fully inhabit it. The experience of Polynesian Latter-day Saints in the 1850s represents the tensions within the restored gospel surrounding the place of Native peoples. Early Latter-day Saints believed that Native Americans would eventually be redeemed and trusted that their missionary work would be the catalyst that allowed that redemption to happen. The inability of the Saints to understand the politics of Indian removal, however, limited their capacity to reach Indian people and to speak intelligently to them when they did have access. In the Pacific, Latter-day Saints discovered that imperial politics shaped their experiences. Their status as Americans allowed them to position themselves outside of the political battles between the French colonial government and the resident British missionaries, at least temporarily. It was their failure to maintain this neutrality that led to their expulsion from the islands and the end of the church's mission in the Pacific.

Latter-day Saints also discovered that their missionary work was shaped by ideas about sexuality and domesticity. As they attempted to transform the lives of Native families, they found that sex was a part of the language of politics. To accuse someone of sexual impropriety was to allege that they were incapable of governing. Many of the sexual tensions the Saints experienced were centered on interracial marriage. By the mid-nineteenth century, Protestant missionaries were suspicious of marriages between white men and Native women, and marriages between white women and Native men were unthinkable. Members of the Church of Jesus Christ of Latter-day Saints, on the other hand, were divided: some, like Grouard, embraced the idea that Latter-day Saints missionaries should become connected to the communities they proselytized among through marriage, while others, like Addison and Louisa Pratt, saw such marriages as dangerous and feared that the men who participated in them would be degraded. That tension came to the fore when some male Latter-day Saints brought Polynesian wives to the United States. These women found that they were not welcome among white Latter-day Saints despite their status as members of a chosen race.

These questions would only become more important as the restored church began to change its understanding of the family. Joseph Smith began to develop an expansive family theology in the 1830s. Polygamy was a part of but not the entirety of this theology. The development of polygamy transformed understandings of the family and their relationships with indigenous people among the Saints. Throughout the second half of the nineteenth century, Latter-day Saints tried to differentiate their marital practices from Native American polygamy. The next chapter focuses on the development of Latter-day Saint polygamy and the strains that it placed among the Saints. The expansive nature of Joseph Smith's understanding of the family offered believers a vision in which their family ties would allow them to progress through the eternities, gaining knowledge and power until they were exalted as gods. His revelations, however, also created the possibility that individuals outside of his immediate retinue would receive messages from God about sexuality, the family, and domesticity. Individuals claimed to receive revelations commanding them to take wives or to abandon abusive spouses. To quell rumors about sexual indiscretions within the Latter-day Saint community and discredit individuals who claimed new revelations, leaders among the Saints began to discipline people whose domestic lives transgressed Latter-day Saint understandings of the family. The Mormon attempt to create a respectable domesticity would lead them to regulate both white and indigenous bodies within Nauvoo.

CHAPTER 4

CREATING POLYGAMOUS DOMESTICITIES

As Nauvoo arose from the banks of the Mississippi River, Latter-day Saints weathered repeated scandals over their sexual practices, periodic outbreaks of violence, and internal dissent. Fears of theocracy led non-Mormons in Missouri and Illinois to view Latter-day Saints with suspicion. On June 7, 1844, dissidents within the Latter-day Saint community published the *Nauvoo Expositor* to publicize claims that Smith had "introduced false and damnable doctrines into the Church, such as a plurality of gods above the God of this universe, and his ability to fall with all his creations; [and] the plurality of wives, for time and eternity."[1]

The Nauvoo City Council, which was comprised entirely of Latter-day Saints, responded by ordering the destruction of the press and all copies of the newspaper. The newspaper's demolition confirmed non- and ex-Mormon fears that Smith had established a theocracy. Shortly after the *Expositor*'s publication, Smith used his powers as general of the Nauvoo Legion to declare martial law to protect the city from outside threats. Newspapers around the state began to call for his arrest. Illinois governor Thomas Ford guaranteed Smith's protection if he agreed to be tried in a court of law. Smith agreed and was arrested for inciting a riot. Despite the governor's promises of safety, a group of armed men, gunpowder blackening their faces to hide their identities, gathered outside of the jail where Smith was held.[2] By sundown the bodies of the thirty-eight-year-old prophet of the Latter-day Saints and his brother lay lifeless on the backs of two wagons being transported back to Nauvoo.

The Latter-day Saints mourned their deaths for months. In a letter to distant friends, one woman described the event as "one of the most horible crimes comited that every history recorded[!]."[3] Businesses closed while Latter-day Saints turned inward to reflect on the fact that God had not intervened to save their prophet. Joseph and Hyrum's deaths were particularly hard on their wives. According to one witness, Hyrum's widow Mary Fielding Smith "trembled at every step, and nearly fell" as she tried to walk toward her husband's body. Faithful Latter-day Saints had carefully washed the bodies before Mary and her family were allowed to see them. When she reached Hyrum, she "clasped her hands around his head, [and] turned his pale face upon her heaving bosom." She then cried out: "Oh! Hyrum, Hyrum! Have they shot you, my dear Hyrum—are you dead? O! speak to me, my dear husband."[4] The image of his father lying in state would become of the first memories of Mary's son Joseph F. Smith. According to the historian Scott Kenney, Hyrum's face had become so mangled and distorted that it was "nearly unrecognizable" when his son first saw it.[5]

Although the Smith brothers had not publicly recognized their plural wives, the loss was often just as difficult for these women as it was for their legal spouses. The same man who described Mary's heartbreak noticed one of Joseph Smith's plural wives standing with "her face covered, and her whole frame convulsing with weeping."[6] The secrecy surrounding her marriage meant that she could not grieve publicly, but she felt her widowhood nonetheless.

Joseph and Hyrum's deaths represented a turning point for the church. In the year after their deaths, Latter-day Saints continued to experience frequent outbreaks of extralegal violence. Although many Latter-day Saints were reluctant to abandon their city and temple, the threat of violence eventually convinced church leaders to do so.[7] In 1846 the Latter-day Saint exodus from Nauvoo began. Their decision to leave Nauvoo for the Rocky Mountains was painful, but it also provided them with enough physical distance from the rest of the United States to create the godly kingdom they had once envisioned arising in Missouri. As Latter-day Saints moved across the Great Plains and settled the valleys of Utah, they were able to live openly as polygamists for the first time. As a result, they created structures of family, kinship, and community while they built the physical structures of Zion.

Latter-day Saints were not the first white people in the American West. Spanish conquistadors, French fur traders, and a variety of scientists and explorers had preceded them. Some of these men entered sexual relationships with Native women, occasionally forming polygamous bonds. Sections of the Great Plains were part of a Métis homeland that stretched from the Canadian provinces of British Columbia, Saskatchewan, Manitoba, and Alberta to what is now Montana and North Dakota. Descended from white fur traders and Native women, the Métis challenged the Canadian Confederation and even created a provisional government. In what would become the American Southwest, the Comanches and Utes wielded enormous power. Their influence shaped international policy and local politics. The exchange of female captives welded Native communities together and created new kinship structures throughout the region.

The Latter-day Saint exodus brought them into contact with these communities. As a result, the Latter-day Saint practice of polygamy developed in conversation with the sexual practices of fur traders, Native Americans, and other indigenous peoples. In 1846 Elizabeth Brotherton Pratt left Nauvoo with her husband Parley and several of his plural wives. A man named St. Clair and his Native wives visited them at one point. Elizabeth briefly recounted the story decades later, calling the women "squaws."[8] It is impossible to know what she thought when she first viewed the women. Did she see any similarities between their experiences and her own? Was she horrified by the possible comparisons that might be drawn between the two Native women and her life as a plural wife?

Like other white settlers, white Latter-day Saints tried to discipline the family structures of Native Americans and other indigenous people, including Pacific Islanders. The difference was that their own understanding of the family was undergoing a radical revision. It was not foreordained that Latter-day Saints would accept polygamy. The secrecy surrounding its practice in Nauvoo meant that the majority of Latter-day Saints had only heard rumors about it. After Smith's death, Brigham Young had to convince his followers of the practice's divinity and establish social norms for how it would be conducted. Latter-day Saint sexual practices could be just as unruly as Native ones. Young disciplined white men who claimed that revelation allowed them to claim women as sexual partners without consulting Latter-day Saint leaders. While they policed the sexual practices of white Latter-day Saints, missionaries representing the church offered their own families as models of domesticity for indigenous converts. Establishing the Kingdom of God required that Latter-day Saints reform both Native and white families and bring them under the authority of the priesthood. It would not be an easy task—either in Utah or on the Great Plains.

The Succession Crisis and its Impact on Latter-day Saint Polygamy

The changes that occurred in Latter-day Saint theology and family life had their origins in the uncertainty that Saints experienced in Nauvoo after Smith's death. His martyrdom exposed a power vacuum among the Saints. Although some had hoped for a dynastic succession in which prophetic power resided in individual members of the Smith family, most believed that God would anoint a successor. Several men arose to claim Joseph Smith's mantle. A Latter-day Saint named James Strang claimed that an angel had revealed the existence of another testament of Jesus Christ to him and ordained him as Smith's successor. A little over a year after Smith's death, he led four of his followers to a tree where they unearthed six brass plates. This reenactment of the church's birth convinced many Saints that God had blessed them with another prophet. Strang's following may have numbered over twelve thousand people at its height, including Joseph Smith's brother William.[9] Sidney Rigdon, an influential theologian among the Latter-day Saints who had once been Smith's confidant and counselor in the First Presidency, also represented an important claim to power. As an early convert to the church, he had baptized many men and women into the faith. Rigdon and his followers rejected polygamy and disciplined any members who had more than one wife.[10]

Individual families frequently split apart as husbands and wives, sisters and brothers, parents and children chose to follow different contenders for Smith's prophetic authority. One of these families was that of Aidah and Albert Clements, whose appearance before the Nauvoo High Council was described in chapter 2. According to family histories, Aidah joined the church while she was living in Fort Ann, New York. Her husband Albert met Sidney Rigdon during a "business trip" and brought home a copy of the Book of Mormon. After Smith's death, Albert decided to follow the man who had initially introduced him to the gospel. Aidah, on the other hand, followed Brigham Young to the deserts of Utah, where two of her daughters eventually married the same man and became sister wives.[11]

Even those families who ultimately chose to follow Young suffered from the uncertainty that followed Smith's death. On the day the Smith brothers died, Addison Pratt was proselytizing in the Pacific. His distance from Nauvoo meant that he did not learn about the event for over a year, when a schooner arrived with a long letter detailing the death of the Latter-day Saint prophet and his brother. Addison wrote in his journal that the accounts caused his "blood to chill in [his] veins."[12] Thousands of miles and an ocean away, he was unable to help his family or even know if they were safe. The separation, however, was harder on his wife Louisa, who at this point had not yet traveled to the Pacific Islands and was still gathered with the Saints in Illinois. Like Aidah Clements, she decided to follow Young from Nauvoo to the American West. During the journey she contracted scurvy and was forced to live in a sod cave in Winter Quarters, Nebraska, a temporary settlement that Latter-day Saints created to wait out the cold winter months. At one point she claimed that she could feel "my flesh waste away from off my bones!"[13] She lost her upper front teeth as a result of her illness, causing her to speak with an "unnatural" voice until she obtained false teeth decades later.[14] Her altered appearance became a marker of the suffering she had experienced as a Mormon woman. In addition to her disfigured face, Louisa's separation from her husband was an ongoing difficulty. Although they had been married for years by the time she traveled to Utah, he provided her with little financial help and failed to protect their family. When she referred to him in her journal, she initially put the word "father" in quotation marks.[15] While she never did the same with "husband," she admitted that "differences of opinion sometimes arose between [them] in regard to certain principles which had been revealed in his absence."[16] She was likely referring to polygamy.

Louisa's experiences suggest that missionary work and the distance it created exacerbated the divisions that Smith's death caused. The succession crisis was experienced by many Latter-day Saints as a deeply personal fissure that threatened their relationships with one another and with the church. It was also a theological crisis. As historians Benjamin Park and Robin Jensen have argued, Smith's thought was not a fully "coherent worldview." Instead, it was fragmentary—"pregnant with possibilities, saturated with inherent tensions and paradoxes, and capable of several trajectories."[17] The various claimants to Joseph Smith's prophetic vision had fundamentally different understandings of revelation. Although early Latter-day Saints emphasized the expansiveness of their faith's theology, some believed that the revelations that Smith had received served as a corpus to which they could turn to judge the prophetic assertions of others. They believed that past revelation bound prophets and helped to maintain a sense of order and stability within the restoration. When John E. Page was confronted with the claims of the Quorum of the Twelve Apostles to authority, he lamented the fact that the revelations the body had received did not seem to conform to Smith's earlier pronouncements. He ultimately rejected the authority of the quorum even though he had previously been ordained a member of it.[18] Park and Jensen argue that the difference was partly geographic. Members who lived within Nauvoo experienced the multiplicity of revelations offered by Smith and others as expanding their knowledge of the Kingdom of God, while those who lived outside of its boundaries did not have immediate access to new revelation. Their understanding of the Restoration was more static and resistant to change as a result.[19]

The theological crisis among the Latter-day Saints was compounded by the existence of what the historian Ron Esplin has called "private gnosis" within the early church.[20] Smith claimed that he had never hidden his teachings from his followers. However, the explanations he gave of his "strongest doctrines"—including polygamy, the multiplicity of gods, and the eventual fate of the priesthood—were often fuller to members of his inner circle.[21] Brigham Young's task as Smith's eventual successor was to bring his more private teachings into public. He introduced many of the Saints to knowledge that had previously been accessible to only a few.[22] While some Latter-day Saints accepted Brigham Young's teachings, others refused to believe that they had come from Joseph Smith or God, including Smith's first wife Emma. Although she mourned her husband, his death allowed her to rewrite the history of the restoration. Emma professed after Joseph's death that he had never taken additional wives and that he had loved her alone.

She was not the only one of his wives to struggle with polygamy. Joseph Smith had married Sarah and Maria Lawrence when they were only seventeen and nineteen years old respectively. The girls had recently lost both of their parents and were his wards. Although it is possible that they loved Smith, any affection they felt for him would have overlapped with ties of obligation. After his death, Sarah married Heber C. Kimball, a man twenty years her senior. Kimball's daughter Helen reflected on her father's marriage to the young woman decades later in a Latter-day Saint newspaper called the *Woman's Exponent*. By that point, Sarah had left Kimball for another man. Helen blamed Sarah's discontent on polygamy and jealousy. In the end, she wrote, Sarah "lost every spark of the gospel" and "became so wicked that when paying her last visit to Salt Lake she denied emphatically ever being connected to Joseph or to my father."[23] For Helen, Sarah's decision to leave Kimball cost her salvation and separated her from Zion. Sarah, however, likely interpreted her decision differently. After Joseph Smith's death, Kimball had married multiple women in rapid succession. To assume Smith's authority and likely his place in heavenly kinship networks, church elites divided the prophet's wives between them. As a result, Kimball had precious little time to visit Sarah or develop a real relationship with her. She likely saw monogamy as an escape from loneliness and eventually entered another relationship. Unfortunately, her new husband could not provide her with what she wanted. He returned to the the gold fields, and they eventually divorced, leaving her to find a way to provide for their children.[24]

Polygamy and the Changing Latter-day Saint Family

Not all Latter-day Saint women sought to abandon polygamy. Some saw it as an awe-inspiring revelation that exalted women through their self-sacrifice. These individuals rejoiced that the Latter-day Saint exodus had allowed them to stop hiding the bonds they had ritually formed with married men. The relative paucity of sources makes it difficult to trace the precise shifts in restoration theology that occurred as people began to openly claim their polygamous spouses. The documents that do survive, however, allow us to make some sense of the changes that occurred.

The Latter-day Saint exodus to Utah began on February 4, 1846, when thousands of Saints fled Illinois because of continued fears of state and federal harassment.[25] It was the first time that many families were able to openly claim each other as kin. Some of Brigham Young's wives found the experience exhilarating. Sixteen-year-old Lucy Bigelow married the Latter-day Saint patriarch on March 20, 1847, in Winter Quarters. Her decision to do so meant that she entered a sprawling family with dozens of wives, several of whom were near her own age. Emeline Free was twenty-one, Emily Partridge was twenty-three, and Ellen Rockwood was just twenty. Several of them lived together in a single tent. This arrangement allowed them to develop close, loving relationships with each other. Lucy's daughter Susa wrote a biography of her mother in the early twentieth century. She emphasized the childlike nature of the women her father had married, calling them "girl-wives"—still rosy-cheeked and eager to please their shared husband.[26] Many were living apart from their families for the first time. The result was the formation of quick friendships. Denied the company of their husband, who was supposed to sustain them and provide them with spiritual nourishment, these women turned toward the other model of femininity available to them—the world of female friendship.

Carroll Smith-Rosenberg's classic description of female friendship emphasizes the importance of letter writing and visiting in sustaining female friendships. Latter-day Saints used these methods to build community, but they also developed bonds through intense, emotional prayer and suffering. The Latter-day Saint community held frequent prayer meetings in the months they camped at Winter Quarters. Although these gatherings began slowly that December, with just one meeting that month, by early June they occurred twice daily.[27] The result was what the historian Laurel Thatcher Ulrich has called a "pentecostal outpouring."[28] Latter-day Saint women met together to bless each other's bodies, speak in tongues, and be engulfed by the Holy Spirit. On April 27, 1847, Patty Bartlett Sessions attended a prayer meeting at the residence of Sister Cutler. Her description of this initial meeting was brief. We "prayed and sung and spoke as the Lord directed," she wrote. Two days later she attended another meeting in which several Mormon sisters placed their hands on her head and began to prophesy. They told her she would "live to stand in a temple yet to be built" where she would see Joseph. The children that she had delivered as a midwife would then ask her to "bless" them, for she had been the first person to hold their bodies.[29] The next day she attended meetings at the homes of Sister Buell, Sister Thompson, and Sister Kimball, where they feasted on the "good things of the kingdom."[30]

Many of the participants in these gatherings were the plural wives of Latter-day Saint leaders. The spiritual gifts they experienced there allowed them to create a female-centered spirituality. Women frequently blessed and healed each other's bodies. One woman remembered the healing power that had been granted to Latter-day Saint women. A child had been unable to speak or see for two days, so several women blessed it by "anointing [it] with oil, and bathing its eyes with milk and water." The sisters celebrated its recovery and "gave God the glory."[31] The same woman described a prayer meeting in which one man "spoke in tongues in an Indian language, and prophesied of the destruction of this nation before the coming of the Savior." She claimed that "the power that rested upon him was so great as to produce such an intense sympathy with those in the room, that they were all wonderfully affected." After he finished, Eliza R. Snow, an important Latter-day Saint poet who was sealed first to Joseph Smith and then to Brigham Young after the former's death, spoke "in the pure language of Adam."[32]

This spiritual flowering was partially a result of the freedom that Latter-day Saints felt in their distance from the rest of the United States. They saw their trek across the American West as reenacting the exodus of the Israelites from Egypt and believed that they would soon come upon the promised land. This revival resulted in a dichotomy among the surviving descriptions of Winter Quarters. As Maureen Beecher has pointed out, the diaries written during this period are generally more optimistic than the reminiscences written later.[33] Snow, who later bemoaned Winter Quarters, wrote in 1846 that the Mormon community felt for the first time "as tho' we could breath more freely and speak one with another upon those things where in God had made us free with less carefulness than we had hitherto done."[34] When Latter-day Saints lived in Winter Quarters, they found a sense of freedom even as they lived in poverty and experienced disease and death. As time progressed, however, the memories of their poverty likely became stronger than their initial sense of freedom.

Ecstatic prayer meetings and the Saints' newfound freedom did not completely ease the transition from monogamy to polygamy. Patty Sessions's diary is one of the most famous accounts of a woman struggling to accept the restoration's changing understanding of marriage.[35] In 1842 she went to the chamber of Newel K. Whitney to be sealed to Joseph Smith as a plural wife in the presence of her daughter Sylvia. She was likely struggling with grief at the time. A little under a year earlier, she had lost her three-year-old daughter Amanda. She had carried the little girl with her as the family fled Missouri after Governor Lilburn Boggs issued an order demanding that Latter-day Saints either leave his state or be exterminated.[36] In 1842 Willard Richards sealed Patty to Joseph

Smith "for eternity."[37] This language meant that she would be bound to Joseph in the afterlife but would remain her earthly husband's until her death.

Around this same time, Patty's husband David married a second woman, Rosilla Cowan. Patty was in her fifties; Rosilla was nearly two decades her junior. The relationship between the two women was difficult. Many of the women who lived as plural wives in Winter Quarters were in their early twenties or even their teens. In contrast, Rosilla was an adult and refused to cede any authority. Patty wrote in her diary that Rosilla "fil[l]ed" their husband's "ears full."[38] The younger woman also refused to share the household duties. Instead of cooking meals with her sister wife, she insisted on preparing her own food and eating it alone. As Patty wrote simply: "She can eat with the rest of us."[39] Although the tension between the two women was difficult for Patty to bear, her husband's response made it even more trying. He initially blamed Patty for the differences between the two women. Patty wrote in one diary entry, "Mr. Sessions has said many hard things to me," only to strike it out.[40] Several of her entries from this period are blotted out, including ones where she admitted that she slept alone.[41] Eventually, Rosilla decided that the marriage could not be salvaged and left the company. She returned to Nauvoo to join the Latter-day Saints that remained.

There were other difficulties as well. The decision to flee Nauvoo before the Latter-day Saints had finished their preparations meant that they had little food for the journey. The lack of food, the constant physical demands upon individual bodies, and the cold weather led to hundreds of deaths from consumption, malaria, and scurvy. The historian Richard Bennett has calculated that over seven hundred people died in Latter-day Saint settlements between June 1846 and the following summer.[42] The infant mortality rate was approximately 35 percent.[43] When the community reached Winter Quarters they were forced to hastily build cabins, sod houses, and whatever other structures they could.[44] Eliza Lyman likely arrived at Winter Quarters in summer 1846. She complained in her journal that fever and "scorching sun" had reduced her to "a skeleton so much so that those who have not been with me do not know me."[45] The descriptions that women offered of this period in their later reflections were bleak. Eliza R. Snow referred to it as "a growling, grumbling, devilish, sickly time."[46] Jane Snyder Richards reflected on her experiences with the simple sentence: "I only lived because I could not die."[47] She had given birth to a daughter she called Wealthy Lovisa while living in Nauvoo, but the little girl died in Winter Quarters. In his history of the Mormon migration, Wallace Stegner imagined the event as one filled with pathos, with "Jane's brothers were prostrated with fever" while her sister wife Elizabeth was "screaming in delirium in the tent."[48] Latter-day Saint missionary work had called her husband Franklin to London. As a result, he would not hear of the little girl's death for months. Stegner ends the scene with Elizabeth's death, who in his words had been "dwindling with tuberculosis and the compounded scurvy that they called black canker."[49]

Other women's experiences were difficult if less horrific. Mary Fielding Smith had a complicated position among the Latter-day Saints as they traveled west. Although she had been married to one of the leaders of the community, Hyrum's death made her just one of several women who found themselves widowed after the martyrdom. Brigham Young and Heber C. Kimball divided the brothers' wives between them. Mary ultimately decided to cast her lot with Kimball, but her marriage to him was likely no more intimate than Sarah Lawrence's. The two never had children, and Mary ultimately decided to live on a farm in nearby Millcreek rather than in Salt Lake City with her husband.[50] In the public imagination, Mary traveled much of the trail alone.

Joseph F. Smith, Mary's son, contributed to the creation of this idea. In 1919 he published an article in the *Young Woman's Journal* on his mother's trek across the Great Plains. Instead of connecting her to Kimball, the article calls her "the widow" and notes that after applying to a local agent of the church for help crossing the plains, she was turned away and told she would "prove a burden to your company."[51] Mary's son portrayed her as forced to rely on her own ingenuity. When her ox becomes ill, she blesses it with the help of her brother and a man named Joel Terry. When they arrived in the Salt Lake Valley on September 24,

1848, Mary treats herself to the "luxury of a bath" before going to see "Brother Brigham and the others preach."[52]

Joseph F. Smith's vision of his mother entered popular culture. The year after he published the article, the Pocatello First Ward displayed a painting by Minerva Teichert. The painting depicts Mary wearing a blue paid shawl over a black-bodice dress. Her arm rests on her son's shoulder. Two sturdy oxen pull a wagon behind her. There are no other living Latter-day Saints in the painting. Mary, though serene, has been left to provide for herself. God, however, has chosen to help the Latter-day Saint widow. A group of heavenly figures wearing breastplates and sitting astride horses accompany her.[53]

Lavina Fielding Anderson, a Latter-day Saint historian and feminist, explored the myths surrounding Mary's trek across the Great Plains in a 1981 article with the wry title, "Mary Fielding Smith: Her Ox Goes Marching On." She points out that despite the imagery of Mary traveling alone, she made the trek with "a household of eighteen people, including her sister Mercy Fielding Thompson; her brother Joseph Fielding; their families; the five children of Hyrum by his previous marriage, including a sixteen-year-old boy; her own son and daughter; three hired men; an unmarried woman who had been living in the Smith household and helping with the homemaking duties since at least 1837; and an older man who was a general handyman."[54]

A letter that Kimball sent to Mary after she decided to travel across the plains belies her son's descriptions of her as completely without resources. Kimball tells her that he hopes that she "will overtake us and winter with us in some good place." He then provides her with specific information about which items will be useful to her and which will only make the journey more difficult, telling her to leave behind any "heavy articles" or "furniture that is of no use" but bring "all the oxen" she could and "any breeding mares."[55] Although Kimball's letter lacks any emotive language or sense of intimacy with his new wife, it does suggest that he considered Mary to be his responsibility and that she was not entirely without help or friends as she embarked on the journey across the Great Plains.

The freedom they enjoyed was double-edged. While Latter-day Saints celebrated their freedom with the overflowing of heavenly tongues, their leaders worried about their ability to control marriage and sexuality. The open, if still unspoken, acceptance of polygamy during the journey made plural marriage possible for ordinary members of the faith. What had been a closely regulated practice in Nauvoo became one in which dozens of men participated. In Iowa a local leader named Henry Davis claimed that "it was the privilege of every Elder, Seventy, etc. to have as many wives as he could get and that he had the right to marry them."[56] Although some Latter-day Saints considered Davis' prophetic claims to be nothing more than "pretended authority," others believed that he spoke the word of God. A man named Conyers took a young woman as his plural wife after embracing the doctrine. Jonathan Wright called it "the strongest case of adultery" in his letter to Brigham Young and told the man's first wife when she asked that her husband should repent and ask forgiveness for his sins.[57] If he continued to have sex with the young woman, "he would be damned."[58] The willingness of Latter-day Saints to accept revelation would have made it difficult for women to know which individuals had a legitimate claim to prophetic authority. Disagreements over the identity of Joseph Smith's legitimate heir overlapped with questions about who had the authority to enter polygamous relationships and who did not. Disentangling these questions was essential. One's position within the community, and perhaps more importantly, one's eternal life, was at stake.

During the journey from Illinois to Winter Quarters, Young routinely condemned men for seducing women with promises of salvation. He claimed that these men twisted Latter-day Saint theology by telling women they could not enter the Kingdom of God without a husband and that there was "no harm for them to sleep together" before they were "sealed" together. Such men often followed their promises with hasty visits to a "clod head of an elder" who sealed the couple—"all done without the knowledge or counsel of the authority of this church."[59] For Latter-day Saint leaders, these marriages represented a challenge to their authority. Young told his followers that he worried that many Latter-day Saints would be "cut off for whoredom" if the "strict letter of the law" was enforced.[60] Some of the couples that engaged in these relationships, however, may have seen them as lawful marriages. Although the United States government had long tried to bring marriage under its control, many men and women living in sparsely settled regions married each other without publishing notice or contacting a public official. They believed that simply living as married individuals legitimized their unions.[61] The introduction of polygamy into the church may have solidified ordinary members' belief that these were righteous marriages rather than whoredoms or evidence of adultery.

Young's statements about marriage represented not so much an indictment of illicit sexuality as a desire to bring marriage under the control of the church. The clod heads that Young mentioned erred by not submitting their marriages to the priesthood; they insisted on their ability to marry individual women by gaining their consent and finding someone to perform the religious ceremony. Young recognized that the establishment of polygamy had created a space for people to challenge many of the assumptions of monogamous marriage, and that they saw the announcement of polygamy as being representative of a greater openness to alternative sexualities. Young, however, believed that it was important to exert control over marriage among Latter-day Saints. Displaying proper understandings of domesticity was important because of the attacks on the Latter-day Saint community that had arisen in the wake of polygamy. Although the practice only circulated outside of the Latter-day Saints as rumor and innuendo, non-Mormons had accused Smith and his followers of condoning sexual immorality, prostitution, and adultery. Young's assumption of leadership had not stemmed these accusations. The attempt to establish polygamy and to control other forms of sexuality was an important part of solidifying the Latter-day Saint community during the westward trek and in Utah. Establishing a polygamous domesticity would not be the only concern of Latter-day Saint leaders; relations with Native Americans would complicate matters still further.

Encountering Native Americans

Latter-day Saints had been in contact with Native American communities since the 1830s. As we have seen, the earliest Latter-day Saint missionary work had focused on the Delawares and Shawnees; in Nauvoo they had met with Native leaders in hopes of convincing them that the Book of Mormon was a record of their ancestors. The few Native people who had converted to the Church of Jesus Christ of Latter-day Saints then served as missionaries themselves. In 1845, for example, the Council of Fifty called upon Lewis Dana to look for new opportunities for settlement in the American West. He was also to serve as a missionary to the Blackfeet. The turmoil among the Latter-day Saints, however, prevented them from engaging in any sustained efforts to convert Native peoples. When Latter-day Saints moved west, they chose to travel north of established routes to avoid harassment from non-Mormons.

Latter-day Saints entered "Indian Country" as they moved across the Great Plains. This land had been given to the Potawatomi and other Indian tribes in exchange for their ancestral homelands. The U.S. government required that Latter-day Saints receive permission to settle on Potawatomi land. In 1846 Brigham Young met directly with Indian leaders to ask them to allow his people to remain on their land in the winter months. Young's question placed the leaders of the Potawatomi in a difficult position. For over a century they had navigated the vagaries of European imperial politics to remain an independent nation. They had fought in the War of 1812, allied with Tecumseh during his rebellion, and ambushed a U.S. military force at Fort Dearborn. Their removal west in 1833 after the Treaty of Chicago was supposed to offer the Potawatomi a new homeland and a respite from imperial politics. The arrival of Mormons in their homelands threatened to disrupt that peace. If Mormons were successful in creating a New Jerusalem, it was possible that the Potawatomi would be forced to move again.[62]

Latter-day Saints accounts of the meeting between their leaders and the Potawatomi emphasize a sense of brotherhood between the two groups. In one report a Potawatomi leader compares the Latter-day Saint exodus to their own expulsion from their households. "The Potawatomi," the man's speech begins, "came sad and tired into this unhealthy Missouri bottom, not many years back, when he was taken from his beautiful country beyond the Mississippi, which had abundant game and timber, and clear water everywhere. Now you are driven away the same from your lodges and your lands there, and the graves of your people."[63] The man then enjoins the Saints: "We must keep one another and the Great Spirit will keep us both."[64]

In this vein, Latter-day Saints came to see their own exodus as part of God's prophetic plan. He had called them out of Nauvoo and, in so doing, had placed them among the Lamanites. On August 1, 1847, almost immediately after arriving with the first Latter-day Saints to Utah, Orson Pratt gave an address to the Saints directly addressing the unexpectedness of the community's exodus west and the effects that it would have on their relationship with Native peoples. He told those who were assembled in the Salt Lake Valley that it was "with peculiar feelings" that he that he had come to stand "before so many of the Saints in this uncultivated region." As he continued, he told his listeners that the Latter-day Saint community had been called to "congregate among the remnant of Joseph" and reimagine their future. Initially, the Saints had anticipated that they would serve as missionaries to Native Americans. Their "wives and children would be built up among the strongholds of the Gentiles" while they sojourned among the Delawares and Potawatomi. Pratt, however, had come to realize that "Jehovah had different purposes." If God had not forced the Saints leave their homes, the gospel would have never been brought to the Lamanites.[65] Pratt's speech argued that the Latter-day Saints' exodus would be the means through God would redeem Native Americans.

It is possible to read Pratt's statement as a radical act. He called for the Saints to identify with Native Americans and to accept that the gospel might collapse the distance between them and their Native brethren. The movement of Latter-day Saints into the Great Basin, however, also turned them into settlers. In Missouri and Illinois it had been possible for them to dream of a day when Native Americans would overturn the U.S. federal government and rule in the Latter-day Saints' anticipated

New Jerusalem. In Utah, however, the Saints would not entertain the possibility of an Indian revolution. Instead, they became the government and expected Native Americans to work within the confines of the law. Just before Pratt suggested that God had "brought [the Saints] out almost as an entire people," Heber C. Kimball asked that a guard be placed in front of the Latter-day Saint cattle to prevent local Indian groups from stealing their livestock.[66]

The latent radicalism of Pratt's statement was rarely realized. White Latter-day Saints entered the Salt Lake Valley not as a people ready to be transformed by their encounters with Ute, Shoshone, and Paiute people, but as colonialists ready to transform the landscape. The Quorum of the Twelve Apostle had originally traveled to the Great Basin with an advance guard of Saints to select a site for the city. After they superintended the exploration of the valley, they started back. On September 9, 1847, the quorum sent a letter to the men they had left behind instructing them on how to prepare for the arrival of the rest of the companies of Latter-day Saints. It encouraged them to finish building the fort they had started and to erect a fence around it to keep in their cattle and horses. The following spring, the men were to plow the cattle yard so that their wives and children would be able to plant gardens when they arrived.[67] These instructions were the beginning of the Latter-day Saint attempt to transform the Great Basin into an area suitable for white farming. God may have called the Saints out of Nauvoo to live among Native people, but he did not intend for them to live like them.[68]

White Latter-day Saint depictions of Native Americans were just exotic as other white Americans. The diaries the Saints wrote as they crossed the plains included rich, ethnographic descriptions of Native American cultures. William Clayton remembered sitting on an Indian grave and gazing at the "splendid view of the surrounding country for many miles." The next day he wrote a thick description of a Native village that was close to the Presbyterian mission station on Plumb Creek. He later reported that there were cachets "large enough to admit a common sized man" and shaped like a thin-necked jug called a demijohn.[69] Caroline Barnes Crosby saw the burials of two Indian children who had been placed in trees. She described them as a "great curiosity."[70] Latter-day Saints sometimes desecrated these graves by stealing grave objects.[71]

Their descriptions of Native Americans could verge on animalistic. On July 27, 1847, for example, Patty Sessions described a group of Native Americans that she saw as coming "like bees."[72] The apostle Wilford Woodruff encountered a group of Ute Indians for what may have been the first time a day later. He was riding on a horse to retrieve a carriage whip that he had lost when he saw twenty men in the distance. At first they looked like bears. As they got closer, however, Woodruff realized they were people. One of the men leapt on his own horse and raced toward the apostle, stopping when he was within twenty rods. They asked Woodruff to accompany them to their camp and smoke a peace pipe.[73]

Many white settlers adopted animalistic language when talking about Native Americans. The radical potential of the Book of Mormon for Native peoples was entangled with racist ideas that emphasized their degradation and savagery. Of course, Latter-day Saint depictions of Native Americans were never uniform. In her journal documenting her trip west, Martha Spence Heywood described her encounter with some Native Americans living near Fort Laramie. She found their "symplicity in living" fascinating and described Native women "drying Buffalo meat & tanning the Skins" while their children played around them. She found their work "clean" and the children "very handsome & smart looking."[74] John Lyman Smith likewise noted approvingly that the Indian women who visited the Latter-day Saint encampment to trade would sing and dance for the community. He wrote that "some of the Squaws looked very tidy."[75]

In many ways, even Latter-day Saints who used "positive" language to describe Native people were willing participants in American colonialism. Heywood's description of the simplicity of Native American culture, for example, drew on a long tradition of casting Native Americans as less sophisticated and cultured than white settlers. Native Americans, while noble, were considered unable to resist the onslaught of European civilization. The language that Saints like Heywood used could be weaponized to justify white settlement and often was.

The Saints, like other white Americans, saw education as a method of assimilation. While they were wintering in Iowa, a few Latter-day Saint women opened a school for Indian children where they hoped to teach pupils "how to sew, knit, spin, read, write, cipher, and spell."[76] One of their sons—a boy named Mosiah L. Hancock—read the Book of Mormon to the Potawatomi and Delawares. In exchange, they would sometimes "fill [his] hat with venison or buffalo meat." He remembered the meat as "dried, and so nice!"[77] Hancock, however, was not convinced that their efforts were fully repaid. Although he fondly remembered a boy named Opteksech, he felt "it was hard to keep the Indian children in school, or even to teach the girls to knit or spin."[78] His autobiography also contained mention of a Métis man who cheated them of hay and Sioux Indians who attempted to trade for a sixteen-year-old girl named Lovina. When he arrived in Utah, the boy briefly served a mission to the Indians but found them "mean." He noted that measles soon "thinned out" the Indians living near his house.[79]

Many Latter-day Saints imagined the homes of Native women as deficient even when they married white men. An English Italian convert named Guglielmo Sangiovanni considered men who had married Native American women, often called "squaw men," to be one of the "great features of the plains."[80] In a description published decades after his 1852 trip across the plains, he acknowledged that these men had been born to white families but remarked on how different their lives had become from their previous existence. His description focused on the dirtiness of the clothes the fur traders wore. He wrote that an imagined individual trapper's clothes consisted "of a greasy slouch hat, long hair and beard—'a la Buffalo Bill,' an old dirty over-shirt and buckskin pants, a butcher knife and revolver in his belt, and moccasins on his feet." His description of the Indian woman who would marry such a man was no kinder. He styled her in "a dirty old buckskin gown . . . [with] a few beads worked on it."[81]

Even Latter-day Saints who rejected the overt racism of Sangiovanni's description of the mixed-race family remarked that living with Native Americans could undermine an individual's whiteness. Clark Davis was only nineteen years old when he joined a Latter-day Saint emigration company. At some point the company came across a group of Arapahoe women who were boiling buffalo meat. As Davis was eating the meat, a man came who did not look either "Indian or white." He wore a "buckskin coat . . . pants made of scotch plaid, a hat on his head and moccasins on his feet." The man asked Davis if he had whiskey, which Davis gave him in a bottle. The next day the same man served as an interpreter and demanded that the Saints pay for "passing through their country" with "salt, sugar, blankets, shirts, and whiskey."[82]

In the Latter-day Saints' imagination, such liminal figures came to represent what could go wrong in the relationships that white people developed with Native Americans. The Saints were not the only ones who described fur traders as wearing buckskin and adopting Native culture. Historians like Adele Perry and Sylvia Van Kirk have pointed out the contempt that many people held for fur traders and their Indian wives.[83] Perry cites an 1862 letter to the editor that claimed that white men who had married Indian women were "almost without an exception . . . degraded below the dignity of manhood." The author described them as "long-haired, badly dressed, dirty faced, [and] redolent of salmon" in one sentence and as "half-inebriated sots" in another.[84] As W. Paul Reeve has demonstrated, white commentators were not reluctant to apply these descriptions to Latter-day Saints who married Indian women.[85] It wasn't without irony, then, Latter-day Saints joined other white Americans in emphasizing the drunkenness of fur traders and their adoption of Native culture, including polygamy. In many ways their descriptions were not substantially different than those of non-Mormons. White Latter-day Saints described fur traders as existing in-between Native and white society. They emphasized their savagery, abandonment of white domesticity, and willingness to raise nonwhite children. What was different was that Latter-day Saints had adopted a family structure that most white Americans would have considered no less savage than those of fur traders. Restoration theology also compelled them to proselytize among American Indians and bring them into God's family. Their task on the Great Plains and in Utah would be to establish a polygamous domesticity that would differentiate them from Native Americans and the Métis families of fur traders.

Defining the White Polygamous Family

The historian Matthew Bowman has argued that Latter-day Saints "practiced plural marriage with all the rectitude they could manage."[86] Although many Americans accused the Latter-day Saints of debauchery, the Saints saw their faith as reflecting the order of heaven and believed that it would ultimately protect women's virtue rather than destroying it. One of their concerns as they began settling the Salt Lake Valley would be differentiating themselves from the white fur traders who had traversed the area before they arrived. They would do so by trying to discipline Native people and positioning themselves as more beneficent missionaries and colonizers than other white Americans had been.

The first years in the valley were difficult for white Latter-day Saints. The advance party that Brigham Young sent from Winter Quarters in 1847 tried to prepare the region for the arrival of settlers. They laid out the city streets in a neat grid, built temporary cabins, and began to plant crops. The number of people who arrived the following year, however, overwhelmed their preparations.[87] People began to eat food that they would normally have considered unfit for whites. Priddy Meeks found himself eating hawks, crows, wolf meat, sego lily, thistle roots, and cattle that he had found "dead" in "the mire holes."[88] The lilies that the settlers ate eventually became a symbol of "LDS grit" and appeared in Mormon art commemorating their entrance into the valley.[89] Latter-day Saints came to see the difficulties that they faced as they carved Zion out of the mountains and recesses of the Great Basin as evidence that they were a godly people. Like the Israelites, they had suffered in their quest to found the Kingdom of God. Somewhat ironically, because this process had caused suffering among followers, this sorrowful language became a part of Latter-day Saint patriotism. When white Americans challenged the hold that the church had on the territory of Utah in the nineteenth century, Latter-day Saints leaders pointed to their ability to create a thriving civilization out of the wilderness as evidence of the rightness of their claim. In 1852 Brigham Young delivered a speech celebrating the fifth anniversary of the entrance of the Saints into the Salt Lake Valley. He described the Latter-day Saint community arriving in the valley "five, and six, and eight" to a wagon "huddled together" on their way to "plant themselves in the wilderness." He asked his listeners: "Would the Methodists thus run the hazard of losing their lives for their religion? Would the Presbyterians, the Baptists, the Quakers, or their old mother, the Roman Catholic church, run the same risk? Would she venture thus in the wilderness?" The answer, of course, was "no."[90]

The decision of the Latter-day Saints to constantly establish new communities meant that they would frequently find themselves living in rough conditions. In 1857, for example, twenty-eight families traveled to southern Utah to establish a cotton mission. They believed that God had inspired their leaders to call them to the area and had foreordained the beginnings of a cotton industry in Utah.[91] However, outcroppings of a black lava called basalt and the presence of lime in the soil made it difficult for them to grow crops.[92] A flood a few years later transformed the orchards they had planted into "debris."[93] The town of Parowan, Utah, also struggled in its infancy despite a belief that the development of an iron industry there would free Utah from dependency on the outside world. Residents faced a shortage of raw materials and experienced frequent floods that overwhelmed their machines. In 1858 the iron works that had represented the town's hopes closed. The town wouldn't be successful until the twentieth century.[94]

These dearly won settlements became a part of the Saints' argument for why they should be able to have their own government. Brigham Young denounced the way that the United States treated Latter-day Saints in an 1857 speech. He warned the U.S. government that they had "better count the cost" before they tried to destroy the Latter-day Saint community. "I have saved," he announced, "the Government hundreds of thousands of dollars, by keeping the Indians peaceable in Utah."[95] Young believed that U.S. settlement of the American West would have cost more lives and money if the Saints had not acted as brokers between the emigrants and Native Americans. Other leaders echoed his thoughts.

In 1868 Orson Pratt told listeners that he doubted the transcontinental railroad would have been built or California settled without the Latter-day Saints. He reminded his followers of "toils" and "hardships" they had experienced and suggested that church members, by asking to be allowed to practice polygamy and to govern their own people, requested nothing more than the "civil and religious liberty . . . guaranteed by the Constitution" of the United States.[96] In Pratt's mind, the work that the Saints had done settling Utah—their willingness to move to the Great Basin when it was still Mexican territory—had purchased their freedom and liberty.

The Latter-day Saints who listened to these talks no doubt found them thrilling. Even now it impossible to read them without imagining the speaker's likely crescendo. Yet equally as important to Latter-day Saint arguments for self-government was their missionary work among Native people. Nineteenth-century Americans imagined westward expansion as a process by which white men tamed the wilderness and made it safe for their gentler and cultivated wives. Part of this transformation involved the physical or cultural eradication of Native peoples. White Americans did not necessarily believe that American Indians would have to be entirely removed from the continent, but they did believe that those who wanted to remain in their homelands would have to assimilate into white society. Latter-day Saints rejected the idea that monogamy was the ideal system for creating families, but they did not completely reject other white ideas about domesticity. They accepted American views about purity and emphasized the importance of rearing godly children. Their argument was not that white America was misguided in its ideals, but that polygamy was a better system for achieving those ideals.

In the 1850s the Saints established missions to Native Americans throughout Utah Territory. Missionaries traveled to the southern edge of the Great Basin in 1854 "to civilize and instruct the Indians in [the] region, [so] that they might . . . inherit the blessings pertaining to them because of the works and promises of their fathers."[97] They believed it was important not to try to transform their "wild habits" too quickly but to change them "by degrees." The first step in this process was teaching them to "labor for their food."[98] At one point, Parley Pratt told the missionaries not to "leave the outside dirty" while they "sweetened . . . the inside."[99] As a result, the seed corn, axes, bushels of wheat, and ploughs that the men brought with them were just as important to their missionary work as their knowledge of the Book of Mormon. The missionaries believed that they would not be able to fully convert Native Americans without civilizing them.[100]

They were not the only the Latter-day Saints in the nineteenth century called to establish model farms or teach Native communities how to cultivate the earth. In 1855 white Latter-day Saints established a mission in central Utah in response to a request from the Pahvant chief Kanosh that the Saints teach his people how to farm like white men.[101] Latter-day Saints also helped to establish an Indian reservation near Spanish Fork, where they worked with federal officials to build a farmhouse for the area's superintendent and to irrigate the fields. And in 1876 the *Deseret Evening News* celebrated the success that returning Latter-day Saint missionaries had in convincing Native Americans in Colorado to irrigate their crops.[102] The work that they did with these communities was in many ways mundane. It involved digging ditches that calloused the hands rather than experiencing spectacular manifestations of heavenly tongues. Many Latter-day Saints, however, believed that it would be impossible to fully convert Native Americans without teaching them how to divert water from streams and labor to bring forth food from an otherwise arid landscape.

Early Latter-day Saints did not confine their missionary efforts to the United States. By the mid-nineteenth century they had developed a transnational vision of the faith in which Polynesians also came to be regarded as descendants of the peoples of the Book of Mormon. The Latter-day Saint mission to the Society Islands, a chain in the South Pacific that includes the island of Tahiti, ended in 1852 because of the French government's decision to expel the Saints. Until the 1890s, when the Saints returned to the Society Islands, Latter-day Saint missionaries turned to the Hawaiian Islands as a potential missionary field. They had originally traveled to Hawai'i in 1850 in hopes of converting white men who had traveled there to participate in the burgeoning whaling industry. Their efforts, however, came to little. Some of the missionaries wanted to abandon the mission as a failed experiment. Others concluded that the Native Hawaiians were part of the same sacred history as American Indians. In reflecting on his experiences as a missionary, George Q. Cannon urged Latter-day Saints to recognize that "the soul of a Sandwich Islander or a Lamanite" was just "as precious in the sight of the Lord as the soul of a white man."[103] He also recounted stories of Native Hawaiians who had their sight restored and their limbs healed through their faith.

Cannon's purpose in emphasizing the spiritual value of Native Hawaiians was to counter the condescension of white Saints toward Native people. Frequently, Latter-day Saint missionary work emphasized the inferiority of Native culture and the need to redeem indigenous people from their savagery. Latter-day Saint missionaries in the Hawaiian Islands would encourage Native people to cultivate sugarcane and other crops, learn to sew, and maintain white standards of cleanliness and domesticity. Cannon and other Latter-day Saint missionaries saw their efforts to save Native Hawaiians from Protestant missionaries, whose immorality they believed was leading to the destruction of the Native Hawaiian community. Mormon missionaries believed that the efforts of other white Americans to civilize Native Hawaiians had done nothing but "[tempt] them with worldly advantages" and teach them "vicious" practices that would lead to their "extinction."[104] Implicit in Cannon's narrative was a contrast between Protestant and Latter-day Saint missionaries. If Protestant missionaries were leading Native Hawaiians to extinction, Latter-day Saint missionaries saw themselves as restoring these people to their place at the center of God's heavenly kingdom as Israelites.

Latter-day Saint missionaries sometimes drew upon the language of the Book of Mormon in describing their missionary work among Native Hawaiians and American Indians. In at least one instance, in present-day Nevada, they even renamed converts, explicitly claiming them as part of the Book of Mormon story. In 1855 Latter-day Saint missionaries arrived at the Muddy River. According to Thomas Brown, one of the missionaries, they had already encountered the restored gospel through rumors that were circulating among Native communities. Over three hundred of them submitted to baptism within a few days. The Latter-day Saint missionaries present wrote down the new converts' "Indian name" before giving them "a new name" from the Bible or Mormon scripture. The missionaries also named some of the converts after Latter-day Saint leaders.[105] Brown had already renamed other Native Americans he encountered in the southern Indian mission.

Missionaries in the Pacific rarely renamed their converts. The same language, however, infused their missionary work. When Edward Partridge returned from the Hawaiian mission in 1885 the secretary to the First Presidency reflected on the meaning of the church's mission to the Pacific. At a Sunday afternoon meeting he reminded the congregation that the ancestors of Native Hawaiians and the Maori had been "brought out of the land of Jerusalem under Lehi, Mulek and others" and had "inhabited this land from about 600 years before Christ."[106]

White Latter-day Saints saw themselves as redeeming Native Americans and Polynesians from the savagery that had become their inheritance because of Laman and Lemuel's disobedience. The Indian farms they established in Utah in the 1850s were meant to train Native Americans in white standards of domesticity. Latter-day Saints in Hawai'i established a sugar plantation that would allow them to gather their Polynesian converts in a single place on the island of Oahu. Latter-day Saints' missionary work, however, was not limited to the establishment of model farms and plantations. In addition to trying to civilize Native peoples through agriculture, white Latter-day Saints began to think about the role that family ties could play in the transformation of Native people.

Latter-day Saints had long thought of heaven as being constructed through the sacred ties they formed in the temple. The Latter-day Saint family was more than a reflection of God's love for humanity; it was the very stuff with which his kingdom was made. In 1852 Orson Pratt, delivering a speech in the adobe brick tabernacle that served as the Latter-day Saint community's meeting space, declared that the "covenant of marriage" was "eternal."[107] For the Saints, "domestic pleasures" were not ancillary to religion but were "necessary for our exaltation to the fulness of the Lord's glory."[108] Latter-day Saint leaders came to believe that bringing Native Americans and Polynesians into Latter-day Saint families would transform them. The ties they created would bind them into the white community. As we shall see in the next chapter, Latter-day Saint leaders encouraged a few white men to marry Native women in hopes these marriages would cement ties between their communities and white Latter-day Saints. This encouragement made individuals who still regarded white men who had married Native women with suspicion uncomfortable. Leaders like Brigham Young were also unwilling to set an example by marrying Indian women. The upper echelon of the church was exempt from intermarriage.

Marriage was not the only way that Latter-day Saints integrated Indian people into their families. On a wider scale, Latter-day Saints adopted Native children, bringing them into their homes in hopes of "civilizing" them. Anson and Mary Call, for example, adopted a Native girl they called Ruth. She eventually married a Latter-day Saint named James Davids and worked as a midwife in Chesterfield, Idaho, where she blessed the bodies of women as they were going into labor and ministered to those near death.[109] Likewise, Amos Warner adopted a boy he called Frank after the Bear River Massacre left the child without a mother.[110] They hoped that the children would adopt white habits and would act as ambassadors to their people. The missions that Frank served in the early twentieth century to the Lamanites seemed to fulfill this promise. Frank was the exception rather than the rule, however. Most adopted Native children struggled to find their place within the white Latter-day Saint community. Although they often adopted white culture as their own, many people continued to regard them with suspicion.

The idea that a family could assimilate indigenous people seemed misplaced in the nineteenth century. Most Americans saw individuals who married Native people as more Native than white and assumed that marriage into Native communities would degrade white bodies, not elevate Native ones. Yet the Latter-day Saint attempt to create Zion required them to domesticate both white and indigenous bodies. As they moved across the Great Plains, the Saints sought to discipline individuals who transgressed developing norms surrounding polygamy. In Utah they continued to regulate plural marriage. They also began to domesticate Native American families. Joseph Smith had always imagined Zion as an expansive family that would bind together all of humanity and unite them with God. The instability of the Latter-day Saint community, however, meant that early leaders rarely had to consider what this system would look like when it was enacted on a large scale. While the Latter-day Saint exodus to Utah allowed the Saints to establish their own society outside the boundaries of the United States, it also required them to face the contradictions within their religious faith.

Not all Latter-day Saints were convinced that it was wise to adopt Indian children. Many people were skeptical of the Native children white Saints had adopted and doubted that they had fully assimilated into white society. White Latter-day Saints viewed these mixed-race children as existing in-between white and Native society. In this way, Latter-day Saint opinions did not substantially differ from those of other white settlers. Restoration theology, however, placed Native Americans at the center of its redemptive narrative and scriptures. Native adoptees, many of whom had experienced trauma, had to navigate the tension between their elevation in restoration theology and the racism they experienced within their communities. White Latter-day Saints began to reflect on their history at the end of the nineteenth century and to try to reconcile the disparate views their faith had about Native Americans. The next chapter focuses on a single community to understand how it did so.

CHAPTER 5

MAKING NATIVE KIN

On October 30, 1900, John T. Garr died in a small log home at the age of seventy-three.[1] Although he was known as a bachelor, he was not childless. Shortly after he arrived in the Cache Valley, he likely fathered two children with a Shoshone woman.[2] He brought one of the children, a boy whom he called Johnny, into his home as a toddler. Johnny died in a wagon accident as an adult, leaving his widow Elizabeth dependent on their family members for support. Garr invited her to share his home, and she probably hoped to inherit the estate after her father-in-law's death. Garr's passing placed her in a precarious position. On June 1, 1903, Garr's siblings used Johnny's illegitimacy to file a claim alleging that they were "sole heirs at law of the deceased" and that Elizabeth had no right to the estate.[3] One of the primary questions in the case was whether Garr had publicly recognized Johnny. A Utah statute declared that an illegitimate child "acquired inheritable blood" if his father "acknowledge[d] himself to be the father thereof."[4] If Elizabeth wanted their children to receive an inheritance she would have to prove that Garr had claimed her husband.

For their part, Johnny's descendants remember the case as the moment when their extended family "denounced" them.[5] One of his descendants has written about the effect of the case on her family, weaving together academic and personal narratives to explore the meaning of these accounts. The court case, she writes, meant that the family's identity was permanently linked to the Cache Valley, not Nauvoo. It became the place where other people had tried to disinherit their family and take their land. She describes her family as continually having to prove their whiteness and worth to the wider community.[6]

The Garr case was not just a family or local story. It called into question the very nature of the relationships that white Latter-day Saints had formed with indigenous people. Although many Latter-day Saints believed that Johnny was Garr's biological son, court testimony raised the possibility that Garr had adopted Johnny. This immediately placed the boy's story in a much larger context. White Latter-day Saints in the mid-nineteenth century had adopted Native children in the Pacific and the American West in hopes of teaching them to live like white people. The quick end of the Tahitian mission, however, had severely limited the numbers of Polynesian children who could be adopted. As a result, most children adopted into Latter-day Saint families were Native American. Like many settlers, the Saints relied on indigenous labor and knowledge when they colonized new areas. During the Saints' first winter in the valley, the Shoshones frequently visited their camp. The intimacies sometimes went beyond friendship.

Latter-day Saints were uncertain about how to approach interracial intimacy and kinship. On the one hand, their theology cast the redemption of Native American people as an important part of the final dispensation of the gospel. In 1875, for example, a Shoshone leader named Pocatello brought his people to Salt Lake to be baptized. The *Deseret News*, a newspaper based in Salt Lake City and run by Latter-day Saints, interpreted his willingness to submit to the authority of the church as the consummation of prophecy. "Surely," the newspaper told its readers, "the promises made to the fathers are being fulfilled."[7] White Latter-day Saints had seen Pocatello as a marauder and a miscreant before his baptism. Afterward, he became a Saint, if only temporarily. Some Saints reveled in the possibilities of Native American conversion. For them, the Book of Mormon called its followers to see the history of

Latter-day Saints as Native history. Brigham Young famously enjoined followers to "take their squaws & dress them up . . . & raise up children by them."[8] He believed that the children born to such unions would ultimately adopt white standards of domesticity, leading to the conversion of entire tribes. When Latter-day Saints entered the Great Basin in the mid-nineteenth century, they encountered a preexisting slave trade in which Ute traders often sold Indian children. Latter-day Saints bought some of these children and adopted them into their families. The trade largely ended in the late 1850s, but Latter-day Saints continued to adopt Indian children for decades afterwards.

On the other hand, the reality of Lamanite redemption was more complex than white Latter-day Saints anticipated. Although many Indian children were only a few years old when they were adopted, they soon became adults with sexual desires. The question of whom they would marry was contentious. Marriage to a Native person risked returning them to Native society and undoing the work that Latter-day Saints had done in "civilizing" them. Marriage to a white person, however, raised the possibility that the whiteness of Latter-day Saint families would be undone. Michael K. Bennion found that fewer than half of adopted Indian children were able to find spouses.[9] For example, an Indian woman named Mary Mountain died of consumption in her mid-twenties. She was unmarried and childless, despite her biographer's insistence that she loved to care for small children within her family and the emphasis among the Latter-day Saints on the importance of marriage.[10] It is difficult, of course, to know how individuals like Mary perceived their own singleness. Did she mourn her inability to marry? Did Mary embrace her singleness and see herself as part of an extended kin network? What we do know is that the singleness of Indian children placed them at the edges of a Latter-day Saint society that stressed marriage.

The presence of adopted Indian children in Latter-day Saint homes raised questions about the nature of family relationships. Sealing practices in Nauvoo had indicated that ritual, not biology, defined who was and was not kin. Ritual adoptions initially did not have material benefits. During the exodus of the Latter-day Saints from Nauvoo, however, the Saints began to organize those traveling west into companies pat-terned after the Kingdom of Heaven. Jonathan Stapley has argued that idea of adoption underlay the Saints' actions in this period. Brigham Young also gave a sermon telling his adopted family that they would eventually provide him with "temporal blessings" instead of relying on his "boarding."[11] In 1852 the Utah territorial legislature tried to define the obligations of white Latter-day Saints toward Native children. It required that Latter-day Saints provide education and clothing for Native children in their homes and limited any term of indenture to twenty years.[12] Some Latter-day Saints saw their relationship with the children they had adopted as one of kinship rather than labor. These Latter-day Saints went beyond providing Native children with clothing. Family histories, for example, suggest that Mary Ann Barzee Boice breastfed a child named Alpharetta with her son. When Alpharetta died, "Nothing was left undone for she was their very own."[13]

Latter-day Saints claimed Native children as kin to varying degrees. The Saints faced a series of uncomfortable questions in the late nine-teenth century about these children's place in their homes: Should these children be considered legitimate members of their communities? Were they kin to the white Latter-day Saints who had raised them? If so, what kind of kin were they? And finally, was it acceptable for Native Saints adopted into the faith to marry their white neighbors? The theology of the restoration foregrounded the redemption of Native people and offered white Saints an expansive understanding of the family. Although many Saints found this narrative compelling, it was unclear what it meant to adopt Native children or to bring people into their families. What claim did Native children have on their families?

These questions became a topic of open discussion during the Garr case when a lawyer accused his sister Eliza of trying to hide her brother's sexual relationship within an Indian woman. Ultimately, the trial raised questions about the place of Native Americans among the Latter-day Saints. Community members made arguments implying that Native children had no claim on their family's estates and suggested that Native children were not full kin. The family's decision to bring the case to trial rather than deal with the matter privately also changed the type of language that could be used to describe Native Americans and their relationship to the Saints. Early Latter-day Saints had emphasized the coming redemption of the Lamanites, that language was absent from court proceedings. Utah's courts required that Latter-day Saints speak about Native Americans using secular language. The Latter-day Saints who testified as part of the case referred to Native Americans not as the children of God but as marginal figures that lived at the edges of white society.

Their testimonies, though secular, reveal tensions about the acceptability of Native children. Martha Hodes has argued that communities often "tolerated" sexual transgressions for decades before questions of inheritance invited public scrutiny.[14] Garr's neighbors recounted the gossip that spread about Johnny's paternity when he arrived in the community decades earlier. The future of Elizabeth's children was at stake in their testimonies. Would she be able to continue living in the house she had shared with her father-in-law? Would her children be able to claim the inheritance they had received after their grandfather? Would they be recognized as rightful members of the Garr family?

Latter-day Saints were called to examine their relationship to Native peoples throughout the nineteenth century. The Garr case made it clear that the theology of the Book of Mormon would be more difficult to implement than the Saints had originally imagined. Although adopting Native children allowed them to participate in the redemption of the Lamanites, it also raised questions about the very nature of their families and what they should look like. Scholars who have investigated the meaning of the family for Latter-day Saints have often focused on polygamy. The Garr case reminds us that Latter-day Saints remade the family in the nineteenth century in more ways than one. They adopted Native children, created expansive kinship networks, and emphasized ritual sealings. These capacious understandings of the family would inspire people to join the Saints and remake their lives; they sometimes collapsed, however, when confronted with the hard realities of inheritance and wealth.

John T. Garr arrived in the Cache Valley in 1855. The area had originally attracted the interest of Latter-day Saints because of its potential for agriculture. In the first decades of the nineteenth century, an American fur trader named Warren Ferris described the valley as a "favorite resort for both men and animals."[15] His description suggested a region whose fertility and mild weather might allow settlers and their livestock a brief respite before they returned to hard labor.[16] The Cache Valley had long been a part of the Shoshones' seasonal rounds. In addition to hunting buffalo and gathering grass seeds, bands camped near the Bear River each year and danced in prayer for warm weather to nourish the plants that maintained human and animal life.[17] The thick grasses that had maintained herds of buffalo attracted the interest of the Latter-day Saints. In 1855 drought followed by a particularly bitter winter decimated Utah's cattle culture.[18] Jane Wilkie Hooper, an English convert who had immigrated to Utah in the mid-1850s, remembered the cattle coming "off the range . . . so poor they could hardly walk."[19] Brigham Young estimated that two-thirds of the territory's cattle died.[20] In the midst of the drought, church leaders sent over two thousand head of livestock to the Cache Valley.[21] Earlier expeditions had suggested that the valley might have the resources to support a significant number of Latter-day Saints; one two-year scientific expedition had described the region as filled with "rich green grass" and willow trees.[22]

Garr was one of the settlers who came to the Cache Valley. He and his brothers had previously worked on a church farm on Antelope Island in the Great Salt Lake and had the skills necessary to work with cattle. The men who traveled with them had similar experience. Samuel Roskelley, for example, had worked for the church as a "teamster."[23] In spite of their skills, the Latter-day Saint settlers did not find the Cache Valley as hospitable as their fur trade brethren had. Frequent blizzards and storms left many of the cattle emaciated by winter's end. In April 1856 Bryant Stringham complained to Daniel H. Wells that the cows were "so weak" that it was difficult "to get enough together to pull a plough."[24] The men, for their part, were only able to survive by killing chickens. Their arrival in late summer and fall meant they had little time to prepare for the coming winter, and as a result, hunger was a constant problem.[25]

Despite these difficulties, other Latter-day Saints and followed and created their own communities. Wellsville, for example, was founded in 1856, Mendon in 1859, and Franklin, Hyrum, and Avon in 1860. Church members in these outposts saw themselves as extending the Kingdom of God. In practice, however, they often failed to live up to the standards of Zion. The minutes of the Cache Valley quorum of high priests, for example, recorded that Peter Maughan, one of the area's founders and a local ecclesiastical leader, reprimanded the group for "teaching wrong doctrine" on February 11, 1861. He demanded they tell him if they "had feelings against him." Although the men responded in the negative, there had been dissent within the community. According to the minutes, "a man at Hiram" had tried "to persuade people that Joseph Smith was a fallen prophet."[26]

Apostasy was not the only problem the communities faced. In occupying the Cache Valley, white settlers had entered Shoshone land. Their claiming of the land threatened Native communities who discovered that the settlement of Latter-day Saints fundamentally changed the environment, and in so doing, threatened the health of their families and loved ones. According to the historian Bradley Paul Hansen, the region's "bunchgrasses" succumbed to "farms of wheat, potatoes, oats, rye, barley, beans, and corn" in the decades after colonization.[27] Purple heads of cheat grass began to color the area.[28] The native grasses that had fed the Shoshones for generations gave way to a new landscape designed to promote European styles of agriculture.

In the Hawaiian Islands, Latter-day Saints had been able to position themselves as the opponents of American colonialism. In the Cache Valley, however, they became its obvious participants. Latter-day Saints grazed their cattle on native grasses that had maintained the Shoshones, resulting in ecological crisis. Native people struggled to support their families in the changed landscape and were often unable to respond to the cries of hungry children. The changes that occurred in the Cache Valley mirrored those occurring in Utah as a whole. In 1854, for example, white Latter-day Saints established a mission in southern Utah. Under the leadership of Rufus C. Allen, David Lewis, and Samuel Atwood, Latter-day settlers cultivated cotton in addition to traditional food crops. The men would also be expected to evangelize local Native Americans. Although he later assisted in the baptism of hundreds of Native Americans near the Muddy River, Thomas Brown felt that the people he encountered paled in comparison to the stories of the Book of Mormon. He bemoaned in his journal how far "Ephraim [had] fallen." He described local Native Americans "greedily" eating "matted ants" before comparing them to "hogs with little or no covering."[29] His description of their poverty was influenced by white understandings of how people should eat, which did not include eating insects or consuming lizards.[30] White Latter-day Saints interpreted the willingness of the Goshutes, Shoshones, and Paiutes to eat these foods as evidence of their degradation. Even if Native Americans had been experiencing a time of plenty when the Saints arrived in Utah, white settlers would have interpreted their lives as stunted and in need of redemption. The devastation that followed in the wake of Latter-day Saint colonization only confirmed their presuppositions about Native life.

The response of Native communities to these hardships varied. The Ute chief Black Hawk, for example, was said to have stolen over two thousand head of cattle in an explicit attempt to disrupt white colonization.[31] In their reminiscences, white settlers in the Cache Valley complained about frequent "Indian scares."[32] Peter Maughan went so far as to have the families of one settlement move closer to his eponymous fort to protect them from possible attacks.[33] From the perspective of Native people, however, raiding cattle made sense. The animals were destroying the landscape that allowed their families to thrive and, in so doing, were starving their children. The cattle also represented a source of food. According to historian John Peterson, hungry Native families "flocked to eat the 'Mormon beef'" after they learned of Black Hawk's raids.[34]

Cattle raids intensified the violence that had marked the relationships between Native Americans and white settlers in this period. The 1863 massacre of the Shoshones was part of a larger pattern of violence against Native Americans in Utah. Two years after the Bear River Massacre, a group of Ute men attacked John Given, his wife, and their children as they slept in the central Utah town of Circleville. Their deaths terrified the white community. A few months later a party of Ute men attacked the settlement, killing several white men who tried to stop them as they rounded up cattle. White settlers increasingly panicked as the violence escalated,. In April 1866 they imprisoned several local Paiutes. When the men tried to escape, the Mormon settlers shot them. Town authorities then took the Native women and children to a cellar, where they held them captive before executing them one by one.[35] Latter-day Saints did not necessarily view their actions as immoral. Indeed, they sometimes adopted the children orphaned by the massacres. After the Bear River Massacre, for example, Salmon Warner took a small child who had been found on the battlefield holding "a bowl of frozen pine-nut gravy."[36] He may have intended to raise him within his household, but he eventually decided to give the child to his brother Amos. They called the boy Frank. Although Frank Warner served missions to the Lamanites in the early twentieth century, he likely bore emotional and physical scars from losing his mother and people.

The violence of the Bear River Massacre and similar events convinced some Native Americans that they could not survive by continuing to hunt buffalo or raiding cattle. In the face of overwhelming environmental change and endemic violence, they came to believe that the future of their communities lay in adopting white methods of agriculture. White agriculture had been controversial among many Native Americans who saw it as incompatible with their knowledge about the land and their culture. Historians have suggested that some Native groups saw farming as the purview of women and believed it femininized their sons.[37] The historian Brigham Madsen has documented the reluctance of some Shoshones to adopt agriculture. An Indian agent assigned to the North-western Shoshones felt that they were more reluctant than other tribes to accept farming as a way of life.[38]

There is evidence, however, that other Shoshone groups more readily turned to farming. Hints of this can be seen in an 1856 parade at Fort Supply in what is now Wyoming. The parade was part of a celebration of the

Mormon entrance into the Salt Lake Valley nearly a decade before. As part of the parade a group of twenty-four Indian men clad in "buckskin pants, blue shirts, and moccasins" carried a banner that proclaimed, "We shall yet be a white and delightsome people."[39] The phrase drew from Book of Mormon imagery promising that Native Americans would become white as they turned away from savagery. After the processional stopped, a Native American man named Boziel stepped forward and said that he would like to speak. According to an account in the *Deseret News*, he told those assembled "that he felt well to see grain growing on the Snake land, for their children could get bread to eat, also butter and milk."[40]

Latter-day Saints interpreted the men's willingness to claim a Lamanite identity as evidence that they had accepted the truthfulness of Mormonism and the superiority of white culture. The men who participated in the parade may not have seen it that way, however. For these Shoshone men, adopting white ways was not necessarily an admission of their superiority so much as a recognition that doing so would provide them with access to food. Another speaker echoed this theme. An Indian man named John praised Mormonism not for offering his people access to the history of their ancestors but for providing them with "wheat, potatoes, beets and peas."[41]

John's statement also suggested what white Saints were unwilling to admit: Latter-day Saint colonization had caused Native suffering. The introduction of European crops and animals into the region fundamentally disrupted Native foodways, leaving Indian families destitute. The descriptions white Latter-day Saints left of life in the mid-nineteenth century overemphasize the deprivations facing the white community and ignore the suffering of the Native Americans they sought to displace. In 1924 an English convert named Thomas Irvins lamented the inability of modern Latter-day Saints to understand how difficult life in early Utah had been. Life for the early white settlers in the Cache Valley required "labor and sacrifice," he wrote. They had to "dig the ditches" and "build the canyon roads," "meeting houses," and schools. Another woman described people going barefoot or wearing moccasins because they had no other shoes.[42]

Stories of white deprivation and loss papered over the destitution of Native families. One of the most harrowing experiences for white Saints living in the Cache Valley was the loss of Rosie Thurston. When the two-year-old girl disappeared in 1868, many assumed that local Shoshones had kidnapped her. Lorenzo Hatch remembered the community's horror over fifty years later. He reported that it had caused "quite a stir in the valley . . . Her mother was broken hearted, and grieved constantly." "Never," he added, "while she lived here could she free herself from the dreadful uncertainty of the fate of her child."[43] Mary Ann Weston Maughan, whose husband would be remembered as almost singlehandedly superintending the community's growth, described the girl as a "bright little child."[44] She claimed that the Shoshones had tried to steal other children as well, including "one of Brother Curtis's little boys."[45] Stories like these allowed Latter-day Saints to shift the focus from Native suffering to their own.

When white Latter-day Saints did acknowledge Native pain, they blamed it on indigenous people themselves, arguing that the unwillingness of Native Americans to perform hard labor prevented them from fully realizing the bounty of the land they lived on. This language allowed Latter-day Saints to divorce themselves from the pain of Native people. Their theology, however, prevented them from fully doing so. The Book of Mormon called them to minister to Native people as the Children of Israel. The Relief Society had been dormant since 1845, but Latter-day Saint women like Amanda Barnes Smith revived the organization to raise money for the purchase of clothing for Indian women and children. In their meetings, these women sang hymns about the coming redemption of Native Americans and worked on rag carpets they hoped to sell as fundraisers.[46] The Relief Society would not be fully reorganized until 1867 when Eliza R. Snow began the work of reestablishing it as a formal organization at the behest of Brigham Young. These smaller societies, however, no matter how short-lived, temporarily transformed the organization from one focused on redeeming the poverty of white Latter-day Saints to one focused on Indian women and children. The impulse was an imperial one. The historian James Vernon has demonstrated that humanitarian narratives had their birth in the nineteenth century's "civilizing mission." In his words, humanitarian narratives could be used to delegitimize societies by demonstrating that they "had failed to protect their subjects and citizens from the ravages of hunger."[47] In Britain these narratives could be used both to critique the British state and to support imperialism. They held the same power in Utah. Latter-day Saints argued that the federal government had failed to provide for Native people and saw themselves as their potential saviors. These Latter-day Saints were determined to end Native sorrow, even if they could not recognize its cause in their own presence in the Valley.

Interracial Kin

Latter-day Saints saw the purchase of Native children in the years immediately following their entrance into the Great Basin as a humanitarian gesture. In the wake of Spanish colonialism in the eighteenth century, Comanche and Ute bands had begun to raid Indian communities for slaves to sell to people in Spanish New Mexico.[48] Their decision to do so mirrored the practices of Americans like Andrew Jackson and southern slaveowners who adopted Indian children in hopes of "civilizing" them. Jackson had adopted a Creek child named Lyncoya after American troops under Jackson's indirect command killed over one hundred and eighty people from the boy's village. Jackson saw his action as one of mercy. He planned to use the boy to show the possibilities of assimilation and groomed him for West Point.[49] Latter-day Saints hoped that their adoptions would be just as humanitarian as Jackson's. Utah law required all white Latter-day Saints who bought Indian children to register them as indentured servants. Consequently, Utah's legal system defined adopted Indian children as separate from biological kin. In these indentures, white Latter-day Saints promised to educate Indian children and provide them with clothing in exchange for them pledging respect for their new white parents. Although the law defined these children as "indentured servants," their status remained ambiguous in practice. Some white families considered these children adopted sons and daughters; others considered them servants.[50]

Regardless of the child's status within the family, white Latter-day Saints saw these indentures as an opportunity to redeem or even "free" Native children. After all, Native children would be raised within the gospel and educated as the brothers and sisters of white Latter-day Saints. In Utah, as in the Anglo-American world, however, the word *freedom* could cover a wide variety of coerced labor. Ephraim and Harriet Hanks lived with three Indian youths, including a sixteen-year-old girl named Delia and an eleven-year-old boy called Jack. Neither attended school in 1859 and no anecdotes remain to commemorate their lives.[51] Likewise, the future mayor of Salt Lake City, Feramorz Little, kept a ten-year-old Indian girl in his household.[52] The 1860 Census lists the girl after his biological children, but before the men who tended his cattle.

Although Latter-day Saints sometimes used the language of adoption to describe their relationship to the Native children in their homes, it is difficult to know exactly what they meant by this term. In the nineteenth century adoption had multiple meanings within restoration theology. The adoption rituals that Joseph Smith developed in Nauvoo allowed individuals to bind themselves to people as kin. These bonds would become part of an ever-expanding kinship network that tied humanity together and to God in the eternities. Some Latter-day Saints hoped that the Native children they adopted would be a part of their earthly and heavenly families. Temple records reveal that at least five families sealed the Native children they adopted to their families, creating ties that they hoped would last into the eternities. Fifteen more performed the rites vicariously after the child's death.[53] Other Latter-day Saints chose not to perform these rituals. The question of what adoption meant for them is open. Did it mean that they saw the children they raised as servants rather than family? Had they once hoped to create new kin but found the presence of Native children in their homes too disturbing to do so? Were the rituals too painful for them to perform? There is likely more than one answer to this question. Latter-day Saints did not have a uniform view of Native children. Their relationships with them could be loving, coercive, and transactional. Sometimes they were an unsettling combination of all three.

Whatever the meaning of adoption, white Latter-day Saints and the Native children they brought into their homes sometimes developed intimate family relationships. In 1854, for example, a white Latter-day Saint named Mary Ann Barzee Boice adopted an Indian girl whose mother had died. Family histories describe Mary Ann coming to love the child as she bathed her body. She eventually nursed the little girl with her own son Albert.[54] George Barber, an English convert who moved to the Cache Valley in 1860, dutifully chronicled the illness of the Native child named Lamoni that he had adopted as an infant.[55] On June 15, 1861, he wrote that Lamoni was "very sick," as was one of his twin boys. The next day, he recorded that he "watched [his] children anxiously all night." Although the other child eventually recovered, Lamoni died a few days later. Barber found it "hard to part with him after having reard [*sic*] him from his infancy" and called it one of the "the saddest days" he had "ever experienced."[56] The emotions that individuals like Boice and Barber used to describe their relationships with their Indian children were no doubt authentic. To paraphrase the historian Dawn Peterson, however, they also transformed the dispossession of Native people into "a family story."[57] The violence that Native people had experienced because of the colonization became a part of the family history of white settlers. White Saints downplayed their role in the systemic dispossession of Native people and emphasized the role that they had played in nurturing Native children.

Not all white Latter-day Saints who adopted Native children narrated their lives using these themes. The different places assigned to Native children within white households indicate the tensions that existed over the proper relationship between Latter-day Saints and the descendants of the people of the Book of Mormon. If Native Americans were to be a part of the redemption of Israel, white Latter-day Saints would need to live among them and teach them the gospel. Latter-day Saint leaders also pushed them to consider marrying Native women both in the Pacific Islands and the American West. It is possible that Latter-day Saint missionaries like Benjamin F. Grouard saw their marriages to Polynesian women partly as a way to "civilize" them and cement their relationships with local communities.

Many white Latter-day Saints, however, were uncomfortable with interracial marriage. In 1855 a Latter-day Saint missionary named Oliver B.

Huntington told his wife Hannah that he was reluctant to take a Native woman as a plural wife because Ute women were "half rotton with the clap from the Spaniards."[58] His statement revealed the Saints' underlying racism. Sexual relationships between Native women and Spanish men were often coerced, but Huntington interpreted them as signs of female licentiousness.[59] In general, white Latter-day Saints were disinclined to marry Indian women. When Brigham Young recommended in the 1850s that some Latter-day Saints consider taking Indian women as their wives, the men's response was telling. They described the potential wife of the one man who had eagerly assented to the injunction as a "haggard mummy looking" woman and considered the marriage "a signal failure."[60]

Even Latter-day Saints who promoted interracial marriage imagined it occurring within defined parameters. The racial mixing Young imagined was explicitly gendered. In reviving patriarchy, Latter-day Saint leaders placed the responsibility for family discipline in the hands of the father. They assured their followers that Native children who were raised in white families would adopt the standards of whiteness. Building upon Joseph Smith's teachings, Young crafted an understanding of the restored gospel in which white men might marry Indian women, but white women would not marry Indian men. Young's counselor, Heber C. Kimball, told followers that if they were to "graft" a "white apple" onto "a red apple tree, it [would] bring forth a white apple."[61] The presence of Indian children within Latter-day Saint homes raised the possibility that interracial marriage might involve white women as well as white men. As adults, some of these children chose to marry white partners. For white Latter-day Saints, the question of whether these marriages would still bear white fruit had not been resolved.

The adoption of Native children also forced their families to confront the terrors of colonization. The children who had survived the Bear River Massacre bore the violence of the encounter on their bodies. Frank Warner's descendants, for example, reported that his shoulder was permanently gnarled by bullets.[62] It is likely that these children also suffered from long-term trauma. Scholars have found that children who experience traumatic events often suffer from anxiety and become hypervigilant about perceived threats.[63] This was even true in the Pacific, where the children Latter-day Saints adopted had not watched white soldiers massacre their parents. After she returned to the United States, Louisa Barnes Pratt adopted a Polynesian boy with the consent of his father. She remembered the child's screams when she separated him from his mother, who was traveling back to the Pacific.[64]

Latter-day Saints in the United States had willingly severed Native children's ties to their natal communities. They were unwilling, however, to fully integrate them into white society. As a result, the children often struggled to create meaningful lives. In her diary, Louisa lamented her inability to completely to "break" the "wandering propensities" of the Polynesian child she had adopted. She considered him to be "bright shrewed, and witty" but also full of "Indian traits."[65] He ran away when he was fifteen to work as a stagecoach driver in Montana.[66] He was not the only adopted child to experience difficulties living in white society. In 1887 a Paiute adoptee named David Monson married Laura Jensen, the daughter of a Danish convert. Monson worked an odd variety of jobs to make ends meet. He sheared sheep, butchered animals, and worked as a teamster. Their family lived in a one-room log house in Spring City, Utah, and, according to his daughter Edith, struggled to do more than "live hand to mouth." Laura did not write extensively about her reasons for marrying Monson, although her early marriage seems to have been a happy one. Edith describes her father as a "gentleman who was fun loving and liked to attend the occasional picnic and dance."[67] In 1912, however, Monson abandoned his family to "shear sheep" in Wyoming. When Monson died in 1925, the local Saratoga Springs newspaper reported there was "common talk" that he "had several sons and daughters" in Utah.[68] Native scholars have argued that Native Americans experienced intergenerational trauma that fractured family ties and led to increased levels of anxiety, depression, and alcoholism.[69] It is possible to read Monson's abandonment of his family as the result of this same trauma.[70]

The historian Michael K. Bennion tells the story of another Indian child who struggled with her place in the Latter-day Saint community. A mixed-raced Latter-day Saint couple adopted Susie Pulsipher when she was a young girl. She later lived in St. George, Utah, where she gave birth to a series of illegitimate children. According to Bennion, she offered an impassioned defense of her morality when she was called before a local judge. "I have a right to children," she insisted. "No white man will marry me. I cannot live with the Indians. But I can have children, and I will support the children that I have."[71] The people of St. George appear to have eventually accepted her as part of their community. A local girl told the historian Juanita Brooks that if she was "going to be an old maid," she would "be a respectable old maid, like Susie, and have children."[72]

Other Native women who transgressed the bounds of propriety were not so lucky. A well-known Parowan physician named Priddy Meeks adopted a captive child that he decided to call Lucy. She was raised as a Latter-day Saint and educated with the other children in Parowan, Utah. One day, however, she told her adopted father she was pregnant and named John McCleve, an Irish convert to the church, as the father. Her father demanded that McCleve take responsibility for Lucy and her child. For his part, McCleve denied that he had sired a baby by an Indian woman and subsequently committed suicide. According to McCleve's sister, "Many of the people blamed the Doctor and some blamed Lucy." After the incident, "There were many ugly stories circulated about her."[73] When her daughter was eight years old, Lucy became sick. As she lay dying, she spoke in her native language for a few moments before telling her family that she believed "it had been a mistake for her ever to suppose that she could be a white girl."[74] Lucy's death and perhaps her life served as a cautionary tale for Latter-day Saints who adopted Indian children, undermining the belief that they could transform Indian children into white ones. Few Native children became fully integrated into white society. Instead, they became liminal figures, neither fully white nor fully Native. Although the church offered a theology in which Native people were at the center of God's redemptive plan, Latter-day Saints were not necessarily kinder to Native people than other white settlers had been.

In the end, the Native children that Mormons adopted forced the communities that raised them to confront two problems: the violence of colonialism and the specter of interracial sex. The Cache Valley would be forced to confront these issues head on when the Garr case came to trial.

Johnny Garr and the Politics of Interracial Marriage

The Garr case highlighted the tensions within the community over interracial marriage and the place of Native children within Latter-day Saint families. In the years immediately following the settling of the Cache Valley, Native Americans frequently visited Latter-day Saint settlements. John Orsmond had been born in South Wales in 1832 and joined the church because he believed that the manifestations of God he witnessed—"speaking in tongues, healing the sick, [and] casting out devils"—proved that the new religion had come from God.[75] Although there were significant tensions between white Latter-day Saints and Native Americans, J. H. Campbell remarked in his reminiscences that "a number . . . were friendly to settlers."[76] Another man claimed that he had particular affection for Indian children and admitted he sometimes gave Johnny's mother presents for her child when she came to camp.[77] For the most part, the relationships between white Latter-day Saints and Native people appear to have been platonic. It is likely, however, that some of them were sexual.

Rumors began to spread about the "intimacy" Garr shared with a Shoshone woman soon after his arrival in the valley. Family histories suggest the woman may have been Susie Wigegee, a Shoshone woman originally from the Ruby Valley of Nevada who eventually settled in Washakie.[78] It was difficult for the first Latter-day Saint settlers to keep secrets from each other. Before the arrival of white families, the men who lived in the valley promoted a rough homosociality in which they "rode together, ate together, slept together and associated generally together" as "cowboys . . . do."[79] The relationships that they formed with each other were not unusual in the American West. Mining, ranching, and working on the railroad created all-male spaces where men lived in proximity and engaged in homosocial and sometimes even erotic behaviors that would have been considered inappropriate in other circumstances.[80]

Many Latter-day Saint settlers in the Cache Valley were familiar with the Shoshones, who regularly visited the area. Many of the men noticed the woman who would become Garr's lover and later remarked on her appearance and attitude in court records. One man described her as "quite heavy" but also "quite good looking."[81] When the Shoshone woman became pregnant, rumors began to circulate as the community tried to figure out who the father might be. Some speculated that it was Garr. Others suggested that the father was a Welshman from Brigham City named Johnny Jones.[82] The woman's pregnancy divided local Latter-day Saints. Inherent in Young's descriptions of interracial sex had been the assumption that white men would marry Native women, bringing them under the authority of the priesthood. Garr's relationship, on the other hand, was clandestine and not sanctified by marriage. It raised questions about whether the priesthood would ultimately be able to contain the sexual urges of its members and the possibility that mixed-race children would be not raised within white Latter-day Saint families but among their Native kin.

Whoever the father was, Garr claimed the child as his own in the late 1850s when the boy was a toddler. It appears that the boy's mother eventually found herself unable to care for the child and brought him to the Garr brothers. According to one story, the mother gave him to Garr's brother William in exchange for some blue blankets and paint. After William took him from his mother, the boy started to cry. He screamed and jerked away from the man who now held him. Ultimately, they spent hours after she left trying to "pacify" the child.[83] The man who reported the story did not believe that the boy was Garr's son. Garr's former fiancée Naomi Campbell told a different story. She claimed that the woman had brought the boy to Garr and insisted that he take care of him. According to Campbell's testimony, the woman feared that the other people living in her camp would "kill it" if Garr didn't agree to take of the child.[84]

Garr's decision to claim the boy, whom he named Johnny, as his son did not end community gossip. People continued to debate the boy's paternity and asked Garr to confirm whether the boy was his son. A difficult conversation about Garr's intentions regarding Johnny, for example, ended his engagement with Campbell. While she was "grind[ing] coffee" one day, the woman asked Garr whether he planned to keep Johnny. His affirmative response ended their relationship. Rather than disowning the boy, he told her that "a father [was] always supposed to take care of their own children." Her unwillingness to "marry a man that had a papoose" made the relationship unworkable and they "quit." At another point, one of Garr's childhood friends inquired about Johnny's origins. "Did you marry that squaw?" he remembered asking. "Is that your son?"[85] Although Garr initially demurred, he eventually admitted that the boy was his.

It is likely that some members of Garr's family accepted his mixed-race child. There is little evidence, however, to reconstruct how they felt about Johnny before the Garr's siblings sued for access to his estate. As Martha Hodes has pointed out, court records disproportionately represent dysfunctional families. Protracted court cases over inheritance, divorce, and adultery tended to bring out matters that had long lain dormant within communities.[86] Johnny's paternity only became a matter of official concern when Garr's siblings brought the case before the Utah courts. What emerged from the testimony given to the court was a family conflicted over Johnny's relationship with them.

After he grew up, Johnny married a white woman named Elizabeth Hulse on December 31, 1890, and she quickly bore him three children, one of whom died as an infant. Elizabeth was pregnant with twins when Johnny died in a wagon accident. To provide for her children, she moved her children into Garr's home. She remembered her relationship with her father-in-law as close. After her husband's death, Elizabeth recalled the elderly man telling her not to "worry or fret, or be a bit alarmed."[87] One neighbor described Garr as a loving grandfather who remarked on how proud he was of his grandchildren and kissed them when they ran up to him. Although individual family members objected to the union, his family tolerated Johnny until Elizabeth sued for Garr's estate. Garr's sister Eliza had once asked Elizabeth to change her last name to Jones after the man they later claimed was Johnny's biological father. Eliza's son admitted that his mother had done so because she did not want a Native man to bear their family name.[88]

The tensions within the Garr family over Johnny were replicated in the larger community. When he died, a letter to the editor about his accident referred to him simply as "one of our citizens." It also reported that "[twenty-one] vehicles loaded with sympathizers accompanied the remains to the cemetery." The image was not that of a reckless Indian man who had met his death but of a family man who left behind a grieving widow with two living children. The letter ended with a statement saying that the contents of his wagon at death suggested "his last thoughts, or nearly so, were for their welfare."[89] The newspaper's empathetic portrayal of Johnny suggests that some people considered him a legitimate member of the community. Further, her marriage to a half-Indian man did not disqualify Elizabeth from obtaining a form of white respectability. She was able to find work as a dairy woman after Johnny's death and eventually married a Swedish convert named John Anderson. Many of her descendants have remained within the Church of Jesus Christ of Latter-day Saints.

Some community members, however, were reluctant to accept Johnny as a member of the community. Johnny had experienced racism from white Latter-day Saints since childhood. According to his cousin Fielding, he hated being referred to as an Indian and once got in a "fracas" with a boy who called him one.[90] Another instance was published in the *Salt Lake Herald*. While he was in a butcher shop in Logan, Utah, a man shouted, "Get out you dog!"—ostensibly at a stray dog who was trying to steal "a leg of mutton on the counter." According to the newspaper, Johnny thought that the man was using the epithet for him and threatened the people in the store with a "large knife."[91] Johnny's position within the community was especially difficult because of the Bear River Massacre. Family histories suggest that his mother Susan was one of the massacre's survivors.[92] Some of Johnny's descendants even believed that his death had not been "an accident."[93] His granddaughter Opal speculated that someone had killed her grandfather because he was a Native man. She told her niece that "they was killing all the Indians. That's why they killed my grandpa." Opal believed that her neighbors knew who was responsible but had decided to remain quiet. She saw her grandfather's death not as an accident but as a kind of lynching.[94]

The Garr case, and Johnny's tenuous position among the Saints, raised important questions about the relationship between white Mormons and Native Americans. Was the restored gospel a faith focused on the redemption of Native peoples or not? What role should Native people play among Latter-day Saints? And ultimately, were the relationships that white Latter-day Saints had contracted with Native Americans legitimate? Behind that last question lay another. Throughout the nineteenth century white Latter-day Saints had emphasized the reality of kinship ties they created through their rites and religious faith. Latter-day Saint leaders had hinted that these sealings might have material effects. The Garr siblings' claim that Johnny shouldn't inherit because he was illegitimate reasserted the importance of biological kinship. They rejected the idea that Garr could claim a child and expect him to be accepted as a member of their family. For them, kinship was biological.

The social and theological implications of the lawsuit meant that it was important beyond the Cache Valley. Newspapers across Utah published the details of the case. The prominence of the men that the two sides hired as their lawyers raised the case's profile. George Q. Rich represented Elizabeth and her children. Called the "Dean of North Utah Attorneys" at his death, Rich had received his degree from the University of Michigan and was the child of an apostle within the church.[95] The influential attorney may also have been personally sympathetic to the mixed-race family he was representing. Members of his extended family had adopted Indian children and considered them kin. A boy named Horace had lived with Rich's sister-in-law for years after her husband's 1878 death and helped with the livestock. When Horace's body was found "mutilated and in several pieces" on the Oregon Short Line tracks near Blackfoot, Idaho, in 1902, members of the family told the public that he was one of their own and they would pursue the murderer.[96] It is possible that his family's willingness to claim their Indian kin influenced Rich when Elizabeth asked him to take her case. His legal arguments emphasized the legitimacy of the relationships that white Latter-day Saints had created with Native Americans and insisted that the Garr family had the responsibility to claim Johnny's children.

His opponent was no less influential. The Garr siblings chose Frank

K. Nebeker, a local attorney who would later prosecute radical labor unionists in Chicago for the U.S. Justice Department. Nebeker had returned to Cache County after graduating from Cornell Law School in 1895. During his time in Utah, he prosecuted Abe Majors—an Oakland criminal variously called a "highwayman" and "desperado"—for the 1899 murder of a police officer who had been tracking him after a series of robberies and arrested horse thieves who had been terrorizing Box Elder County.[97] The residents of Cache Valley may have leaned in with anticipation when they heard of the upcoming court case.[98] The trial testimony promised to reveal sexual secrets and to open the Garr family's personal lives to scrutiny.

The case opened with the interrogation of John C. Dowdle, who had been one of the first men to live with Garr in the Cache Valley. Garr's former fiancée Naomi Campbell testified about the role that his unwillingness to give up his son had played in unraveling their relationship. Garr's sister Eliza and her son Fielding raised questions about Johnny's paternity and called witnesses who testified that Garr had considered the boy a drunk and did not mourn his death. Conversely, a woman named Sarah Weaver testified that Garr had excitedly told her about the birth of Johnny's children and referred to them as his grandchildren. Although Nebeker did not raise the point during her testimony, she likely sympathized with Johnny and Elizabeth. Her husband Frank had adopted an Indian child before he moved to the Cache Valley and brought the child with him.[99] Latter-day Saints like Sarah Weaver adopted Indian children out of a belief that these children were redeemable and an important part of the Mormon story. Theological musings about the role of Native Americans in God's redemptive plan had no place within Utah's courts. Instead, these ideas remained an unspoken subtext of the proceedings.

The court initially found for Garr's siblings on December 19, 1904. In his decision, Judge T. D. Lewis wrote that he was unconvinced that Johnny was the child—"illegitimate or otherwise"—of John T. Garr.[100] As a result, he decided that the estate should be split between Garr's siblings and their descendants.[101] Utah newspapers are frustratingly silent on Elizabeth's reaction, but she soon filed an appeal on her children's behalf. In 1906 the Utah Supreme Court reversed the decision after reviewing testimony, declaring that Garr had fathered Johnny and claimed him as his own. It dismissed the exchange of blankets for the infant as an attempt to cover up the "disreputable offense" of a "member of a family mingling in social intercourse and possessed of commanding influence in the community."[102] In the end, Elizabeth's children would inherit the estate. The original decision was "reversed, with costs."[103]

Ultimately, the lawsuit reflected the tensions that existed for decades among Latter-day Saints surrounding the adoption of Native children. Restoration theology relied heavily upon the idea that American Indians would be redeemed before the Second Coming of Jesus Christ. White converts to the faith had spoken in Indian tongues and participated in imagined baptisms in which they pretended to become "Indians." Native Americans who converted to the restored gospel also participated in its sacred rituals and adopted some of its language concerning their history; for example, the Pahvant chief Kanosh was one of the first Native Saints to participate in the endowment ceremony.[104] By the late nineteenth and early twentieth centuries, the creation of kinship networks between white and indigenous Saints provided white people with a way to participate in this redemption. As the research of the historian Ardis Parshall suggests, a white woman named Georgianna identified her husband Frank who had served multiple missions to Native American reservations as the "one mighty among them" mentioned in 2 Nephi 3: 24 who would bring "restoration unto the house of Israel."[105] She was not the only white person to be thrilled by the possibility of participating in the salvation of the Lamanites. Mormon missionaries such as Benjamin F. Grouard and John Layton had married Polynesian women. They likely did so while fully believing in the promises of the Book of Mormon.[106]

Not all Latter-day Saints believed in the power of their religion to transform Native peoples. The *Salt Lake Herald* referred to Johnny's birth as Garr's "disgrace."[107] The *Vernal Express* approvingly quoted a man who called Wild Bill Johnson "a murderer, cow and horse thief, squaw man and notoriously tough man."[108] After the court case, Johnny's descendants concealed their family history. Johnny's daughter Merle only told her own daughter about their ancestry when the girl called the local Shoshones "dumb Indians"[109] The family only began to speak openly about their past when Johnny's wife Elizabeth died in 1947.[110]

Her death allowed them to tell stories about how John T. Garr had allowed his grandchildren to braid his beard, and how Johnny destroyed "a brand new saddle" when his family locked him in a granary as a punishment.[111] They even spoke of Johnny's mother. Opal was convinced that the elderly woman had visited her as a child. She remembered "quilting with her mother and her aunt Leone . . . when an old Shoshone woman came to the door." The woman was "frail," even "fragile," but walked long distances to see the Garr family. One day she gestured toward Opal and her siblings and said something emphatically in the Shoshone language. Her aunt told the confused child that the woman was her great grandmother.[112]

Opal's family members eventually began to search for more information about Johnny's mother in hopes that it would allow them to perform the "soul-saving temple work" they believed she would need in the afterlife.[113] The story of John T. Garr represents one of the stories that can be told about the aftermath of Utah's colonization. It focuses on the children lost to Native communities. Johnny's mother visited her son after she was forced to give him to Garr and may have even visited her grandchildren and great-grandchildren. They could not understand her, however. The Shoshone culture was lost to them.

Johnny's story also reveals the tension among Latter-day Saints about the place of Indian children within white families. Latter-day Saints did not agree on the possibilities of integrating Native children into their society. Some Latter-day Saints breastfed Indian children and performed temple rites to bind these children to them for the eternities. Others used the courts to disclaim any connection to their Indian kin and created alternative stories about who may have fathered individual children. The story of Indian children is not the only story that can be told about colonization and the place of Native Americans among the Latter-day Saints.

After the Bear River Massacre, many of the Northwestern Shoshones were in a difficult position. Several descendants of the people that were slaughtered at Bear River converted to the church. In 1873 a Shoshone elder had a vision telling him that "the 'Mormons' God was the true God, and that he and the Indians' Father were one."[114] The vision compelled several of the Shoshone leaders to seek out the Latter-day Saint missionary George Washington Hill that same year and ask to be baptized. They wished to follow the command within the vision that they "be baptized . . . and learn to cultivate the earth and build houses, and live in them."[115] The historian Gregory Smoak has argued that we should understand these conversions through the lens of traditional Shoshone religion: the Shoshones understood the restoration's embrace of visions, prophesying, and faith healing as echoing their own religious beliefs. Conversion allowed them to incorporate that community's religious power into their existing life of faith.[116]

It also, however, represented a rupture. The Shoshones hoped that their adoption of the restoration would be a way forward and would provide them with an opportunity to learn white methods of agriculture. For their part, white Latter-day Saints saw the Shoshones' embrace of their faith as evidence of its veracity. Although white Latter-day Saints had been able to create an orderly polygamous domesticity, they found it more difficult to control the Indian children they had adopted or the half-Indian ones they had birthed, who would always remain not quite white and not quite Indian. The failure of the Saints to fully assimilate Indian children did not end their attempts to transform Native Americans into a "white and delightsome people." Around the turn of the century they turned their attention to communities of Native Saints. Located in the Intermountain West, these communities suggested that the restored gospel could fulfill its promise to Native people without the intimacies of bringing Native children into white families. The experiences of the Native Hawaiian and Shoshone towns that Latter-day Saints founded in the late nineteenth and early twentieth centuries, however, would be just as fraught as the experiences of the Native children brought into Latter-day Saint homes.

CHAPTER 6

NATIVE ZIONS

On February 11, 1872, apostle Orson Pratt stood in the tabernacle in Salt Lake City, Utah. His focus that Sunday was on the place of the Lamanites within the Church of Jesus Christ of Latter-day Saints. He began his speech by "contemplat[ing] the vast number of millions that must have swarmed over this great western hemisphere in times of old, building large cities, towns and villages, and spreading themselves forth from shore to shore from the Atlantic to the Pacific, from the frozen regions of the north to the uttermost extremity of South America."[1] He told those assembled that God had not abandoned "these nations," leaving them "deprived of the light of revelation from Heaven." The Book of Mormon stood as a testament to that. Pratt believed that the Lamanites from other parts of the world would "sing with joy" as they "wafted in ships to their promised land" to be reunited with their Native American brethren.[2]

The vision that Latter-day Saints had of Zion included both Polynesians and Native Americans. They believed that both groups were integral to the building of Zion and that they were both peoples of the Book of Mormon. Although Native Americans and Polynesians had distinct histories, the church's theology flattened the distinctions between them, transforming both into the "seed of Israel."[3] Native Americans and Polynesians thus became a part of the church's imperial project. White Saints hoped that they would be able to transform the domestic, cultural, and religious practices of the Lamanites. They believed that the priesthood would ultimately bring order to the lives of indigenous peoples and bind them to the Kingdom of God.

Latter-day Saints had initially hoped that adopting Native children would hasten the deliverance of Native communities, but the practice raised uncomfortable questions about interracial intimacy and the nature of kinship. Latter-day Saints were unwilling to let go of the image of a Native Zion. The establishment of communities for Native Saints in the American West and the Pacific in the late nineteenth century offered the promise of a Native Zion without raising concerns about interracial intimacy. In 1865 the Church of Jesus Christ of Latter-day Saints purchased land on the island of Oahu to serve as a gathering place for Native Hawaiian Saints. Such a community fulfilled spiritual and practical needs. For Native Hawaiians, the decision of the Hawaiian monarchy to institute private land ownership had devastated their political and religious practices.[4] The founding of Lāʻie allowed Native Hawaiians to reconstruct a sense of sacred space and community. It could not, however, facilitate participation in the temple rituals that defined the faith. In 1889 a group of Native Hawaiians worked with white church leaders to establish the town of Iosepa, Utah, to provide Saints from the Pacific with access to the Salt Lake Temple. Limited numbers of Pacific Islanders had been moving to Utah since the 1850s, but the racism they had experienced in Salt Lake City made Mormon leaders reticent to encourage large-scale immigration. Iosepa was meant to provide Native Hawaiians with refuge from the racism of Latter-day Saints as well as the ability to perform temple rites. Residents would progress in knowledge—gaining "precept upon precept" in the words of the Book of Mormon—until they were exalted.[5] Native Hawaiians created Lāʻie and Iosepa as sacred spaces, a kind of Pacific Zion.

While Native Hawaiians were founding Iosepa in Tooele County, Shoshone Saints were creating a similar community in the Cache Valley. In the wake of the Bear River Massacre, the displaced Northwestern

Shoshones established their own stake of Zion near the Idaho border where they raised sheep and cattle, trapped rabbits, and harvested grain. They called it Washakie.[6] In the late nineteenth century it became the nucleus of a reinvigorated Northwestern Shoshone Nation. According to Natalie Larsen, Washakie served as an "alternative" to the Fort Hall Indian Reservation in southeastern Idaho.[7] In 1868 the Shoshone had signed a treaty agreeing that they would relinquish their claim to much of southeastern Idaho and would consider 1.8 million acres near Pocatello to be their homeland. By the late nineteenth century the reservation had a day school that encouraged the Shoshones and Bannocks who resided there to give up their culture. Larsen argues that Washakie allowed the Northwestern Shoshones to continue their "traditional ceremonies" and learn the Shoshone language.[8]

The town had been borne out of the violent dislocations of the nineteenth century and was regarded by its inhabitants as sacred. It was a space where the Northwestern Shoshones experienced God in their communal actions as a people. As they attended church, they learned about the scripture, fasted, and taught their children about God. In Washakie the Shoshones came to recognize themselves as a chosen people. To borrow Jonathan Z. Smith's understanding of sacred space, Washakie was "a place of clarification (a focusing lens) where men and gods [were] held to be transparent to one another."[9] The communal aspect was important. Individual men and women in Washakie did not just come to understand God; they came to understand themselves as Shoshones. In 1967 Frank Timbimboo connected the faith of the Shoshone Saints with their decision to "settle down" in Washakie. He felt that the tribe's conversion had fundamentally changed them, just as he believed that faith could "turn a drunk into a pretty faithful man."[10]

For Northwestern Shoshones, Washakie presented a turning point in their relationship with God. Although they believed that God had always interacted with their community, their conversion represented a moment when they turned from one way of life to another. The communities that Pacific Islanders formed in the Hawaiian Islands had a similar meaning for Polynesian Saints. Although northern Utah and

Hawai'i were geographically distinct, they had both been subjects of American colonialism. Juxtaposing the two spaces allows historians to see how Native communities responded to the pressures of colonialism.

Latter-day Saints, of course, occupied a different position in the Hawaiian Islands than they did in Utah. In Hawai'i they could position themselves against colonialism. Adopting the same stance was more difficult in Utah, where they had been enthusiastic participants in settler colonialism. The status of Native Hawaiians also changed as they immigrated to Utah. As Hokulani Aikau has pointed out, Native Hawaiians who traveled to Utah changed from indigenous people to participants in settler colonialism when they moved from Hawai'i. Examining the creation of Native spaces in Hawai'i and Utah allows historians to more fully understand the complexities of Latter-day Saint imperialism. As white Latter-day Saints moved between imperial spaces, their relationship to power to changed. The same was true of Native Hawaiian Latter-day Saints. Although Native Hawaiians were marginalized in Utah, they occupied a different position within the Latter-day Saints' empire there than they had while living in the Hawaiian Islands.

The communities that Latter-day Saints created also had different meanings for white and Native Saints. Polynesians and Native Americans saw Lā'ie, Washakie, and Iosepa as sacred spaces where they were known to God and each other. White leaders of the church, in contrast, saw these communities as opportunities to change how Native Latter-day Saints lived and acted. Like many Americans, white Latter-day Saints believed that Native people would be transformed—both spiritually and materially—through agricultural labor. When a journalist from the *Los Angeles Times* visited Washakie in 1911, he discussed the settlement with the white Latter-day Saint bishop who had been called to oversee the community. As he observed the community of Washakie, the journalist found a people who seemed to represent "civilization." There were "log cabins, cooking stoves, and farm wagons and one man who owned stock in a Mexican rubber company." The journalist relished the irony that it might be among the Latter-day Saints—a hated people—that civilization would ultimately be found among the Indians.[11]

Native Saints, meanwhile, invested the religion with their own meaning. Many accepted the Book of Mormon as a record of their ancestors and saw its promises to the Lamanites as assurance of their future. The Northwestern Shoshones had long regarded the land that the Latter-day Saints chose for the Logan Temple as sacred. One Northwestern Shoshone man told an interviewer that the land was "known as the most sacred place of worship" and the Shoshones had experienced "many miraculous healings" there.[12] The church's decision to place the temple there reaffirmed the Shoshones' belief that they were a chosen people, and that Mormonism was a part of their heritage.[13]

At the same time, Native Americans had to confront the meanings that white Latter-day Saints placed on their community. Throughout the twentieth century Polynesian and Native American Latter-day Saints were asked to participate in parades and pageants that portrayed their cultures as belonging to the past. Native Saints never severed their relationship with their indigenous past, but they were sensible of the meanings that white Latter-day Saints placed on their church membership. To be Native and a Latter-day Saint was to be aware of the religion's racial politics. Creating separate communities gave Native Saints a place where they could create their own understandings of the restoration.

The contradictory meanings of these communities are at the heart of this chapter. Native Americans and Polynesians created a version of the restoration in the mid- to late-nineteenth century that empowered them and allowed them to remake families that had been destroyed by colonialism. Temple rituals knit communities together and offered Native participants an expansive vision of a future in which they would be claimed as God's chosen people and exalted as gods. The church's belief in healing also allowed them to participate in indigenous spiritual practices that white Protestantism had outlawed. Yet white Latter-day Saints were uncomfortable with the spiritual identities that Native Saints created and tried to discipline these communities. While the restored gospel offered Native Americans and Polynesians a way to reinvigorate their communities, it also perpetrated racism. The communities Native Saints created were frequently marginalized and, in the case of Iosepa and Washakie, eventually disbanded. This chapter weaves together the lives and stories of Native converts to the Church of Jesus Christ of Latter-day Saints to demonstrate how they fashioned new identities and embraced certain aspects of settler colonialism as a matter of survival—even as they challenged others.

Forging Native Hawaiian Space at Lāʻie

Latter-day Saint missionary work began in Hawaiʻi in 1850 when several men who had been mining in San Francisco traveled to the islands. They initially intended to build a congregation among the islands' white residents but found them unresponsive. Some of the men considered abandoning the mission. One of the missionaries famously received a revelation, however, that Native Hawaiians were descendants of the peoples of the Book of Mormon and that God considered them a "chosen people."[14] Reading the correspondence and dairies of white missionaries from the earliest years of the Hawaiian Mission reveals the degree to which Native Hawaiians contributed to and sustained the mission. A Native Hawaiian woman named Nalimanui offered three of the missionaries—James Keeler, George Q. Cannon, and Henry Bigler—hospitality. It was in her home that God "revealed himself to [Cannon] as he had never done before." He believed that he developed "a friendship" with God that would "never be broken or diminished."[15] William Uaua, who later served as in the Hawaiian legislature, preached and baptized people throughout the Hawaiian Islands.[16] In 1853 he returned home to find that his wife had died a few hours earlier. As her family mourned her death, "He anointed her and laid hands upon her." According to Cannon's journal, "She recovered instantly."[17]

Members like Nalimanui and Uaua fashioned a Native Hawaiian face for the church. Although white Latter-day Saints held several important leadership positions within the church in Hawaiʻi, Uaua and other Native Hawaiian missionaries provided a sense of continuity when white missionaries returned to the United States to be replaced by new men. Native men also traveled to the various Latter-day Saints communities on the islands and exhorted Native Hawaiians to embrace the restored gospel. The missionaries attracted individuals who were disaffected with the ascendant Congregational Church. Protestant missionaries had arrived in the islands in the first decades of the nineteenth century and managed to convert the royal family. Their church discouraged certain indigenous practices, such as healing the sick through miracles and practicing polygamy. Many Native Hawaiians, in contrast, saw the restored gospel as a Native faith that allowed them to create an alternative Christianity that privileged their needs. Latter-day Saints relied on Native converts to teach them the Hawaiian language and frequently traveled with Hawaiian men as they preached the gospel.

In 1857 Latter-day Saint leaders responded to James Buchanan's decision to send federal troops to Utah by calling people back to the heart of Zion; distant settlements were abandoned, and white missionaries returned home. In their absence, Native Hawaiians maintained the church by continuing to preach the gospel and organizing meetings. In 1861 Young sent a man named Walter Murray Gibson to the Pacific as a as a "roving missionary" in hopes of reestablishing control over Latter-day Saints in the region.[18] Gibson was able to gain control of the local Hawaiian Church. Some of his followers later accused him of proclaiming himself "King and God."[19] They claimed that he had incorrectly assumed power and allowed no dissent within his congregation. Brigham Young sent emissaries from Utah in 1864 in hopes of marginalizing Gibson. These men, including Joseph F. Smith, convened a church council that excommunicated the errant missionary and disavowed the practices he had introduced.[20]

Young's representatives now faced a challenge. Gibson's excommunication had left many members of the church in Hawai'i disillusioned and impoverished. Under Gibson's guidance, many had given their homes and livestock to the church.[21] They eventually decided to create a new gathering place to provide the community with fresh spiritual and physical sustenance. Individual Hawaiians would be able to work on the plantation and it would serve as the locus of a revived Hawaiian church. The land for Lā'ie was purchased in 1864.[22] The missionaries also demarcated fields for cultivating sugarcane and raising livestock and included land for Native Hawaiians to build their homes.[23]

The establishment of Lāʻie in the 1860s occurred within a larger debate about the nature of American colonialism. The first American missionaries to be sent to the Hawaiian Islands, Burma, and China had seen themselves as called to live "among a heathen people."[24] Although they saw themselves as advocates for the Hawaiian people, their actions led to the disenfranchisement of Native Hawaiians. In the late 1840s the Hawaiian government declared the land a commodity. This action, which was often referred to as the Māhele, severed the spiritual relationship between Native Hawaiians and the *ʻaina,* or land. The descendants of the first American missionaries benefited from this action. land. One missionary's daughter noted in 1878 that the family was beginning to see a return from a thousand-dollar investment they had made in a sugar plantation twelve years earlier.[25] These financial gains, of course, often came at the expense of Native people.

The intentional dispossession of the Hawaiian people from the mid to late nineteenth century meant that creating Native Hawaiian communities like Lāʻie was a political act. The Hawaiian royal family visited the Latter-day Saint community several times, commenting on the success of their Relief Societies and the health of the plantation's residents. In so doing, they offered it as a model community. Lāʻie also offered spiritual sustenance. Native Hawaiians may have seen the Latter-day Saint religion as restoring their connection to the *ʻaina.* Although white Latter-day Saints did not see themselves as kin to the land, their understanding of Zion as a physical place sacralized the landscape in similar ways. They reprinted the lyrics of a hymn that proclaimed "the mount of God" would be established "on mountain tops and above the summit of hills" in their hymnal.[26] Parley P. Pratt believed that prophecy foretold a day when "the twelve tribes of Israel" would be "concentrated from all nations in their own land" and would recognize "Jerusalem" as "the capital of political government, the seat of knowledge, and the shrine of worship." He did not believe that the Kingdom of God was a spiritual concept with no physical reality. Rather, he believed—along with other

Latter-day Saints—that the Kingdom of God would be something that individuals could touch and see.[27]

White Latter-day Saints set Zion against the secular power of the United States. They told stories about the coming apocalypse, which would destroy secular governments. For Native Saints, however, Zion was not a political entity that required them to disavow the Hawaiian monarchy. Instead, they combined their faith in the restored gospel and their allegiance to the monarchy. In 1906 a Mormon elder named Abraham Kaleimahoe Fernandez wrote to Samuel Woolley that he had baptized Lydia Kamaka'eha Lili'uokalani. He explicitly called Lili'uo-kalani the queen in spite of the recent establishment of the Hawaiian republic. This defiance of the Bayonet Constitution, which had over-thrown the monarchy and established a Hawaiian republic, delegitimized the American annexation of the islands. Fernandez's claim asserted the sovereignty of the Hawaiian people and politicized the restored gospel. In claiming to baptize Lili'uokalani, he joined the Hawaiian monarchy to the new gospel and suggested that to truly be a Latter-day Saint was to be loyal to the Hawaiian monarch.[28]

This claiming of Native Hawaiian identity was at odds with white Latter-day Saint understandings of the Hawaiian Islands. White Latter-day Saints believed that conversion would transform Native Hawaiians by teaching them proper forms of domesticity and industry. When white Latter-day Saints originally traveled to the Hawaiian Islands in 1850 they argued that lengthy contact with white Protestants had led Native Hawaiians to fall into sin and flagrant immorality.[29] The domestic practices of Native Hawaiians would have to be remade as they accepted the gospel and learned to live as members of the Kingdom of God.

White Latter-day Saints sought to transform the domestic habits of their indigenous converts by teaching them how to clean their homes and care for their children. Susa Young Gates chronicled the difference she saw in the community for a Utah audience in an October 1888 article she wrote for *Juvenile Instructor*, the church's youth periodical. Adopting the pseudonym "Homespun," she told white Latter-day Saint children that she wished they could see how Native Hawaiian women

J. A. Gonsalves

129 Fort Street,
Honolulu, H. I.

FIG. 2. Susan Young Gates with her family in Hawai'i, ca. 1889. Photo courtesy Church History Library, Church of Jesus Christ of Latter-day Saints, PH 286.

and children prepared for the Relief Society's fair. If they could, they would observe "black-haired, dark-skinned women and children all busily, quietly, eagerly working at mats, tidies, baby hoods and socks, crotchet work for pillow-slips and clothes, [and] shoulder shawls."[30] Gates portrayed Native Hawaiians as willing pupils. Having adopted the restored gospel, these converts now learned how to darn socks and knit hats.

White Latter-day Saints also identified culturally specific practices such as the consumption of the mild narcotic 'awa as reflecting the degradation of Hawaiian culture. In June 1873 Frederick Mitchell arrived in the Hawaiian Islands to serve as the mission's president. He was horrified that Native Saints used 'awa in their cultural and religious rituals and sold it for commercial purposes. The Native Hawaiian community saw the use of the plant as integral to their culture, and other Latter-day Saint missionaries allowed its use to continue. Mitchell, however, was unwilling to be lenient. He was a deeply religious man who found it difficult to accept laxity in others. In California, for example, he had noted happily that a fire, which he interpreted as divine judgment, had destroyed the homes and property of several people he had seen "wallow[ing] in abomination and filth" the day before.[31] Mitchell saw the use of 'awa as violating the Word of Wisdom, the dietary code that God had commanded all members of the church to follow. Shortly after he arrived in the Hawaiian Islands, he announced that the entire 'awa crop Native Hawaiian members had produced would be burned. In response, several native Hawaiian members of the church bought land in nearby Kahana and openly defied Mitchell by establishing their own rival community.[32] Mitchell's decision to destroy the crop highlighted the distance between white and Native Hawaiian understandings of the restored gospel. Where some white Latter-day Saints saw a violation of the Word of Wisdom, Native Saints saw a vital part of their community.

Claiming Lāʻie as a Native Hawaiian space allowed individuals like Abraham Kaleimahoe Fernandez to blend the restored gospel and indigeneity. White Latter-day Saints, however, frequently adopted understandings of Lā'ie that were at odds with indigenous interpretations of the space. For Native Hawaiians, the creation of Lā'ie had allowed them to rebuild their culture and identity. White Latter-day Saints, on the other hand, saw Lā'ie as the beginning of a process in which Native Hawaiians and other indigenous people would be fundamentally changed—transformed into Saints and chosen people.

Lā'ie had another meaning for white Saints, who saw the town was a temporary sojourn, even a place of refuge. When Susa Young Gates arrived with her second husband Jacob in Lā'ie in 1885, she doubted her ability to be a good wife and struggled to regain her sense of competence. For her, the islands offered a space of convalescence and self-invention. Susa also developed a close relationship with the other white men and women within the community. The journals and diaries of the Mormon men and women who lived in Lā'ie document frequent trips to the beach and excursions to visit volcanoes. They also enjoyed each other's hospitality and created sumptuous dinners for each other. In one entry, Susa describes the food she had prepared for their evening meal: "Three roast chickens, mashed irish and baked sweet potatoes, plum pudding, floating island and fruit cake." A Native Hawaiian woman named Hana had come earlier that day and "made a lei for the cake."[33] Another time they held a massive feast to celebrate the anniversary of the Saints' entrance into the valley, cooking a meal that included poi as well as roast beef. The speeches that day were given in Native Hawaiian and the feast was held in "Native fashion."[34]

The wives of white missionaries also sent each other loaves of bread, oranges, and other small gifts of food to supplement what food they were able to purchase in nearby villages or on the plantation. They visited each other while they sewed religious garments for their husbands and clothes for their children. Relationships between the white missionary wives were sometimes tense. For example, Susa likely contributed to the friction after she wrote a letter protesting Joseph's decision to appoint Sister Noall as a counselor in the Relief Society. Her letter demanded to know whether she had "inferior qualifications" to a woman who was little more than "a young girl" or if Noall was somehow a "better and nobler woman" than she was.[35] These tensions threatened to undo the sense of refuge white Latter-day Saints sought in Lāʻie.

In their journals, white Latter-day Saints depicted life in the community as idyllic. The fact that the United States did not yet have official sovereignty over the Hawaiian Islands allowed them to reestablish domesticity and normalcy in a period when polygamists were being forced to hide from prosecution. Despite stereotypes of absent nineteenth-century fathers, the home was frequently an important part of white male identity in this period. Contemporary understandings of domesticity demanded that men see themselves as existing within the family and that they be emotionally attached to their wives and children. They were expected to confine their sexuality to the marital bed. Lāʻie offered Joseph F. Smith an opportunity to strengthen his relationship with his wife Julina, whose diary offers readers a picture of domestic normalcy. She describes making mincemeat pies, sewing pillowcases and dresses, and ironing clothes.[36] The domesticity they established, however, was a monogamous one.

The domesticity Julina established also came at the expense of Native Hawaiians. The diaries of Julina and other white Latter-day Saint women frequently ignored the meanings of the community for Native people. Indeed, references to Native Hawaiians in their journals were rare. It is likely that Native Hawaiians helped to prepare meals, fetched water from nearby streams, washed the clothes that the missionaries and their families had dirtied, and scrubbed dishes and floors. In one entry, however, Julina reduces their labor to a single sentence: "The native girles helped me and did the work often."[37] Far more frequent are the references to the multiple pillowcases, dresses, and aprons that she sewed. The separation between the two communities is also visible in the structure of the community itself. Although white Latter-day Saints had initially lived in Native Hawaiian communities when they served as missionaries in the islands, they began to build houses that mirrored building styles in the continental United States. The proximity of these houses facilitated the creation of a white community. Latter-day Saint women could visit each other easily while remaining close to their own families and homes.

In many ways, the Mormon denial of native labor resembles the interactions between middle- and upper-class families and their servants in the United States and Great Britain. Although servants were ubiquitous within middle-class homes, they were also supposed to be invisible. In nineteenth-century novels they appear as "the silent messenger," pouring tea or dusting the furniture with nothing more than a "yes, ma'am" or "no, sir" to mark their presence.[38] This silence allowed middle-class men and women to perpetuate the myth that their homes were self-contained and to efface the labor that was required to maintain them.

The colonial contexts found in the American West, the Hawaiian Islands, and the tropical outposts of the British Empire, however, made the presence of servants within white domestic spaces even more fraught than they had been in metropolitan cities and country estates. The increased anxiety white Americans experienced in these places was partially related to climate. White Americans had long feared that "hot climates" would cause them to become as degenerate as the people who lived there.[39] Descriptions of people living in India and other colonized spaces as effeminate and licentious reflected an anxiety among white, middle-class Britons and Americans about their possible seductiveness. As the historian Sudipta Sen points out, colonial officials like Robert Orme believed that the limbs and features of Indians were supposed to be "more delicate" and "softer" than those of even the most refined European woman.[40] Contained within the descriptions of tropical spaces was the fear that white men and women who came into contact with them would leave noticeably marked and changed.

Absent from these discussions was the question of what would happen to brown bodies that traveled to temperate climates. Few people feared what would happen to people of color who worked as servants in Great Britain or elsewhere. Scientific discourse about climate assumed that white bodies were more malleable than indigenous bodies. Instead, popular literature tended to portray them as a contagion. Any threat that the conversion of Native Hawaiians might have presented to the white Latter-day Saints in the mid-nineteenth century would have seemed distant. Most white Mormons knew of the Hawaiian Islands only through the missionary letters published in church newspapers. The founding of Iosepa in the late nineteenth century, however, changed that by bringing Native Hawaiians to northern Utah.

Gathering to Utah

Although Native Hawaiians saw Lāʻie as a place where their sacred connections to the land and to their community could be restored, it was not complete. According to the church's emerging ritual tradition, the ceremonies that bound family members together for the eternities had to be performed in a Latter-day Saint temple or endowment house. Lāʻie contained neither at the time, meaning that Native Hawaiian Saints could not redeem their family members or bind themselves into the family of God. Individual Native Hawaiians like Jonathan Napela traveled to Salt Lake City to gain access to the keys and ordinances for their exaltation, but a broader solution was needed to extend temple rituals to other indigenous converts.

By the 1880s several Native Hawaiians had purchased land a mile and a half away from Temple Square. Although the temple was not yet complete, the purchase of this land allowed them to anticipate its completion and placed them physically near the center of the Latter-day Saint community.[41] The Native Hawaiian community had faced significant discrimination. Many white residents in Utah feared that the community harbored leprosy and represented a public health threat. In 1889 white Latter-day Saints worked with Native Hawaiians living in Utah to choose a site for Iosepa. The town, which was seventy-five miles from Salt Lake City, would provide Native Hawaiians with access to temple rituals.

It also brought Native Hawaiians and other Polynesians out of the Pacific and to the land where Latter-day Saints had established their American Zion while providing them with shelter from white racism.[42] As Native Hawaiians moved from Lāʻie to Iosepa, the meaning of the community shifted. The creation of Iosepa in the late nineteenth century took what had been Native land and recreated it as a Hawaiian space. The Goshutes had inhabited the area between the Oquirrh Mountains in northern Utah to the Steptoe Mountains in Nevada.[43] In 1863 they had signed a treaty allowing for the construction of transportation infrastructure.[44] The federal government would eventually confine the Goshutes to a reservation just thirteen miles away from Iosepa. Although white Latter-day Saints believed that Native Hawaiians and American Indians shared a destiny as peoples of the Book of Mormon, the residents of Iosepa frequently adopted the language of white settlers to describe their presence on the land.

In 1904 the *Honolulu Star-Advertiser* printed an article describing a celebration the community had organized for the fifth anniversary of its founding. Those present had a feast where they ate "poi, puaa . . . and other native luxuries." White ranchers from the area joined in the celebration and, after the feast, they held a dance "in which natives and whites freely participated, mingling together without distinction of race or color." The newspaper and the participants labeled the celebration a "pioneer day."[45] In so doing, they compared the founding of their colony to the entrance of Brigham Young and his followers into the Salt Lake Valley and adopted the language of settler colonialism to describe their presence in Utah.

In a letter to the editor published in the *Hawaii Herald*, another resident explicitly adopted the language of assimilation to describe Iosepa. He told a reporter: "We Hawaiians in Utah are doing as the white people do. We own our homes and try to be independent. We own cattle, horses, sheep, swine, wagons, buggies and surreys, and our mothers, sisters and wives do the housework. We do not believe in being idle for, as you know, laziness is a cardinal sin with the Hawaiians in Utah."[46] Another of the city's residents worked as a contractor for the federal government building homes on the nearby Goshute Reservation.[47]

In some ways, the language that Native Hawaiian Saints used was a way to claim the restored gospel for themselves. Eating poi on Pioneer Day suggested that the holiday was not reserved for whites. Instead, it was a holiday that held meaning for all Latter-day Saints regardless of their racial identity. An obituary published in the *Woman's Exponent* similarly claimed the gospel for Native Hawaiians. Kapala Pahupu died in Iosepa in 1897. Her obituary emphasized her commitment to the church. It reported that she had "attended all of the meetings punctually and was a logical and dignified speaker." Before she died, she "had her nice linen burial robes all ready and looked when laid out just like one in a graceful sleep." The suggestion was that she had been a faithful sister and would be called forth in the resurrection. Beyond securing her own salvation, she had worked for the church—serving as Relief Society President in Hilo, Hawaii, and using her skills as "a fine needlewoman" to help finish the pioneer quilt that the Iosepa Relief Society had decided to make for Wilford Woodruff while he was ill.[48] Although the obituary spent little time on Pahupu's identity as a Native Hawaiian woman, the obituary served as a claim that Native Hawaiian women were as much Latter-day Saints as their white sisters.

Iosepa, however, was not merely a capitulation to white colonialism. The scholar Patrick Wolfe has argued that countries like the United States, Canada, and Australia relied on the disappearance of Native peoples to make their control of the land appear legitimate. [49] Iosepa challenged the idea that Native Hawaiians would disappear. The community was fundamentally a Hawaiian community. Residents painted sea turtles on nearby boulders and named the streets after important figures within the history of the church in the Hawaiian Islands. The streets bore the names of early Hawaiian converts like Jonathan Napela and J. W. Kaulianamoku.[50] One resident told a Hawaiian-language newspaper while he was visiting the islands that Iosepa would be "a place where Hawaiians will multiply once again." Far from disappearing, the Hawaiian community would be revitalized, and Utah would become a place filled with "true Hawaiians."[51] Although Samoan and Maori Saints also lived in the town, the Salt Lake Tribune reported in 1915 that the area had been renamed "Hawaiian valley."[52]

Iosepa ultimately occupied an ambiguous place within the Saints' empire. On the one hand, the Native Hawaiians living there adopted white standards of domesticity and industriousness. They accepted the dispossession of Utah's Native people and remade Goshute land into a community for Latter-day Saints. On the other hand, the residents of Iosepa refused to accept that Native Hawaiians should be erased.

Instead, they saw Iosepa as a place where their children would be educated and create families of their own. Rather than disappear, Native Hawaiians would "[progress] very nicely," in the words of one Hawaiian Saint.[53] Native Latter-day Saints also rejected the idea that they were less civilized than their white coreligionists. Pahupu's obituary emphasized her equality with other Latter-day Saint women. She was dressed in her temple robes at death, waiting for the resurrection.

For their part, white Latter-day Saints read Iosepa as evidence of the success of Latter-day Saint colonialism. The language that Utah's newspapers used to describe the colony suggested that the community could be used as a model of progress. The *Salt Lake Herald-Republican* reported in 1915 that town "ought to be exploited as a mecca for tourists, for in no one-day drive can such diversity of stupendous mountains, impressive lake and weird mysterious desert be seen."[54] It also informed readers that the community had "a fine school" and that one of its students was working as a "stenographer for the first presidency of the church."[55] That same year, the *Salt Lake Tribune* reported that Iosepa had been named "a model of cleanliness."[56]

The tensions between the visions that white Latter-day Saints and their Native brethren had for Native Mormon spaces can be seen in the experiences of two people who died in 1918. Both had been involved in the formation of Iosepa in Utah. Hannah Kaaepa's life was spent between Utah and Hawai'i. Born in the Hawaiian Islands in 1873, Kaaepa immigrated to the United States as a young woman. In 1899 she addressed the Triennial Congress of the National Council of Women on behalf of Native Hawaiians. She also represented her chosen faith, standing as an example of the strength that the restoration gave to its women. Her conversion to the restored gospel did not lead her to abandon her belief in the sovereignty of the Hawaiian people. On her deathbed she told her husband, "Give my aloha to the Prince Kalaniana[']ole, stand by him, stand by the church and stand by the flag."[57] Her words connected her faith in the restored gospel to her loyalty to the Hawaiian monarchy. More broadly, they represented the sense among Native Mormons that the faith offered them an opportunity to revitalize their communities and resist white colonialism.

That same year, Joseph F. Smith died in Salt Lake City. As the founding prophet's nephew and the last Latter-day Saint apostle to be born in the first generation of Mormonism, he had been one of the closest living links to Joseph Smith. At fifteen years old he was called to the Hawaiian Islands to serve as a missionary. Soon after his death, the *Logan Republican* praised his early missionary service, claiming he had saved "hundreds of souls" by offering "his simple, childlike, yet divine message" to the Hawaiian people.[58] The Hawaiian Islands had a multitude of meanings for Joseph F. Smith. Hawai'i was where he had been forced to become an adult and learned to submit to God's will. The islands succored him as an adult by offering him a space of refuge during the federal prosecutions of polygamists in the 1880s. They also allowed him to reconnect with his wife Julina, who moved there with him, and to create a monogamous domesticity that would have been impossible in Utah. Kaaepa's eventual return to Hawai'i and deathbed affirmation of the bonds between the church and the Hawaiian monarchy point to the ways in which Native Hawaiians saw their spiritual and national identity as intimately linked. Native Hawaiians, of course, were not the only people to struggle with what it meant to be indigenous and a member of the Latter-day Saints in the nineteenth century. The residents of Washakie, Utah, would ask similar questions as they tried to build their own indigenous community.

Washakie: Contested Space, Contested History

On January 29, 1863, a group of American soldiers attacked a Shoshone encampment on the banks of the Bear River. By the time that the morning ended, over two hundred and fifty Shoshones were dead. Like many white people who lived in the Cache Valley, Amy Davis Phillips remembered the 1863 Bear River Massacre even though she was only a child at the time. According to a 1936 interview conducted by the Works Progress Administration, Phillips said that Colonel Connor had "attacked the Indians in the ravines on Battle Creek" and that "only a few women squaws . . . and a number of children" had survived. For Phillips, the massacre represented the death of the Northwestern Shoshones as a people. Afterward, she reported, "the spirit of the Indians was broken."[59]

Her description of the massacre's aftermath reflects the ways that white historians and settlers alike have interpreted the event. In the stories that white people tell about the American West, Native Americans disappear from the land after the end of the Indian Wars in the late nineteenth century. The removal of American Indian populations to reservations represented the end of their existence as a people. Members of the Northwestern Shoshone Nation, however, remember the event differently. For them, the Bear River Massacre was an integral part of their identity as a community. The Northwestern Shoshones did not see the Bear River Massacre as a story about the demise of their people but as a record of their survival. For example, in 2003 the Utah State Historical Society published a history of Utah's Native American communities in consultation with the Bureau of Indian Affairs. The entry on the Northwestern Shoshones was written by a tribal historian named Mae Parry. Although Parry chronicled the devastation her people had experienced, she did not end the story there. She also described the community's conversion to Mormonism, their relocation to Corinne, Utah, and their continued survival in the twentieth century.[60] When her niece Patty Timbimboo-Madsen spoke about the effects of the Bear River Massacre on the Northwestern Shoshones in 2012, she emphasized their continued presence in Utah. "We're still here," she said, "and we never left."[61]

The Shoshone people's conversion to restored gospel and the eventual formation of the town of Washakie near the Idaho-Utah border were important parts of that survival. White settlement had destroyed Native foodways and decimated their communities, and the 1863 massacre intensified the Northwestern Shoshones' destitution. Unable to bury their dead, the community pushed the bodies of their kin into the Bear River.[62] Uncertain of their future, the tribe signed a treaty with the U.S. government that exchanged their claims to some of their homeland for a small annuity of $5,000, an amount that could never support the entire community. In the years after the treaty, people frequently commented on the poverty of the Northwestern Shoshones. The *Corinne Reporter* contained frequent stories about American Indians begging local white settlers for food. In 1869 the *Deseret News* scoffed that Chief Pocatello's name meant "give-us-another-sack-of-flour-and-two-beeves."[63]

Their mocking—though derisive and condescending—pointed to the real hunger that Native communities in northern Utah and southern Idaho were facing. When George W. Dodge became an Indian agent in the early 1870s, he commented on the "entire destitution of provisions" among many Shoshone communities and sought to provide for them. He began issuing weekly rations of beef, but the needs of his charges were overwhelming.[64] It was during this time that a Shoshone man named Ech-up-way claimed to receive heavenly visitors. They told him "that the 'Mormons' God was the true god, and that he and the Indians' Father were one; that he must go to the 'Mormons,' and they would tell him what to do; that the time was at hand for the Indians to gather, and stop their Indian life, and learn to cultivate the earth and build houses, and live in them."[65] Ech-up-way's vision called the Shoshone people to live in a new way. Instead of gathering pine nuts and building sagebrush corrals, they would learn to cultivate crops and adopt whites' methods of ranching. Ech-up-way had adopted a conception of the restored gospel similar the one that some Native Hawaiian converts to the church embraced. Native Hawaiian Saints had believed that Lāʻie and Iosepa would become places where the Hawaiian people would multiply—revitalizing their community and restoring their sense of themselves as God's people. Ech-up-way hoped that something similar would happen for the Shoshones. Conversion to the restored gospel would provide his people with a respite from the relentless assaults of colonialism and allow them to regenerate.

On August 1, 1873, George Washington Hill, a Latter-day Saint missionary assigned to the Shoshones, baptized dozens of Shoshone men and women.[66] For these Native converts, the gospel of the Latter-day Saints offered a compelling sacred narrative. Contained within Ech-up-way's vision was the promise of prosperity. He suggested that Native Americans, rather than vanishing from Utah, would adapt to white methods of farming and be able to feed their families. The restored gospel may have also offered the Northwestern Shoshones a way to bind their families together and recreate the kinship networks that settler colonialism had destroyed. On March 3, 1885, Alma Shoshonitz was baptized in the name of several of his male family members, including his father Widg-e-gee-an-tach-gwits, his brother Puo-pitch, and a son named Twid-gee-gee. On that same day, Manasseh Hootchew and Pans-a-gootsey Weatuts were baptized for their dead kin as well.[67]

For a community that had lost dozens of individuals to starvation, disease, and the Bear River Massacre, the ability to ensure that relationships would be preserved after death must have been particularly meaningful. Temple records held at the Church History Library in Salt Lake City underscore this point. In addition to the baptisms mentioned above, the records contain information about temple rituals performed for dozens of individuals who died at the Bear River Massacre or in the difficult years surrounding it. Put together, their names became a litany of the dead. Anno-tz-do-bey, Tabby-Woot-te-gwa, Co-ro-boits-e, No-ro-nug-in-jo, Tin-nam-bey, Pooa-took-unt, Ko-be-no, and Nin-nan-goit-zah-ny all died in 1863. Widg-e-gee-an-tach-gwits, Pah-gah, and Mode-zi-yah passed away in 1864. As one reads the pages, names pile on top of names. Tzuk-qua-nun-gah, Po-wip, Mo-so-wy, Wah-wut-te-gah, Me-tuk-ut-se, Mo-qua-a-tutz. All had died. All were baptized. No-yo-zach-wa, Nek-u-wat, Yee-gum, Tidz-a-pah. These sons, grandfathers, fathers, and nephews were lost before being reclaimed in the temple. The records also contain examples of women being baptized for their female kin. Pa-pa-ris Brown baptized her mother, aunts, and mother-in-law.[68]

Interviews conducted in the mid-twentieth century suggest the continued resonance of participation in temple rituals to resist colonialism. In one 1945 interview, a Shoshone woman discusses a vision she received while in the temple telling her the names of those who had died in the massacre. She sees how "their bodies had been disposed of" and "where they were killed."[69] Her vision is undated and told in the third person, but it points to the difference between white and Shoshone understandings of massacre. As we saw in chapter 5, white Latter-day Saints had celebrated the massacre, seeing the hand of God in the removal of an obstacle to Latter-day Saint settlement. For Shoshone Latter-day Saints, however, God sympathized not with white settlers or the U.S. Army but with murdered children and the women who had been raped by white soldiers. Mormon temple rituals offered Native Americans the chance to reform families that had been split apart by massacre and kidnapping. Shoshonitz and his brethren had experienced the horrors of colonization and had their family members taken from them. In 2013 Shoshone Latter-day Saints read the names from the temple records at the site of the Bear River Massacre. That same year, the Smithsonian returned two bodies of the massacre's victims that it had held in its collections.[70] Ironically, it was in the temple of the Church of Jesus Christ of Latter-day Saints, which had served as the inner sanctum for the people who had stolen their land and destroyed their families after the massacre, that they were allowed to reclaim their kin.

Shoshone Latter-day Saints, however, needed physical as well as spiritual sustenance. Ech-up-way's vision offered them a way forward: the Shoshones would adopt whites' methods of agriculture and make them Shoshone. The restoration's emphasis on creating "stakes of Zion" meant that the Shoshones would also need to create a separate community. Instead of integrating into white society, they would have their own community, their own bishops and Relief Society presidents, and their own schools. In short, they would be able to be *Shoshone* Latter-day Saints.

The task of creating a Shoshone town was difficult. The first Shoshone Latter-day Saint settlement was near Corinne, Utah, sixty miles north of Salt Lake City. Their resources were meager. In 1875 George Hill, the Latter-day Saint missionary who had first baptized the Shoshones two years before, sent several letters to Brigham Young about the settlement and described a community desperate to do well with little. In one letter he told Young that, using "their own horses," the Shoshone men sometimes "hold the ploughs themselves" when they worked the fields.[71] It was difficult, however, for the men to labor in the fields all day when they had little food. It is impossible to read Hill's letters to Young without sensing the community's desperation. Hill would later write Young about Chief Washakie's plans to come to the settlement with his band to be baptized.[72] Although the occasion would have created excitement among the small community, Hill was concerned that the party would arrive with "very little supplies" and the Latter-day Saint community would be forced to draw on already meager resources. He ended this letter with a plea that Young spare any cattle he had. For the Northwestern Shoshones, Washakie's visit would have been an opportunity to show their hospitality and renew their relationship with their Newe kin. They were willing to share what few provisions they had. The poverty that followed, however, would not have been any less devastating for their willingness.

The existence of a Shoshone Latter-day Saint community played on preexisting non-Mormon fears about the church's collusion with Native Americans. On July 17, 1860, the *New York Times* published an article describing Brigham Young's policy toward Utah's Native community. Although the author ultimately thought that Young tried to prevent violence, he recognized that it was a "general belief that the Mormons leaders [were] accustomed to tampering with the Indians and inciting them to hostility towards other whites than the Mormons."[73] In 1872 the *Salt Lake Tribune* told its readers that Latter-day Saints believed Native Americans were "their cousins" and that "the triumph of one" would ultimately be "the triumph of both."[74] Three years later the *New York Daily Herald* warned readers that Latter-day Saints missionaries had been "baptizing the Indian by the hundred all through Utah and the adjoining territories." "The red skins," it continued, "believe that the spirits of their forefathers have visited some of the leading chiefs in Southern Utah, and told them to cling to the Mormons." These comments appeared under the title "Threatened Indian War" and directly referenced the possibility that Native Saints had encouraged American Indians living in Nevada to attack white settlers.[75] Other newspapers, including the *Washington Union, Western Kansas Ensign, Tennessean,* and *Detroit Free Press,* included similar insinuations.[76]

The 1857 Mountain Meadows Massacre, in which white Latter-day Saints donned Native costumes and murdered an emigrant train, only deepened their concerns. Newspapers continually reported on Mountain Meadows, but in the initial decades after the attack it was unclear if white Latter-day Saints had murdered the emigrant train of white

Protestant settlers by themselves, if they had convinced local Paiutes to participate, or if Native American tribes had acted on their own initiative. It would later become clear that the first possibility was the reality.[77] In the nineteenth century, however, people were afraid that the massacre was an example of the dangers of Latter-day Saint and Native collusion, which could prevent the incorporation of the American West into the United States. Stories of Paiute and Latter-day Saint men slaughtering white women and children chilled non-Mormons—despite later evidence that there was little to no Indian participation in the event.[78] In 1882 the U.S. Congress passed a resolution asking the secretary of the interior to investigate whether Mormons encouraged Native Americans to attack white settlers.[79]

Corinne, Utah was a locus of the area's non-Mormon community, and these inhabitants also feared the presence of Native Saints. Residents worried that white Latter-day Saints were colluding with the Shoshones to destroy the town. The articles that the local newspaper published about the Indian community over the summer of 1875 were increasingly paranoid and feverish. On August 9, 1875, the *Corinne Mail* printed an article with the headline: "Mormons Meddling with the Indians! Mountain Meadows to be Repeated!" The newspaper played upon racism and longstanding concerns about Mormon settlement. White residents worried about the Native American presence near Corinne despite a lack of a tribal affiliation between the Paiute and the Northwestern Shoshone.

In mid-August a group of U.S. soldiers visited the Shoshone community to determine whether it represented a threat to nearby white residents. Although George Hill tried to defuse the situation, one of the officials read a prepared statement telling the gathered Shoshones that they must either return to their reservations or be forced from the land. Hill's protests that the community's residents had never belonged to a reservation were ignored. The Northwestern Shoshones, perhaps still haunted by memories of the Bear River Massacre, decided to leave the land they had cultivated rather than face forced removal. Some chose to go to Fort Hall, where a reservation had been created for the Shoshones and Bannocks. Others moved to nearby towns or to the Cache Valley.

Just after the dispersal of the Northwestern Shoshones, Hill published an article in the *Deseret News* defending the Shoshones' progress. He said residents had sown "one hundred acres of wheat, about twenty-five of corn, five and one-half to six of potatoes, [and] three to four of melons, peas, beets, and other vegetables."[80] They had already dug a ditch and made a new dam. The soldiers, however, had refused to listen to reason and had stolen "beaver traps," "copper kettles," "axes," and even the "rabbit skin robes" the Shoshones used to "[wrap] their children."[81] Over the next five years, the Northwestern Shoshones cooperated with Mormon leaders to found two other Indian farms, including one at a place called Lemuel's Garden.[82] Each time, however, they were forced to abandon their homes.

In 1880 they were finally able to establish a lasting Shoshone Latter-day Saint community. Washakie was in the Malad Valley in Idaho, just a few miles away from Portage, Utah. It initially consisted of just 1,700 acres but eventually encompassed around 18,000. Members of the community homesteaded the land but embraced the communal nature of the Mormon faith. They consecrated their property to God and voluntarily gave any excess materials to the local bishop to redistribute to the poor.

Over time, white Latter-day Saints approved of the community as an example of what they believed Native Latter-day Saint communities should look like. Descriptions of the town appeared in newspapers in Salt Lake City, Ogden, and Logan, apprising white readers of the community's progress. The articles used language that closely mirrored white descriptions of Native Hawaiian Saints. When Matthias Cowley visited the settlement, for example, he described the congregation as "neat and clean."[83] An 1883 article published in the *Utah Journal* enumerated the items that the author had found within the community's school, including "a full set of Cornell's outline maps, Payson, Dunton and Scribner's writing charts, and also reading charts."[84] These descriptions presented Native Americans who had embraced the restored gospel as willing pupils who had accepted their inferiority and their need to change.

The conflict between white and Shoshone understandings of the gospel, however, was deep. Shoshone Latter-day Saints saw their conversion as a turning point. They recognized that they had accepted a new religious tradition and that they had been forced to abandon their previous way of life. Their conversion, however, did not represent a rejection of what it meant to be Shoshone. Instead, it was a way to preserve the community and allowed it to thrive. The restored gospel offered the Shoshones a religion that privileged their experiences as the descendants of the Book of Mormon and promised that they would be redeemed as a chosen people and participate in the building of a new Jerusalem. It also provided them with a version of Christianity that accepted the prophetic visions and spiritual healings that had been such an important part of their previous religious experiences.

White Latter-day Saints, however, saw Native Americans' conversions as the beginning of a faith journey that would lead Natives to abandon their earlier practices for a more "faithful" existence. In this case, faithfulness was synonymous with whiteness. In 1882, for example, a correspondent of the *Ogden Daily Herald* told readers that "education [would] dispel a great deal of their tradition and superstition, thereby causing [the Indians at Washakie] to leave off many of their present habits, and adopt instead the customs of the more enlightened race."[85] Native Saints who refused to follow white counsel could be accused of apostasy. The *Utah Journal* included a story about a man named Tope who had criticized the United Order, a church cooperative program. According to that article, a local storekeeper confronted him with his apostasy after hearing him claim to be a Latter-day Saint, which caused Tope to retract his criticisms.[86] To explain why Tope had been so willing to recant his earlier statements, the newspaper recorded him—using a faux-Indian accent—as saying: "Me talk two ways; that's all right, me two kinds of friends."[87] It is possible, however, that Tope feared being cast out of the church because of the retaliation that might ensue and was willing to forget his complaints as a result.

Interviews from the twentieth century give a sense of the ongoing tensions within the community. According to Phoebe Zundell Ward, whose father had been the bishop of Washakie while she was a child, those who apostatized from the church faced dire consequences. She told an interviewer that a man named Turnapitch "ridiculed the sacrament." Eventually, church authorities held a council meeting. The man defended his position and then declared that if he was wrong, "The Lord [may] strike *me* and *my children*." It wasn't long until the man and his children were dead. The members of the community who followed him were likewise "curse[d]." They begged God for forgiveness, however, and were made "whole" through rebaptism.[88]

In the white Latter-day Saint imagination, the Native Americans at Washakie remained only partially civilized despite their conversion to the restored gospel. Fulmer Allred, a white Latter-day Saint who had lived in Washakie in the mid-twentieth century, interpreted the decision of community members to frequently visit Blackfoot, Idaho, as a desire to "rove." He told an interviewer that the Shoshone "didn't like to be tied," adding the phrase "any of them" to emphasize his point.[89] In the same interview in which she described Turnapitch, Phoebe noted that it had been difficult for Shoshone women to completely adopt white understandings of domesticity and that the women she knew hunted for pine nuts, serviceberries, and a vegetable called *yampa*.[90] In the early twentieth century, white Americans increasingly encouraged Native Americans throughout the American West to abandon their indigenous foodways for white agricultural practices. Federal officials in Montana established a fair in 1904 to encourage the Crow to adopt farming.[91] Although Crow Fair allowed individuals to participle in foot races and wear traditional clothing, it also displayed the progress that they had made in adopting white agriculture by displaying Native handicrafts and produce. White Latter-day Saints saw the work they were superintending at Washakie as a spiritual version of the progress the Crow Fair promoted. For them, Washakie was ultimately a place where Native Americans would learn the arts of civilization. Indigeneity would be erased, not preserved.

Nineteenth-century understandings of the restored gospel had long marginalized Native peoples even as it placed them at the center of its theology. White Latter-day Saints interpreted the statement in the Book of Mormon that Native Americans would be made "white and delightsome" as a promise that they would be assimilated both culturally and physically into white society. Understandings of the place of Native Americans in restoration theology changed in the twentieth century. As white Latter-day Saints agitated to be fully included within white, middle-class American society, they marginalized the theological threads that had emphasized the role Native Americans would play in the redemption of humanity. Utah newspapers sought out Native correspondents who would report on the happenings in Washakie, and people like Willie Ottogary and Leona Peyope complied, providing both humorous stories and serious reports from the community. A 1938 column by Peyope contained a story about a Native woman from Fort Hall whose inability to remember "how to say Baking Powder" led her to mistakenly purchase and back with face powder.[92] Peyope's columns included information about the Shoshones' stops at the Logan Temple and the visitors that the community had entertained. Readers of her columns would have gained a sense of what the Shoshone version of the restored gospel looked like. Her stories, however, appeared alongside articles designed to portray Native Americans as part of the history of the Church of Jesus Christ of Latter-day Saints instead of its present. In 1935, for example, the *Ogden Standard-Examiner* informed its readers that the upcoming Box Elder County Fair would contain "street scenes . . . reminiscent of the old west, with cowboys and Indians, the latter from the Washakie Reservation."[93] These depictions were overwhelmed by the sheer number of stories about white Mormons and their understandings of the world. As a result, the Shoshones appeared as an oddity—an amusement meant to entertain white Latter-day Saints readers rather than prompting them to engage in a serious discussion of Native Saints.

It is important, however, not to overemphasize these tensions. What emerges from a reading of Shoshone sources is the "normalcy" of life at Washakie. The sports columns of local newspapers contained announcements about games that the town's baseball team was playing with nearby Garland. Peyope's columns described children singing songs after they finished the school year. She created a sense of identity for Shoshones that was American, Latter-day Saint, and Native. The stories that the

Northwestern Shoshones told about Johnny Garr's mother emphasize this point. According to one history of her life, she testified to the truth of the Latter-day Saint gospel during church and expressed her thanks for "her papa Nephi-Lehi who shine[d] on Cheyenne paper." The same history identifies her as living in "a little frame house" with "white sheets and . . . beautiful pillow cases."[94] The residents of Washakie took pride in their identity as members of the Shoshone Nation and saw it as being inseparable from their faith as Latter-day Saints. Johnny Garr's mother saw herself as a descendant of Nephi-Lehi, an identity only available to those who identified as both Latter-day Saint and Native.

This identity was at odds, however, with an increasingly mainstream white Church of Jesus Christ of Latter-day Saints. These tensions came to a head in the mid-twentieth century. The economic opportunities offered by World War II enticed many young Shoshones to leave Washakie to work in local industries. Few returned. According to Mae Parry Timbimboo, the community dwindled until the LDS Church decided to burn the remaining homes and sell the property. In an article she published with the Utah Division of State History, Timbimboo wrote that many Shoshone Latter-day Saints felt that the church "had defaulted on a promise."[95] Geneva Alex Pacheco, for example, testified that she had been "scraping [a] deer hide" when she saw a man "start a fire by Elias Pubigee's home." The fire then began to spread and threatened her "mother's gooseberry patch."[96] She confronted the man but was told that a local church official had ordered the burning. Leona Peyope described returning from Bannock Creek to discover that local Latter-day Saints had burned her home. Her papers and the "records of [her] people" had been inside. Everything—her "blankets, clothing, mattresses, beds, stove, dishes, cupboard, refrigerator, table and chairs, and even [her] food"—had been destroyed. When she saw the state of her home, she "cried out loud."[97] One of Mae Parry Timbimboo's relatives, Amy Timbimboo, summarized the sorrow that many in the community felt in a 1967 interview: "The church, they took their land . . . and they [had] no place to farm and stay."[98] The result was diaspora. According to an interview that Martin Seneca conducted with Amy and her husband, some of the residents dispersed to nearby states with substantial Indian communities, settling in Nevada, Wyoming, and Idaho. Others moved to Brigham City, Ogden, or Salt Lake City. Whatever their ultimate destination, the result was the same: "Everybody went."[99]

Washakie and Iosepa are now ghost towns. Although Iosepa was called "the most progressive city in Utah" in 1911, the LDS Church called the residents of Iosepa to return to Hawai'i to help build a temple in Lā'ie in 1917.[100] The towns' desolation is a reminder of the tensions within the restored gospel surrounding the place of indigenous people and the desire among many white Latter-day Saints in the twentieth century to be accepted by mainstream society. Although nineteenth-century Latter-day Saints had partaken in American colonialism, dispossessed Native American tribes, and associated whiteness with godliness, it had also been a religion predicated on the redemption of the peoples of the Book of Mormon. Its scriptures were fundamentally a story about the descendants of "papa Lehi-Nephi."[101] After all, Orson Pratt had rested his faith partially in the idea that God would convert the millions of people who had lived in the Americas before the arrival of Europeans, as he described to an audience in Salt Lake City. The mixed race and indigenous communities these narratives had created were increasingly marginalized in the twentieth-century United States. There is, of course, an exception: the story of Lā'ie in the twentieth century was one of success. The construction of the Hawaiian temple in 1919 gave the community a sense of purpose and called the Native Hawaiians living in Utah back to the islands. In the 1950s the Church of Jesus Christ of Latter-day Saints began construction on what would eventually become Brigham Young University–Hawai'i. This community, however, did not threaten white understandings of the restored gospel. Lā'ie's geographical remoteness provided white Latter-day Saints the opportunity to continue their work among "the Lamanites" without endangering their own white respectability. The distance between Hawai'i and Utah also provided Native Hawaiian Saints with the geographic remove they needed to create their own community without daily interference. Lā'ie survived, in part, because it was already at the margins.

EPILOGUE

In 1909 the Northwestern Band of the Shoshone Nation traveled to Logan, Utah, to participate in its semicentennial celebration. Photographs from the event show the teepees, erected on an open green in town, where the Shoshones stayed. In one image, white people huddle around a teepee where a Native man and his wife stand with their two children. The man is wearing a loosely fitting suit and his hat is cocked back. The little boy in front of him looks as though he might burst into tears at any moment. The man's wife stands emotionless by her husband's side. The boy seems to know that he is on display and finds the experience intensely discomforting. At some point during the celebrations the Shoshones participated in a parade. A man wearing a headdress and sitting atop a horse is surrounded by Shoshone men sporting a wide variety of outfits in one photograph. One of the Shoshones dons a cowboy hat; another has his hair loose down his back. It is impossible to know what spectators thought as they saw the Shoshone men riding their horses down Logan's streets. Some of the onlookers may have met the participants when they had traveled to the city to help build the temple decades earlier, or perhaps they had read about the community in the frequent reports given on its status in the newspaper. It is likely, however, that the parade was meant to portray Utah's past. One float

FIG. 3. A 1909 parade held as part of a semicentennial celebration in Logan, Utah. Photo courtesy Church History Library, Church of Jesus Christ of Latter-day Saints, Shoshone Latter-day Saints photographs, 1909, PH 9714.

consisted of a wagon drawn by two oxen with the words "Pike S Peke or Bust" written crudely on the side. The photographer Alma Compton snapped a picture of Shoshones participating in the celebrations while men wearing military uniforms stood in the background—a cruel decision given the history of the Northwestern Shoshones.[1]

Logan was not the only town to mark its semicentennial that year. Mount Pleasant held its own celebrations on July 5. Hilda Madsen, a thirty-one-year-old woman, dressed as the goddess of liberty. Four plumed horses led her carriage, and American flags jutted out from the float. The imagery represented the absorption of Utah into the United States and displayed a patriotism that would have been impossible just a few decades earlier. The celebrations also featured a drum corps comprised of veterans from Utah's Indian wars and the erection of a monument to the pioneers who had built the town fifty years earlier. John A. Averett

FIG. 4. A float from the 1909 semicentennial celebration parade in Logan. The words "Pike's Peke or Bust" refer to an 1859 gold rush near Pike's Peak, Colorado. Photo courtesy Church History Library, Church of Jesus Christ of Latter-day Saints, Shoshone Latter-day Saints photographs, 1909, PH 9714.

also led a "band of Indians" in the parade. It is likely that these "Indians" were played by white men.[2]

For white Latter-day Saints, these celebrations marked the end of Utah's existence as a frontier space and the beginning of its identity as a progressive, modern community that participated in national politics and affairs. Gone were the banners declaring that Native Americans would soon be a "white and delightsome" people.[3] Latter-day Saints' parades instead depicted Native Americans as part of their faith's history, not as vital parts of its theology and future. For Native Saints, however, the parades had a different meaning. Participating in parades allowed Native communities, which mainstream Latter-day Saints had sidelined, to make their story and presence known.[4] They also presented a sense of conviviality among the Native Saints who participated. The same set of

FIG. 5. It was common for Native families to camp overnight at the grounds of parades and celebrations in which Native nations agreed to participate. As suggested by this photo from Logan's 1909 semicentennial parade, these camps could become tourist attractions. Photo courtesy Church History Library, Church of Jesus Christ of Latter-day Saints, Shoshone Latter-day Saints photographs, 1909, PH 9714.

photographs that show white Latter-day Saints crowding around Native families as though they were an ethnographic exhibit demonstrate the togetherness that such gatherings could create among Native people. Traveling to state fairs, rodeos, and parades allowed Native people to see family members, dress in special clothing, and celebrate their tribal identity. Native Americans transformed ceremonies that were meant to mark them as part of Utah's past into a celebration of their place in the present.

Pacific Islanders occupy an interesting place within Utah society. In the twenty-first century they have become a significant minority within the state. In 2014 there were almost thirty-eight thousand Polynesians living in Utah. This number is almost 3 percent of the total number of

FIG. 6. This photograph shows members of the Northwestern Shoshones at the Logan semicentennial parade positioned in front of men dressed like soldiers. Although it's unclear what the photographer intended when he took this photo, it immediately brings to mind the Bear River Massacre. Photo courtesy Church History Library, Church of Jesus Christ of Latter-day Saints, Shoshone Latter-day Saints photographs, 1909, PH 9714.

Pacific Islanders living in the United States. Although they are a significant proportion of Utah's population, many Pacific Islanders feel disconnected from Latter-day Saint society. The remnants of Iosepa allow Polynesian Saints to lay claim to a place in Utah's history. Polynesian Saints in present-day Utah sometimes hold a festival on Memorial Day commemorating the men and women who settled Iosepa. In addition to a luau, they carve Tahitian drums out of coconut wood, hold an exhibition in which Samoan men dance with fire knives, and place flowers on the graves in the town's cemetery. For them, Iosepa represents the beginnings of an identity that fuses deep faith in the restoration with their ethnic identity.[5]

FIG. 7. A tree near the Bear River Massacre site. Visitors sometimes leave objects and remembrances in the trees near the site in commemoration of the massacre's victims. Wikimedia Commons.

Latter-day Saints have celebrated the history of their missionary work in the Pacific. During a research trip to the Church History Library in Utah, I heard an elderly missionary tell visitors that the murals that greeted visitors were copied from the walls of the Latter-day Saint temple in Lāʻie. White missionaries who traveled to the Hawaiian Islands in the nineteenth century as Saints are remembered as beloved figures who cared deeply for Pacific Islanders and their community. Several years after Joseph F. Smith's death in 1918, the U.S. Senator and Latter-day Saint apostle Reed Smoot wrote that he did not "believe it [was] possible for human beings to love a man more than did the natives of the islands love President Joseph F. Smith."[6]

White Saints, however, have been more reticent to celebrate the history of their interactions with Native Americans. Early twentieth-century Latter-day Saints began to move away from the elements that had marked them as distinct from mainstream Protestantism in an attempt to integrate into dominant American society.[7] This movement required them to jettison their polygamous past and emphasize their fundamental whiteness.[8] Although the church issued a manifesto temporarily suspending the practice of plural marriage until U.S. law could be changed, members of the church leadership quietly authorized certain individuals to perform plural marriages. In 1904 Joseph F. Smith read a letter in the church's general conference prohibiting church officials from contracting new plural marriages. Anyone who participated in such a marriage would "be deemed in transgression against the Church and will be liable to be dealt with . . . and excommunicated therefrom."[9] The statement represented the church's further movement away from a practice that had defined it for decades.

The decision of the Church of Jesus Christ of Latter-day Saints to deemphasize the place of Native Americans in restoration theology can be partially read as an attempt to distance themselves from a racially ambiguous past. It can also be seen, however, as a response to the pushback that the church received to its policies concerning Native Americans. American Indian activists have frequently critiqued the community. In 1973 members of the American Indian Movement (AIM) asked the church to donate $1 million to programs led by Native Americans. The church denied them entrance to the meetings of its annual general conference and prohibited them from entering Temple Square.[10] AIM members met with church leaders on the sidewalk outside of the square and offered them flowers. They told them that their appeal was made in a "spirit of love."[11] AIM's activism made many Latter-day Saints uncomfortable. It belied the church's narrative about the role white Latter-day Saints would play in "redeeming" Native communities.

Much of the criticism that Latter-day Saints received centered on the church's Indian Placement Program. The program began in 1947 as a way to educate the children of migrant farm workers. Selected families fostered Indian children who they introduced to white Mormon culture through enrollment in local public schools and church attendance.[12] Approximately fifty thousand children participated in the program. Although some Navajo children had fond memories of the program, others criticized the effects that it had on Indian families. The removal of Indian children from their homes during the school year made it difficult for them to learn about Navajo culture or to develop deep relationships with their extended families. Many of the children who participated remembered the loneliness that they experienced. Tona Younce Hangen has documented the experiences of some of the children who participated in the program. She describes one Navajo boy who remembered being picked up in a Cadillac. She notes that he saw the car as a contrast to the poverty of the Navajo reservation. Although his foster parents tried to help him overcome his loneliness, he remained aloof. He remembered getting into their pool and going over to the corner because he was so overwhelmed. "I just went over to the corner and stayed there," he told an interviewer. "I wouldn't come out of my corner."[13] Another child who participated in the program remembered crying as her foster family drove her from Provo, where they had processed the children, to Ogden. They bought her ice cream to try to calm her, but she still refused to talk to them for a while. "I knew how to talk English," she remembered. "I guess I was just really shy."[14]

In many ways, the Indian Placement Program continued earlier attempts by the Latter-day Saints to domesticate American Indians by incorporating them into white families. Nineteenth-century Saints had adopted Indian children in the belief that doing so would transform their cultural habits while saving them from slavery. Female Latter-day Saints played an important role in these adoptions, teaching Indian children how to cook, eat correctly with utensils, and create the skirts and stays that dressed their bodies. Although the Indian Placement Program emphasized the temporary nature of its foster placements, it drew on similar imagery and rhetoric as earlier Latter-day Saint practices. Both nineteenth- and twentieth-century Saints believed that the redemption of Native Americans would occur through their incorporation into white families. In both cases, it was the home that served as the place where indigenous people would be culturally whitened. As a result, female Latter-day Saints played an important role in the program. They were to serve as mothers to the Indian children they fostered, ensuring that they received a proper education and learned how to behave within white society.

White Saints did not see this transformation as a loss of indigenous identity. They believed that Native Americans, in adopting Mormonism and the habits of white culture, were returning to their original heritage. Nevertheless, Native American activists attacked the program as a form of cultural terrorism. The anthropologist Martin Topper wrote that the program was "neither a successful missionary practice nor a means of reducing the strain of acculturation on the Navajo child."[15] A Native American advocate named Beth Wood went further and called the program an "adoption racket." One person that she quotes in the article refers to the education that Native children received in the homes of white Latter-day Saints as "brainwashing."[16] Opposition from Indian activists combined with opposition on Navajo reservations led to the program slowly being phased out. The last student graduated from the program in 2000. The controversy surrounding the program was symptomatic of a larger discomfort surrounding the position of American Indians within the Church of Jesus Christ as Latter-day Saints. Perhaps the most famous incident concerning the identity of Native Saints centered on George P. Lee, a Navajo man who had participated in the placement program as a child and became the first Native American to be named a general authority, one of the highest leadership positions in the church. For much of his tenure Lee was seen as a symbol of the success of Latter-day Saint programs concerning Native Americans. Lee's career, however, ended in disgrace when he was convicted of raping a twelve-year-old girl.[17]

The disillusionment that many people felt after Lee's dismissal deepened the uncertainty about the place of Native Americans within the church. Before his excommunication, Lee had been an important advocate for Native Saints. He advocated that the church invest money in programs for Native youth and take seriously injunctions within the Book of Mormon to redeem the Lamanites. Even before Lee's excommunication, some members of the Quorum of the Twelve Apostles rejected his claims. The Latter-day Saint apostle Bruce R. McConkie told faithful members that the idea that white Saints would be of "assistance" to the Lamanites in the creation of Zion was a "whiff of nonsense."[18] They likely saw Lee's excommunication and conviction as evidence of the rightness of their interpretation of the Book of Mormon.

Several white Latter-day Saints have recognized the role that Christian missionary work played in destroying Indian communities. In an article on the Indian Placement Program, Hangen describes visiting a Navajo ward during her field research. As she sang the verses of a common Latter-day Saint hymn—"They, the Builders of the Nations"—she found it difficult to reconcile the celebration of white Latter-day Saint pioneer heritage with being surrounded by the people that white Saints had dispossessed. Unable to navigate the meaning of the hymn, she dissolved into "awkward giggles."[19]

The discomfort that she experienced is less prominent in Mormon discussions of the role that Polynesians play within the Church of Jesus Christ of Latter-day Saints. Although Pacific Islanders have advocated for the decolonization of the islands they live on, Utah's Latter-day Saints have been less aware of this activism. Instead, they tend to celebrate the church's missionary work in the Pacific Islands as an unambiguous success. This lack of awareness of Polynesian activism may be responsible for the differences in how contemporary Latter-day Saints perceive the two groups. The restored gospel has also found a wider acceptance among the Polynesian community than it has among American Indians.

This tradition has continued into the present. In the 1960s the church founded the Polynesian Cultural Center (PCC) to preserve the cultures of the Pacific while entertaining white tourists. Many of the people who left their homes to work there saw their callings as religious ones. Emosi Damuni, who served as a cultural expert for the center's Fijian village and worked at the PCC for decades, told an interviewer in the 1980s, "I think I was chosen to come here by our Heavenly Father . . . I think I was brought here on purpose . . . to help . . . build up the Fijian Village and help the students learn the dancing and the cultures of Fiji."[20] Damuni's statement reflected how the PCC blended cultural tourism and religious calling. According to Hokulani Aikau, he was not the only employee to do so. Mangers at the PCC frequently "blurred the boundary between what constituted work for the center and what was a calling for the church."[21] Students were given college scholarships for agreeing to dance for tourists, and faculty members were encouraged to work at the center. Although there was some dissent from Polynesian faculty members about the willingness of the church to ask students to display their bodies at the center to please tourists, many of the people who worked there saw their employment as a type of missionary work in which people would be converted through their exposure to the joys of Polynesian culture.[22]

The geographic distance of many white Latter-day Saints from the Pacific Islands allows them to ignore the critiques that Polynesian scholars have raised of the PCC. Instead, the Pacific Islands have become an idealized space where Mormon relationships with indigenous people are unrestrained and uncomplicated.[23] A 2014 issue of the *Ensign*, an official church magazine, celebrated Tonga as "a land dedicated to God." It describes the conversion of one of the descendants of 'Iki Fulivai, an elite Tongan who invited Latter-day Saint missionaries to proselytize in the islands in the early twentieth century.[24] Although the *Ensign* frequently published articles lauding the conversion of people from a variety of cultures, Polynesians are often depicted as especially faithful. For many Polynesians, their faith in the restoration and their cultural heritage are intertwined. The country's motto, "God and Tonga are my inheritance," reflects a general sense that Tongans—and many Polynesian nations—are dedicated to God.[25]

The embrace of a Polynesian Latter-day Saint identity as natural allows white Saints to see Pacific Islanders as fulfilling the Book of Mormon's promise to the descendants of American Israelites. It has also created an often unrecognized dynamic within the church in which many of restoration's socially conservative ideas are imported to Hawai'i without being adapted to its progressive politics. Members of local Latter-day Saint congregations protested the passage of the Equal Rights Amendment in the mid-twentieth century and ensured its defeat nationally, in spite of the larger support for the amendment within Hawai'i.[26] Decades later, the church's opposition to same-sex marriage in Hawai'i became a precursor to a much more highly publicized contest in California over the same issue.[27] Native Hawaiian Saints adopted a definition of marriage, sexuality, and domesticity that closely mirrored that of their white coreligionists. Their decision to do so was based on their belief that the church was a mouthpiece for God. They saw their acceptance of Latter-day Saint ideas about domesticity not as a concession to whiteness, but as an embrace of godliness. For them, there was little tension between their faith and their Polynesian identity.

White Latter-day Saints have tended to view the place of Polynesians within the church as unproblematic. This embrace of "Polynesian Mormonness" is part of a global shift away from an emphasis on converting Native Americans. The pictures within modern printings of the Book of Mormon frequently use Latin American motifs to represent Lamanites and Nephites. The emphasis on converting specific groups of American Indians is absent in comparison.

This silencing of Native Americans in Utah is part of a more general movement within the Church of Jesus Christ of Latter-day Saints toward the American mainstream. The historian Paul Reeve has argued that the social transformations that occurred within the church in the early twentieth century caused American views of the church's racial identity to shift. In the nineteenth century, he argues, Latter-day Saints were seen as racially suspect—as almost nonwhite. As the twentieth century progressed, however, Latter-day Saints were increasingly accepted into mainstream society. Members of the church embraced the eugenics movement, arguing that polygamy strengthened the bodies of children and created a newer, more vital race. By the 1960s, the Saints, with their carefully kept hair and beardless faces, were seen as "too white."[28] Although Latter-day Saint whiteness did not preclude missionary work among American Indians and other indigenous peoples, it did mean that the experiences of nonwhite Latter-day Saints became less central to the stories that Saints told about themselves to wider American society.

As this process occurred, the identification of Polynesians as naturally religious became a way to celebrate an indigenous Latter-day Saint identity while avoiding discussions of the Mormons' role in American colonialism. According to the anthropologist Jane Desmond, the Hawaiian Islands have often served this role for white Americans, who can imagine a tropical paradise where racial mixing occurs with few of the tensions that have plagued the mainland United States.[29] This vision of Hawai'i, of course, ignores the sexual violence that white men had frequently enacted upon Polynesian women. Native Hawaiian surfers in early twentieth-century Waikiki frequently challenged American soldiers who became sexually aggressive with Native Hawaiian women.[30] This sexual violence, however, is forgotten in favor of a whitewashed version of Hawaiian history where Native Hawaiians welcome white Americans to the islands.

The ambivalence of white Saints toward Native Americans reflects a shift in how Latter-day Saints remember their history. Although missionary work is an important part of contemporary Latter-day Saint culture, it is relatively absent from studies of the nineteenth-century restoration. Instead, the history of the restoration is told as a relatively straightforward narrative in which violence drives Latter-day Saints from New York to Missouri, Illinois, and finally to Utah. Although Latter-day Saint women are present in this narrative, they are relatively absent from the faith's missionary work and the colonization of Utah. The attempts to recast this narrative have not been integrated into the full history of the Church of Jesus Christ of Latter-day Saints. This book has been an attempt to reframe the history of the restoration by exploring the effects that Latter-day Saint missionary work had on the settlement of Utah. Doing so allows historians to understand how the church has interacted with American Indians and Pacific Islanders more fully. Placing these ideas together forces us to examine the restoration's emphasis on the family in light of the frequent absences of male Latter-day Saints and how the Saints incorporated Native Americans into their families. These are unexpected pieces of Mormon history, but they remind us that Mormonism has always been engaged in missionary work and that their experiences abroad affected their lives within Utah.

This book was partially an attempt to highlight those stories. It is important to remember, however, that these stories are not new to Native

Saints. Johnny Garr's descendants, for example, have continued to tell his story. John T. Garr's descendants posted information about Elizabeth and Johnny on websites well before I learned about their story in court records. Their description of Susan Wigegee as a Shoshone woman who danced the Charleston in the twentieth century provides an insight into how the Northwestern Shoshones remember themselves than is available in traditional historical records.[31] Likewise, the communities of Iosepa and Lāʻie have worked to preserve their history and ensure that it is part of the larger historical narrative about the church. Recently, white historians have begun to pay more attention to these stories and incorporate them into their own narratives. That should not blind us to the fact that these stories have been present all along.

This book began as an attempt to understand how missionary work affected the development of Latter-day Saint polygamy and the experiences of Native Saints. Its dual focus on Latter-day Saint polygamy and missionary work has highlighted the tensions among the Saints over the faith's emphasis on the family and the requirement that men temporarily leave their families to spread the gospel. It also asked how Latter-day Saints' interactions with indigenous people were different from those of other Christian missionaries. In addition, it has attempted to understand how Native Saints understood their faith and its relationship to their identity as indigenous people. In asking these questions, this book has sought to provide a history that goes beyond the pioneer narratives that have so often shaped how the story of the Latter-day Saints is told. This is ultimately a history that reminds us that the story of the restoration is as much about people like Mae Timbimboo Parry, Hannah Kaaepa, and Johnny Garr as it is about Wilford Woodruff or Emma Smith.

NOTES

INTRODUCTION

1. Brown and Mackay, "Fall and Winter Movements," 873–85.
2. Rose, "Native History"
3. Mercado, "Reexamining the Bear River Massacre."
4. Crawford, "The People of Bear Hunter Speak," 48.
5. Mims, "Bear River Massacre Stirs Tears."
6. Quoted in Fleisher, *The Bear River Massacre,* 64.
7. Thanks to W. Paul Reeve for pointing out Connor's promotion. See also Fleisher, *The Bear River Massacre,* 42.
8. Rose, "Native History."
9. Cited in Madsen, *The Northern Shoshoni,* 90. "Beeves" was used in this period as a plural form of "beef." Information about size of annuity also comes from Madsen.
10. Parry, "Mae Timbimboo Parry."
11. Quoted in Parry, "Mae Timbimboo Parry."
12. Fleisher, *The Bear River Massacre,* 321.
13. Parry, "Mae Timbimboo Parry."
14. Parry, *The Bear River Massacre,* 4.
15. Loether, "Shoshones," 182.
16. Hill, "An Indian Vision," 11. Also quoted in Christensen, *Sagwitch,* 84; and Smoak, *Ghost Dances and Identity,* 126.
17. Cannon, *My First Mission,* 65.

18. The Permanent Forum of the United Nations has released a statement on the need to decolonize the Pacific. See UN Economic and Social Council, Study on the Decolonization of the Pacific Region (advanced unedited version), E/C.19/2013/12, May 21–30, 2013, https://www.un.org/esa/socdev/unpfii/documents/2013/E_C19_2013_12.pdf.

19. Park and Jensen, "Debating Succession, March 1846," 181–205.

20. Walker, "Seeking the 'Remnant,'" 1–33.

21. Formal sealings did not begin in the Nauvoo temple until 1845. Gordon Irving has argued, however, that the idea that the human family would be knit together through ritual came much earlier. See Irving, "The Law of Adoption," 291–314.

22. Morgan, "Some Could Suckle Over Their Shoulder," 167–92.

23. Walker, *Pulling the Devil's Kingdom Down*, 237.

24. Quoted in Walker, *Pulling the Devil's Kingdom Down*, 237.

25. Koven, *Slumming*, 25–87.

26. Lyons, *Sex Among the Rabble*, 3–4.

27. [Lieber], "The Mormons," 234. See also Reeve, *Religion of a Different Color*, 229, 239.

28. [Lieber], "The Mormons," 234.

29. Reynolds v. United States, 98 U.S. 145 (1878), 98; Reeve, *Religion of a Different Color*, 240.

30. Kaplan, *The Anarchy of Empire*, 2.

31. Kaplan, *The Anarchy of Empire*, 6.

32. Kaplan, *The Anarchy of Empire*, 6.

33. Gordon, *The Mormon Question*.

34. Reeve, *Religion of a Different Color*.

35. Shipps, *Sojourner in the Promised Land*, 21.

36. Jeter, "Cephalopods 4 of 4."

37. "History, 1838–1856, volume A1 [23 December 1805–30 August 1834]," 359, JSPP; see also Reeve, *Religion of a Different Color*, 65.

38. See, for example, "The Mountain Meadows Massacre—Pursuit of the Murderers—Heart-Bending Details," *Louisville Daily Courier,* July 8, 1859, 1; "Details of the Mountain Meadows Massacre in Utah—Rescue of Children—Escape of the Murderers," *Holmes County Republication* (Millersburg OH), July 14, 1859, 2; "Return of the Survivors of the Mountain Meadows Massacre: Meeting of Citizens of Carroll County: Resolutions, &c. &c.," *Arkansian* (Fayetteville AR), October 7, 1859, 2.

39. "Washington," *St. Albans (vt) Daily Messenger,* August 13, 1875, 3.

40. Orson Pratt, "Evidence of the Bible and Book of Mormon Compared," JD, 22.

41. Orson Pratt, "Evidence of the Bible and the Book of Mormon Compared," JD, 22.

42. Lorene Washines, "Lee Neaman Oral History," cited in Keitzer, *The Washakie Letters of Willie Ottogary*, 4.

43. McConkie, *A New Witness for the Articles of Faith*, 519, quoted in Grua, "Elder George P. Lee and the New Jerusalem."

44. Madsen, *Chief Pocatello*, 97.

45. Madsen, *Chief Pocatello*, 101–2.

46. "Mormon Recruiting in India; Reports forwarded by Governor of India," East India Office, IOR/L/PJ/6/160, File 1487, British Library, London, UK.

47. Joseph Cotton Wood, "Peninah S. Cotton Wood," 2, *Family Histories, circa 2000*, CHL. See also Taylor, "Elder Nigeajasha and Other Mormon Indians Moving Westward," 111–24.

48. Taylor, "Elder Nigeajasha and Other Mormon Indians," 114–15.

49. "Council of Fifty, Minutes, March 1844–January 1846; vol. 2: 1 March–6 May 1845," [377], JSPP.

50. "Council of Fifty, Minutes, March 1844–January 1846; vol. 1: 10 March 1844–1 March 1845," [377], JSPP.

51. "Interview #2: Patty Timbimboo-Madsen, Northwestern Band of the Shoshone Nation, Cultural Resource Director," *We Shall Remain*, KUED.

1. THE RACE AND SEX OF GOD

1. Phebe Carter Woodruff to Wilford Woodruff, May 9, 1840, folder 33, Wilford Woodruff Collection, CHL.

2. "John Whitmer, History, 1831–circa 1847," 26, JSPP; Givens and Grow, *Parley P. Pratt*, 51.

3. Josiah Jones, "Historian of the Mormonites," *Evangelist* (Carthage OH), June 1, 1841, 135.

4. Pratt, *Autobiography of Parley Parker Pratt*, 65.

5. 2 Nephi 30: 6.

6. Ulrich, *A House Full of Females*, xi–xxxvi. Thanks to Samuel Brown for the imagery of seeds.

7. See Reeve, *Religion of a Different Color*.

8. Isaac, *The Transformation of Virginia, 1740–1790*, 154, 165–66, 171–72.

9. Johnson and Wilentz, *The Kingdom of Matthias*, 13–48.

10. Kern, *An Ordered Love*; Foster, *Religion and Sexuality*; and Foster, *Women, Family, and Utopia*.

11. Hatch, *The Democratization of American Christianity*; Butler, *Awash in a Sea of Faith*; Taves, *Fits, Trances, and Visions*; Isaac, *The Transformation of Virginia, 1740–1790*; and Wigger, *Taking Heaven by Storm*.

12. Joseph Smith, "Extracts from the History of Joseph Smith, the Prophet," Church of Jesus Christ of Latter-day Saints, accessed November 2, 2014, https://www.lds.org/scriptures/pgp/js-h/1.18?lang=eng.

13. D&C 129: 4–8.

14. Webb, *Jesus Christ, Eternal God*, 243–71.

15. Mormons frequently argued against the idea that God was "without body, passions, or parts." This idea was set forth explicitly in the 1647 Westminster Confession. Brigham Young explicitly referenced this phrasing in his July 24, 1853, sermon titled "Effects and Privileges of the Gospel." See Brigham Young, "Effects and Privileges of the Gospel," *jd*.

16. Pratt, *Key to the Science of Theology*, 161.

17. Pratt, *Key to the Science of Theology*, 59.

18. Park, "Salvation through a Tabernacle." See also Park and Watkins, "The Riches of Mormon Materialism," 159–72. Early conversations with Samuel Brown influenced my thought here.

19. Givens, *The Viper on the Hearth*, 82.

20. "Vision, 16 February 1832 [D&C 76]," 6, JSPP; See also D&C 76: 58, quoted in Givens, *Wrestling the Angel*, 103.

21. "The King Follett Sermon," *Ensign* (April 1971), accessed July 3, 2015, https://www.lds.org/ensign/1971/04/the-king-follett-sermon?lang=eng.

22. Park, "Salvation through a Tabernacle," 2.

23. Quoted in Juster, "Mystical Pregnancy and Holy Bleeding," 259.

24. Warner, *A remarkable dream, or vision*, 6, 8.

25. Warner, *A remarkable dream, or vision*, 8.

26. "Miscellaneous," *York (pa) Gazette*, September 3, 1833, 1. Reeve, *Religion of a Different Color*, 112.

27. Reeve, *Religion of a Different Color*, 112

28. Reeve, *Religion of a Different Color*, 112.

29. Reeve, *Religion of a Different Color*.

30. "Try the Spirits," *Times and Seasons* 3, no. 11 (April 1, 1842): 743.

31. "Try the Spirits," 744.

32. "Try the Spirits," 744.

33. See Pratt, *Key to the Science of Theology*, 157. Other Latter-day Saints employed similar language in their writings. The title of Parley P. Pratt's *The Key to the Science of Theology* (1855) revealed his assumptions about the relationship

between theology and natural world. For Pratt, revealed knowledge was just as scientific as "astronomy" or "physical geography." He imagined a future world in which people would come to know "millions of worlds . . . their physical features and boundaries, their resources, mineral and vegetable; their rivers, lakes, seas, continents and islands." In astronomy, "vast systems of suns and their attendant worlds, on which the eyes of Adam's race, in their rudimental sphere have never gazed, [would] then be contemplated, circumscribed, weighted in their balance of human thought, their circumference and diameter weighed." Although humans would never know the vast worlds that awaited their exploration until after death, Pratt believed that the beginnings of this knowledge would be received in the here and now.

34. Hegel, *Hegel's Philosophy of Right*, 263–64, cited in Koziak, *Retrieving Political Emotion*, 5.

35. 1 Corinthians 11: 1–16; Pratt, *Key to the Science of Theology*, 166.

36. W. W. Phelps, "Come to Me," *Times and Seasons* 6 (January 15, 1845): 783. There is some evidence that Joseph Smith had preached this idea as early as July 1839. Zina D. H. Young, for example, claimed that Smith had referred to the idea of a mother in heaven when she asked if she would ever see her earthly mother again. Smith had assured her that she would and that she would also meet her Heavenly Mother at the same time. See Gates, *History of the Young Ladies' Mutual Improvement Association*, 15–16. For a full explanation of the origins of this idea, see "Eliza R. Snow, 'My Father in Heaven,' October 1945," note 5, *The First Fifty Years of Relief Society*, https://www.churchhistorianspress.org/the-first-fifty-years-of-relief-society/part-1/1-14?lang=eng.

37. Eliza R. Snow, "My Father in Heaven," *Times and Seasons* 6, no. 17 (November 15, 1845): 1039.

38. Heitzenrater, *Wesley and the People Called Methodists*.

39. Job 38: 4–8.

40. Gordon, *The Mormon Question*, 178.

41. Givens, *The Viper on the Hearth*, 82.

42. Givens, *The Viper on the Hearth*, 93.

43. Shipps, *Mormonism*.

44. Cave, "Canaanites in a Promised Land," 277–97; Cogley, "John Eliot and the Origins of the American Indians," 210–25; Hoberman, *New Israel/New England*.

45. Givens, *The Viper on the Hearth*, 99.

46. Bennett, *The History of the Saints*, 151.

47. "The Mormon War," *The Columbian Democracy* 11, no. 31 (1838): 2.

48. Howe, *Mormonism Unvailed*, ix.

49. "In the Name of the Prophet Smith," *Household Words* 3 (1851): 385.

50. For a discussion of this announcement, see Whittaker, "The Bone in the Throat: Orson Pratt," 293–314.

51. Orson Pratt, August 29, 1852, JD, 60.

52. Twain, *Roughing It*, 101.

53. Quoted in Cracroft, "Distorting Polygamy for Fun and Profit," 282–83.

54. Cracroft, "Distorting Polygamy for Fun and Profit," 282.

55. Thomas Fitch, "Fitch on the Cullom Bill, A Speech by Hon. Thomas Fitch, of Nevada, Delivered in the U.S. House of Representatives, February 23, 1870," *Latter-Day Saints Millennial Star* 32, no. 14 (April 5, 1870): 210.

56. Jarman, *U.S.A., Uncle Sam's Abscess, or Hell upon Earth*, 169.

57. Bennett, *The History of the Saints*, 151.

58. Givens, *Viper on the Hearth*, 148.

59. Corinna Aldrich Hopksin, "Under the Pear Tree," *Atlantic Monthly* 11, no. 65 (March 1863): 356.

60. Nicol, *Introductory Book of the Sciences*, 142.

61. Iversen, *The Antipolygamy Controversy in U.S. Women's Movements, 1880–1925*, 102.

62. Doyle, *A Study in Scarlet*.

63. French, "The Politics of Sexual Restraint," 60.

64. Dixon, *White Conquest*, 193.

65. Dixon, *White Conquest*, 195.

66. Kane, *A Gentile Account of Life in Utah's Dixie*, 5.

67. Kane, *A Gentile Account*, 22.

68. Quoted in Givens, *Viper on the Hearth*, 59.

69. Quoted in Givens, *Viper on the Hearth*, 59.

70. Johnson, "Becoming a People of the Books," 42.

71. 1 Lehi 8: 37–38.

72. Mosiah 10: 12.

73. Mosiah 10: 17.

74. Hendrix-Komoto and Stuart, "Race and Gender in Mormonism, 1830–1978."

75. Deloria, *Speaking of Indians*, 25.

76. Jacob 2: 23, 2: 28.

77. W. W. Phelps, "The Indians," *Latter-Day Saints Messenger and Advocate* 2, no. 4 (January 1836): 245–48.

78. Pratt, *A Voice of Warning*, 174, quoted in Thayne, "Indian Removal, Zion, and the Westward Orientation of Early Mormonism."

79. For information on Mormons and Indian Removal, see Underwood, *The Millenarian World of Early Mormonism*, 82–83; Givens and Grow, *Parley P. Pratt*, 37, 44, 111.

80. Pratt, *Autobiography*, 59.

81. W. W. Phelps to Brigham Young, August 12, 1861, Brigham Young Papers, CHL; also cited in Compton, "Fanny Alger Smith Custer," 80.

82. "Mormonism—Nos. 8–9," *Ohio Star* 11, no. 49 (December 8, 1831), reprinted in Howe, *Mormonism Unvailed*, 200.

83. Pratt, *The Journals of Addison Pratt*, 439, 560.

84. McGrath, *Illicit Love*, 2.

85. Maude, "Beachcombers and Castaways," 254–93; and Campbell, "Gone Native."

86. Mosiah 20: 1–5.

87. Private communication with David Grua, historian with the Joseph Smith Papers Project, November 12, 2014. See also, Alley Jr., "Prelude to Dispossession," 104–23.

88. "Celebrations," *Deseret Evening News*, August 13, 1856, 8.

89. Maffly-Kipp, "Assembling Bodies and Souls," 51–76.

90. Brigham Young, "Proper Treatment of the Indians, Etc.," JD, 327.

91. Brigham Young, quoted in Turner, *Brigham Young: Pioneer*, 212, 213.

92. Brigham Young, "The United States Administration and Utah Army," JD.

93. Thanks to Jana Riess for pointing out the similarities between the language that Brigham Young and Lilburn Boggs used. She also pointed me to the passage from Young's speech in the bowery.

94. 3 Nephi 1: 27; Mormon 1: 18.

95. Journal History of the Church of Jesus Christ of Latter-day Saints (chronological book of typed entries and newspaper clippings, 1830–present), May 16, 1851, 1; Reeve, *Religion of a Different Color*, 78; Mueller, *Race and the Making of the Mormon People*, 174.

96. Aikau, *A Chosen People, A Chosen Land*.

97. The term Great Basin Kingdom comes from Arrington, *Great Basin Kingdom*.

2. THE BONDS BETWEEN SISTERS

1. Weber, "Skulls and Crossed Bones?," 3.

2. Newell and Avery, *Mormon Enigma*, 42.

3. D&C 42: 61; 2 Nephi 38: 30.

4. Spencer, "Was This Really Missouri Civilization?," 105.

5. D&C 133: 8.

6. Louisa Barnes Pratt frequently referred to herself as a widow in her writings. See Pratt, *The History of Louisa Barnes Pratt.*

7. Pratt, *The History of Louisa Barnes Pratt*, 65–66.

8. Radke [now Radke-Moss], "We Also Marched," 153.

9. See for example, Ryan, *Cradle of the Middle Class*; Lystra, *Searching the Heart*; Cott, *Public Vows*; Coontz, *Marriage, A History*; Lawrence, *One Family Under God.*

10. Cited in Lystra, *Searching the Heart*, 53.

11. Cited in Lystra, *Searching the Heart*, 25.

12. Cited in Lystra, *Searching the Heart*, 53.

13. Pratt, *Key to the Science of Theology*, 166.

14. Sarah Griffith Richards to Levi Richards, April 28, 1849, folder 7, box 1, Richards Family Collection, Harold B. Lee Library, Brigham Young University, Provo UT.

15. D&C 132: 7.

16. The importance of sealing rituals to early Latter-day Saints meant that some women whose husbands were not members of the faith felt free to be sealed in the temple without first seeking a divorce or waiting for their spouses to die. Joseph Smith and other Latter-day Saint leaders occasionally promised to female Latter-day Saints whose husbands were still living but unwilling to convert to the church. One such woman was Sarah Granger Kimball. Joseph Smith proposed sealing to her in 1842, but she refused to participate in the ritual. See Jenson, "Plural Marriage," *Historical Record* 6 (July 1887): 232.

17. Gordon Irving, "The Law of Adoption."

18. Stapley, "Adoptive Sealing Ritual in Mormonism," 64–66.

19. Underwood, *The Millenarian World of Early Mormonism*, 11–23.

20. Belnap, "Those Who Receive You Not," 81–127.

21. Phebe Peck to Anna Pratt, August 10, 1832, quoted in Johnson, "Give Up All and Follow Your Lord," 93.

22. Ulrich, "The Early Diaries of Wilford Woodruff, 1835–1839," 294.

23. Ulrich, "The Early Diaries of Wilford Woodruff, 1835–1839," 294.

24. Ulrich, *A House Full of Females*, 410.

25. Ezra, August 1838, Phoebe [Phebe] Whittemore Carter Woodruff, Autograph Book, 1838–1844, n.p., CHL.

26. Ezra, August 1838.

27. Allgor, *Parlor Politics*; Dunbar, "Writing for True Womanhood," 299–318.

28. Dunbar, "Writing for True Womanhood," 299–318.

29. This type of relationship was not unknown in the nineteenth century either in the United States or in Great Britain. See Hemphill, *Siblings: Brothers and Sisters in American History*; Davidoff, *Thicker than Water*.

30. Esplin, "Joseph Smith and the Kirtland Crisis," 261–90.

31. Mary Fielding Smith to Mercy Fielding Thompson, ca. August–September 1837, Mary Fielding Smith Collection, CHL.

32. Mary Fielding Smith to Mercy Fielding Thompson.

33. Vicinus, *Independent Women*, 1–4.

34. Yeo, "Virgin Mothers," 41.

35. Van Wagoner, "Sarah M. Pratt," 70.

36. Van Wagoner, "Sarah M. Pratt," 70.

37. Turner, *Brigham Young*, 66.

38. Radke-Moss, "I hid [the Prophet] in a corn patch" 25–40.

39. Radke-Moss, "I hid [the Prophet] in a corn patch" 25–40.

40. Johnstun, "A Victim of the 1838 Mormon-Missouri War: The Tragedy of Hannah Kinney Johnstun."

41. Alice Merrill Horne autobiography quoted in Radke-Moss, "Silent Memories of Missouri," 69–70.

42. Radke-Moss, "Silent Memories of Missouri," 69–70.

43. Radke-Moss, "Silent Memories of Missouri," 69–70.

44. Olive B. Hale to Martha Hale, 1841, cited in Johnson, "Give All Up and Follow Your Lord," 81.

45. Melissa Dodge to William T. Morgan, June 1839, cited in Johnson, "Give All Up and Follow Your Lord," 81.

46. Lucy Mack Smith, History 1844–1845, [11], [miscellany], JSSP. Newell and Avery, *Mormon Enigma*, 61.

47. Newell and Avery, *Mormon Enigma*, 61.

48. Quoted in Corbett, *Mary Fielding Smith, Daughter of Britain*, 43.

49. Newell and Avery, *Mormon Enigma*, 61.

50. Anderson, "Mary Fielding Smith," 91–100.

51. LeSueur, *The 1838 Mormon War in Missouri*; Baugh, *A Call to Arms*; and Gentry and Compton, *Fire and Saved*.

52. Corbett, *Mary Fielding Smith*, 80.

53. Hyrum Smith to Mary Fielding Smith, March 20, 1839, Mary Fielding Smith Collection, folder 1, CHL.

54. Hyrum Smith to Mary Fielding Smith, April 11, 1839, Mary Fielding Smith Collection, folder 1, CHL.

55. Mary Fielding Smith to Hyrum Smith, September 14, 1842, Mary Fielding Smith Collection, folder 1, CHL.

56. Mercy F. Thompson Autobiographical Sketch, 1880, MS 4580, CHL.

57. Don Carlos and William Smith to Hyrum and Joseph Smith, March 6, 1839, JSPP.

58. I read the pronouns as referring to Mercy but have encountered plenty of other people who think the passage refers to Mary.

59. Don Carlos Smith to Hyrum Smith, April 11, 1839, JSPP.

60. Smith-Rosenberg, "The Female World of Love and Ritual," 1–29.

61. Smith-Rosenberg, "The Female World of Love and Ritual," 4.

62. Smith-Rosenberg, "The Female World of Love and Ritual," 7.

63. "Letterbook 2," 8, JSPP.

64. Mary Fielding to Hyrum Smith, April 11, 1839, Mary Fielding Smith Collection, CHL.

65. Marcus, *Between Women*, 15.

66. "Nauvoo Relief Society Minute Book," 5; for the text of the hymn, see "Collection of Sacred Hymns, 1835," 120, JSPP.

67. "Nauvoo Relief Society Minute Book," 7, JSPP.

68. Derr, Cannon, and Beecher, *Women of Covenant*, 34–35.

69. Derr, Cannon, and Beecher, *Women of Covenant*, 35.

70. "Reminiscence of Elizabeth Terry Kirby Heward," in *In Their Own Words*, ed., Madsen.

71. "Reminiscence of Margaret Gay Judd Clawson," in *In Their Own Words*, ed. Madsen.

72. "Nauvoo Relief Society Minute Book," [122], JSPP.

73. Derr, Cannon, and Beecher, *Women of Covenant*, 67–68.

74. Allgor, *Parlor Politics*.

75. Taylor, *Nightfall at Nauvoo*, 180, quoted in Hales, "Emma Smith, Eliza R. Snow, and the Reported Incident on the Stairs," 63–75.

76. See, for example, Hales, "Emma Smith, Eliza R. Snow, and the Reported Incident on the Stairs," 63–75.

77. Mary Ann Barzee and John Boice, "Record," 174, LDS Church History Library, Salt Lake City UT, as compiled by Hales, in *Joseph Smith's Polygamy Documents*, https://josephsmithspolygamy.org.

78. Boice, "Record," 178–79.

79. Smith, *Revelation, Resistance, and Mormon Polygamy*, 58–101.

80. Bradley and Woodard, *Four Zinas*, 115.

81. *Relief Society Minute Book*, March 17, 1842, JSPP.

82. Compton, "Fanny Alger Smith Custer: Mormonism's First Plural Wife?," 174–207.

83. Newell and Avery, *Mormon Enigma*, 66; Compton, "Fanny Alger Smith Custer," 182.

84. Bushman, *Rough Stone Rolling*, 324.

85. Compton, "Fanny Alger Smith Custer," 203.

86. Quoted in Newell and Avery, *Mormon Enigma*, 65.

87. Newell and Avery, *Mormon Enigma*, 153.

88. The Joseph Smith Papers lists the cause of Robert Thompson's death as a "severe lung infection." "Thompson, Robert Blashel," *The Joseph Smith Papers*, http://www.josephsmithpapers.org/person/robert-blashel-thompson.

89. Mercy Rachel Fielding Thompson, "Reminiscence," in Madsen, *In Their Own Words*,194–95.

90. Woodward, "Mercy Thompson and the Revelation on Marriage."

91. Bergera, "Identify the Earliest Mormon Polygamists, 1841–1844," 28; Catherine Philips Affidavit, November 7, 1902, CHL.

92. Corbett, *Daughter of Britain*, 153.

93. Catherine Phillips Affidavit, November 7, 1902, CHL.

94. Catherine Phillips Affidavit, November 7, 1902, CHL.

95. Bushman, *Joseph Smith*, 539; Lyndon Cook, "William Law, Nauvoo Dissenter," 47–72.

96. Dinger, *The Nauvoo City Council and High Council Minutes*, 446.

97. "Nauvoo vs. Albert Clements and Nathan Tener, December 17, 1842" and "Nauvoo vs. Albert Clements, Henry Tener, and Albert Tener, December 20 and 22, 1842," Nauvoo Records: Judicial Proceedings: Mayor's Court, box 4, CHL.

98. Dinger, *The Nauvoo and High Council Minutes*, 446.

99. Dinger, *The Nauvoo and High Council Minutes*, 440.

100. Thompson, *Customs in Common*, 404–66.

101. Dinger, *The Nauvoo and High Council Minutes*, 440.

102. Dinger, *The Nauvoo and High Council Minutes*, 465.

103. Dinger, *The Nauvoo and High Council Minutes*, 389.

104. Van Wagoner, *Mormon Polygamy*, 30, 92–95.

105. Compton, *In Sacred Loneliness*, 235.

106. Ulrich, *A House Full of Females*, 79–80.

107. "A Rumor—Holy Joe Demanded," *Sangamo Journal* (Springfield IL), July 29, 1842, 2.

108. Daynes, *More Wives Than One*, 64.

109. Quoted in Daynes, *More Wives Than One*, 64.

110. Brigham Young, "Building Up the Kingdom of God, Etc.," JD.

111. *New York World*, November 17, 1869, quoted in Iversen, *The Antipolygamy Controversy in U.S. Women's Movements, 1800–1925*, 66.

112. Bradley and Woodward, *Four Zinas*, 113.

113. Henry B. Jacobs to Zina D. Jacobs, August 19, 1846, CHL.

114. Sarah Griffith Richards to Levi Richards, April 28, 1849, folder 7, box 1, Richards Family Collection, Harold B. Lee Library, BYU.

115. Alexander Smith, "Second Coming of Christ," *Zion's Ensign* 14, no. 53 (December 31, 1903): 7.

116. The term "emotional regime" comes from William Reddy. For a discission of the term, see Plamper, "The History of Emotions," 237–65.

3. REDEEMING THE LAMANITES

1. "Journal, December 1842–June 1844; Book 2, 10 March 1943–14 July 1843," [221], JSPP.

2. "Letter to Emma Smith, 4 June 1834," 58, JSPP.

3. There are several accounts of Smith finding the skeleton that offer conflicting pieces of information. For an exploration of the primary sources, see Godfrey, "The Zelph Story," 32–56. Fair Mormon offers a chart of the various primary sources at https://www.fairmormon.org/answers/Question:_What_is_the_story_of_Zelph%3f.

4. Bushman, *Rough Stone Rolling*, 286–93.

5. Givens, *By the Hand of Mormon*, 94–99.

6. "Letter from Oliver Cowdery, 12 November 1830," 207, JSPP.

7. Pratt, *Autobiography of Parley Parker Pratt*, 49, 61.

8. Taylor, "Elder Nigeajasha and Other Mormon Indians," 111–24.

9. "A Mission to the Lamanites," *Revelations in Context* (2016), https://www.lds.org/manual/revelations-in-context/a-mission-to-the-lamanites?lang=eng.

10. "Letter from Oliver Cowdery, 12 November 1830," 207, JSPP.

11. Pratt, *The Autobiography of Parley Parker Pratt*, 49.

12. Bowes, *Land Too Good for Indians*, 125–33. For a short history of the Seneca, see the Wikipedia entry: https://en.wikipedia.org/wiki/Seneca_people.

13. The Delawares use the term "refugee" on their official tribal website in a republished excerpt from Obermeyer, *Delaware Tribe in a Cherokee Nation*, 37–48, 52–58. "Removal History of the Delaware Tribe," *Delaware Tribe of Indians*, http://delawaretribe.org/services-and-programs/historic-preservation/removal-history-of-the-delaware-tribe/. I use the language here and have reconstructed this history partially from their tribal website.

14. Weslager, *The Delaware Indians*, 369–71.

15. See, for example, Rubin, *Tears of Repentance*.

16. Romig, "The Lamanite Mission," 26–27.

17. Thank you to Jana Riess for this example. For a popular article describing Smith's life, see Ryan, "A Huntington's Mohegan Mission."

18. "The Indians," *Latter-day Saint Messenger and Advocate* 2, no. 4 (January 1836): 245.

19. Parkin, "Lamanite Mission of 1830–1831," 803.

20. Pratt, *The Autobiography of Parley Parker Pratt*, 60.

21. Pratt, *The Autobiography of Parley Parker Pratt*, 60.

22. Romig, "The Lamanite Mission," 29.

23. Custer, "Kannekuk or Keeanakuk," 48–56.

24. Untitled article, *Miners' and Farmers' Journal* (Charlotte NC), April 7, 1837, 2.

25. I have been unable to locate a response currently. It is, of course, possible that it exists in an archive somewhere.

26. Romig, "The Lamanite Mission," 29–30.Romig also notes no response in "The Lamanite Mission."

27. "History, 1838–1856, vol. A-10, 123, JSPP.

28. "Peninah S. Cotton Wood," *Family Histories, circa 2000*, LDS Church History Library, Salt Lake City, Utah; see also, Taylor, "Elder Nigeajasha and Other Mormon Indians," 111–24.

29. Taylor, "Elder Nigeajasha and Other Mormon Indians," 114–15.

30. "Council of Fifty, Minutes, March 1844–January 1846; vol. 2: 1 March–6 May 1845," [28], JSPP.

31. William Clayton, *Journals, 1842–1845*, cited in "Council of Fifty, Minutes, March 1844-January 1846; vol. 1: 10 March 1844–01 March 1845," [372], JSPP.

32. "Appendix 2: Council of Fifty, Minutes, 27 February 184," [1], JSPP.

33. Doxey, "The Church in Britain and the 1851 Religious Census," 107–38.

34. See Mauss, *All Abraham's Children*.

35. Manktelow, "Missionary Families and the Formation of the Missionary Enterprise," 134–76; Thomas, *Islanders*, 37–40.

36. Directors of the London Missionary Society, "Counsels and Instructions for the Regulation of the Mission," quoted in Lansdown, *Strangers in the South Seas*, 128.

37. Elbourne, *Blood Ground*, 344.

38. Elbourne, *Blood Ground*, 344.

39. See Ryan, *Women in Public*; Fraser, "Rethinking the Public Sphere," 56–80; Vickery, "Golden Age to Separate Spheres?," 383–414; Hall and Davidoff, *Family Fortunes*; Kelley, *Learning to Stand and Speak*.

40. Seton, *Western Daughters in Eastern Lands*, 12.

41. Ballantyne, *Entanglements of Empire*, 142.

42. Elbourne, *Blood Ground*, 217–23, 231, 314.

43. See Manktelow, "Missionary Families and the Formation of the Missionary Enterprise"; Maffly-Kipp, *Religion and Society in Frontier California*, 148–80.

44. Ballantyne, *Entanglements of Empire*, 142.

45. Gunson, *Messengers of Grace*, 159–60; J. M. Orsmond to the directors of the LMS, January 1, 1829, jacket A, folder 1, box 7, Incoming Correspondence, South Seas, Council for World Missions/London Missionary Society (hereafter CWM/LMS), SOAS. It is important to take these accusations with a grain of salt. Samuel Crook and Charles Wilson were accused of escaping the South Seas Academy grounds to receive a native circumcision, and a few others were expelled for sexual misconduct. Although these actions scandalized people at the time, they can also be interpreted as the children of missionaries partially rejecting the morality of their parents. Premarital sex, tattooing, and circumcision did not have the same meaning within Tahitian society as they did within the British middle class.

46. David Darling to the Directors of the London Missionary Society, September 29, 1818, quoted in Tagupa, "Missionary Lamentations," 168.

47. Quoted in Gunson, "The Deviations of a Missionary Family," 36.

48. Maffly-Kipp, "Assembling Bodies and Souls: Missionary Practices on the Pacific Frontier," 72–73.

49. Pratt, *The Journals of Addison Pratt*, 276–77.

50. The race of the individuals involved in these marriages is not noted, but it is likely that the men were either white or partially white. "Mehaho– Marriages," Records of the Church . . . at Toobooai [*sic*], CHL.

51. Colin Newbury adopted the term "Tahiti Nui" in his book of the same name to describe this region. I use it in the same sense in this book, but Tahiti Nui can also refer to a specific island.

52. Gunson, *Messengers of Grace*, 32.

53. Gunson, "An Account of the Mamaia or Visionary Heresy of Tahiti, 1826–1841," 213–15.

54. For a history of Tahiti, see Newbury, *Tahiti Nui*.

55. These rumors are recorded in the letters that members of the London Missionary Society sent to their directors in London during the war. See, for

example, Letter, Alexander and William Howe to the Directors of the LMS, February 8, 1843, jacket C, folder 4, box 23, Incoming Correspondence, South Seas, CWM/LMS, SOAS.

56. Benjamin F. Grouard Journal, June 1843–September 1846, 37, CHL.

57. Britsch, "The Establishment of the Church in French Polynesia, 1844–1895," 28.

58. Maffly-Kipp, "Looking West: Mormonism and the Pacific World," 49.

59. Edward Leo Lyman mentions some of these marriages. See Lyman, *San Bernardino*, 154.

60. Grouard, Journal, May 14 and May 24, 1844, 34–37, cited in Woods, "Latter-day Saint Missionaries Encounter the London Missionary Society in South Pacific, 1844–1852," 106.

61. See, for example, Henry Petty-Fitzmaurice to A. Tidman, July 1843, Letters Additional Collection, Cadbury Research Library, University of Birmingham, Birmingham, UK.

62. John Barff to the Directors of the LMS, June 27, 1845, jacket B, folder 3, box 18A, Incoming Correspondence, South Seas, CWM/LMS, SOAS.

63. John Orsmond to William Ellis, copy sent to the LMS, July 30, 1845, jacket D, folder 2, box 18A, Incoming Correspondence, South Seas, CWM/LMS, SOAS.

64. Pratt, *The Journals of Addison Pratt*, 263.

65. Ellsworth, ed., *Dear Ellen: Two Mormon Women and their Letters*, 12.

66. Grouard, Journal, May 14 and May 24, 1844.

67. Binney, "Whatever Happened to Poor Mr. Yate?," 154–68.

68. Binney, *The Legacy of Guilt: A Life of Thomas Kendall.*

69. Addison Pratt to Willard Richards, 20 September 1844, folder 4A, Addison Pratt Family Collection, CHL.

70. Addison Pratt to Willard Richards, 20 September 1844, folder 4A, Addison Pratt Family Collection, CHL.

71. Pratt, *The Journals of Addison Pratt*, 169–70.

72. For the correspondence concerning Simpson's case, see boxes 16–18A, Incoming Correspondence, South Seas, CWM/LMS, SOAS. Manktelow has also written an article about the case. See Emily Manktelow, "Rev. Simpson's Improper Liberties: Moral Scrutiny and Missionary Children in the South Seas Mission," 159–81. For these particular quotes, see C. Wilson, Testimony, March 21, 1843 and Elizabeth Darling, Testimony, June 20, 1843.

73. Letter, LMS Foreign Secretaries to T. Joseph, March 5, 1844, and LMS Foreign Secretaries to A. Simpson, March 5, 1844, box 3 (1843–1846), Western Outgoing Letters, South Seas, CWM/LMS, SOAS.

74. Letter, Mr. Henry to Mr. Buzacott, June 8, 1846, appended to a letter from William Henry to the directors of the LMS, January 15, 1847, jacket A, folder 1, box 20, Incoming Correspondence, South Seas, CWM/LMS, SOAS. See also Manktelow, "Rev. Simpson's Improper Liberties: Moral Scrutiny and Missionary Children in the South Seas Mission," 159–81.

75. Letter, T. Joseph to the Directors of the LMS, June 24, 1843, jacket C, folder 1, box 16, Incoming Correspondence, South Seas, CWM/LMS, SOAS.

76. Pratt, *The History of Louis Barnes Pratt*, 139.

77. Pratt, *The History of Louisa Barnes Pratt*, 138–39.

78. Pratt, *The History of Louisa Barnes Pratt*, 141.

79. Pratt, *The History of Louisa Barnes Pratt*, 142.

80. Pratt, *The History of Louisa Barnes Pratt*, 157.

81. Brown, *Giant of the Lord*, 249.

82. O'Reilly and Teissier, *Tahitiens: Répertoire biographique de la Polynésie Française*, 234.

83. Lyman, *San Bernardino*, 297.

84. Lyman, *San Bernardino*, 312.

85. Lyman, *San Bernardino*, 311.

4. CREATING POLYGAMOUS DOMESTICITIES

1. "Resolutions," *Nauvoo Expositor* (Nauvoo IL), June 7, 1844, 2.

2. Bicknell, *America 1844*, 171.

3. Sally Randall to My Dear Friends, Letter, July 1, 1844, reprinted in Watkins and Harper, "It Seems That All Nature Mourns," 97.

4. Carter, *Organization of the Church of Jesus Christ of Latter-day Saints and Their Belief*, 38. See also Kenney, "Before the Beard," 21.

5. Kenney, "Before the Beard," 21.

6. Newell and Avery, *Mormon Enigma*, 197.

7. Flanders, *Nauvoo*, 330.

8. "Autobiography of Elizabeth B. Pratt," *Woman's Exponent* 19, no. 13 (December 15, 1890): 102.

9. See Quinn, "The Succession Crisis of 1844," 194–96; Noord, *King of Beaver Island*; Foster, *Women, Family, and Utopia*, 170–92; Speek, *"God Has Made Us a Kingdom."*

10. Quinn, "The Mormon Succession Crisis of 1844," 188–93; Van Wagoner, *Sidney Rigdon*.

11. Andrea G. Radke, "We Also Marched," 151. For an example of these family histories, see http://ancestry.smithplanet.com/documents/Albert%20clements%20and%20aidah%20winchell%20clements.pdf. The

Daughters of the Utah Pioneers have also collected several family histories as part of the group's attempt to document the ancestry of people descended from the initial white Mormon settlers of Utah.

12. Pratt, *The Journals of Addison Pratt*, 238.

13. Pratt, *The History of Louisa Barnes Pratt*, 88.

14. Pratt, *The Journals of Addison Pratt*, 359.

15. Pratt, *The History of Louisa Barnes Pratt*, 99.

16. Pratt, *The History of Louisa Barnes Pratt*, 100.

17. Park and Jensen, "Debating Succession, March 1846," 182.

18. Park and Jensen, "Debating Succession, March 1846," 189–91.

19. Park and Jensen, "Debating Succession, March 1846," 190–91.

20. Esplin, "Joseph, Brigham and the Twelve," 304.

21. Esplin, "Joseph, Brigham and the Twelve," 304.

22. Esplin, "Joseph, Brigham and the Twelve," 304.

23. Helen Mar Whitney, "Scenes and Incidents at Winter Quarters," *Woman's Exponent* 14, no. 15 (January 1, 1886): 18.

24. Whitney, "Scenes and Incidents at Winter Quarters," 18.

25. Allen and Leonard, *The Story of the Latter-day Saints*, 229–30.

26. Susa Young Gates, "Life Story of Lucy Bigelow Young," 36, folder 6, box 1, Susa Young Gates Papers, Utah State Historical Society, Salt Lake City.

27. Beecher, "Women at Winter Quarters," 17.

28. Ulrich, *A House Full of Females*, 179.

29. Sessions, *Mormon Midwife*, 82.

30. Sessions, *Mormon Midwife*, 82.

31. "A Venerable Woman: Presendia Kimball," *Woman's Exponent* 12, no. 1 (June 1, 1883): 2.

32. "A Venerable Woman," *Woman's Exponent*, 2; also quoted in Beecher, "Women at Winter Quarters," 17.

33. Beecher, "Women at Winter Quarters," 12.

34. McKenzie, "Mormon Women on the 1846 Iowa Trail," 50; Bennett, *Mormons at the Missouri*, 81.

35. Many people have written about Patty Sessions' experience with polygamy. See Bowman, *The Mormon People*, 132, and Smith, *Revelation and Resistance*, 231–42.

36. Karras, *More than Petticoats*, 3.

37. Sessions, *Mormon Midwife*, 276–77.

38. Sessions, *Mormon Midwife*, 61.

39. Sessions, *Mormon Midwife*, 62.

40. Sessions, *Mormon Midwife*, 58.

41. Sessions, *Mormon Midwife*, 58.

42. Bennett, *Mormons at the Missouri*, 137.

43. Beecher, "Women at Winter Quarters," 16.

44. Bennett, *Mormons at the Missouri*, 133.

45. Journal of Eliza Maria Lyman, July 14, 1846, quoted in Bennett, *Mormons at the Missouri*, 133.

46. Diary of John Pulsipher, 13, quoted in Bennett, *Mormons at the Missouri*, 135.

47. Quoted in McKenzie, "Mormon Women on the 1846 Iowa Trail," 50.

48. Stegner, *The Gathering of Zion*, 89.

49. Stegner, *The Gathering of Zion*, 89.

50. Mary Fielding Smith's home is currently located at This Is the Place State Park, where it was moved in 1972. For information about the cabin, see "Mary Fielding Smith Home," *This Is the Place*, https://www.thisistheplace.org/heritage-village/buildings/mary-fielding-smith-home.

51. Joseph F. Smith, "How One Widow Crossed the Plains," *Young Woman's Journal* 30, no. 3 (March 1919): 165.

52. Smith, "How One Widow Crossed the Plains," 171.

53. Teichert, Minerva, *Not Alone*, 1920.

54. Anderson, "Mary Fielding Smith," 95.

55. Letter, Heber C. Kimball to Mary Fielding Smith, ca. 1846, folder 8, box 1, Mary Fielding Smith Collection, CHL.

56. Bennett, *Mormons at the Missouri*, 198.

57. Jonathan Wright to Brigham Young, February 11, 1848, Journal History of the Church, vol. 24, CHL.

58. Jonathan Wright to Brigham Young, February 11, 1848.

59. Lee, *Journals of John D. Lee, 1846–1847 & 1859*, 80, quoted in Bennett, *Mormons at the Missouri*, 197.

60. Bennett, *Mormons at the Missouri*, 197.

61. See, for example, Cott, *Public Vows*, 27–76; Godbeer, *Sexual Revolution in Early America*, 227–263.

62. This history follows that set out by the Pokagon Band of Potawatomi. See "History," *Pokagan Band of Potawatomi*, accessed October 10, 2021, https://www.pokagonband-nsn.gov/our-culture/history. It also uses "War of 1812 and the Bloody Battle of Dearborn," Citizen Potawatami Nation, July 26, 2022.

63. Tullidge, *History of Salt Lake City*, 33.

64. Tullidge, *History of Salt Lake City*, 33.

65. Clayton, *An Intimate Chronicle*, 370.

66. Clayton, *An Intimate Chronicle*, 370.

67. Journal History of the Church, September 9, 1847.

68. Journal History of the Church, August 1, 1847.

69. William Clayton Diary, January–December 1847, Mormon Pioneer Overland Travel Database, https://history.lds.org/overlandtravel/sources/4402 /clayton-william-diary-1847-january-december?lang=eng. William G. Hartley discusses the Presbyterian mission in his edition of John Lowe Butler's journal. See, Butler, *My Best for the Kingdom*, 210.

70. Crosby, *No Places to Call Home*, 72.

71. Coates, "Cultural Conflict: Mormons and Indians in Nebraska," 298.

72. Journal History of the Church, July 27, 1847.

73. Journal History of the Church, July 28, 1847.

74. Heyward, Journals 1850–[1860], vol. 1, 3–14, Mormon Pioneer Overland Travel Database, https://history.lds.org/overlandtravel/sources /14061369700045576594-eng/heywood-martha-spence-journals-1850-1860-vol -1-3-14?firstName=Edward&surname=Hunter&lang=eng.

75. John Lyman Smith, Autobiography and Diaries, 1846–1895, vol. 1, 26– 31, Mormon Pioneer Overland Travel Database, https://history.lds.org /overlandtravel/sources/6417/smith-john-lyman-autobiography-and-diaries -1846-1895-vol-1-26-31?lang=eng.

76. Mosiah L. Hancock Autobiography, undated, 34, CHL.

77. Mosiah L. Hancock Autobiography, 34.

78. Mosiah L. Hancock Autobiography, 34.

79. Mosiah L. Hancock Autobiography, 46.

80. G. G. R. Sangiovanni, "Overland Trips Across the American Desert," *Young Woman's Journal*, May 1912, 244–46, Mormon Pioneer Overland Travel Database, https://history.lds.org/overlandtravel/sources/6433/sangiovanni-g-g -r-overland-trips-across-the-american-desert-young-woman-s-journal-may-1912 -244-46?lang=eng.

81. Sangiovanni, "Overland Trips Across the American Desert."

82. Davis Clark, Autobiography, in Erold Clark Wiscombe, *Descendants of Maria Burr, John Clark, and William West Lane* [1975], 12–14, Mormon Pioneer Overland Travel Database, https://history.lds.org/overlandtravel/sources/11443 /clark-davis-autobiography-in-erold-clark-wiscombe-the-descendants-of-maria -burr-john-clark-and-william-west-lane-1975-12-14?lang=eng/.

83. Van Kirk, *Many Tender Ties*; Perry, *On the Edge of Empire*.

84. Perry, *On the Edge of Empire*, 70.

85. Reeve, *Religion of a Different Color*, 75–105.

86. Bowman, *The Mormon People*, 128.

87. Arrington, *Great Basin Kingdom*, 48.

88. Quoted in Arrington *Great Basin Kingdom*, 48.

89. Campbell, *Charles Ellis and the Erotic Mormon Image*, 24.

90. Brigham Young, "The Pioneers (August 24, 1852)," JD, 145.

91. Brooks, "The Cotton Mission," 202.

92. Brooks, "The Cotton Mission," 202.

93. Brooks, "The Cotton Mission," 210.

94. For the town's history, see Dalton, *History of the Iron County Mission* and Shirts and Shirts, *A Trial By Furnace*.

95. Brigham Young, "Movements of the Saints' Enemies (September 13, 1857)," JD.

96. Orson Pratt, "The Opposition of Wickedness to Righteousness, Persecutions of the Saints, Misrepresentations (October 6, 1868)," JD.

97. Brown, *Journal of the Southern Indian Mission*, 10.

98. Brown, *Journal of the Southern Indian Mission*, 24.

99. Brown, *Journal of the Southern Indian Mission*, 35.

100. See, for example, Tinker, *Missionary Conquest*; Stanley, ed., *Christian Missions and the Enlightenment*; Twells, *The Civilising Mission and the English Middle Class, 1792–1850*; Curtis, *Civilizing Habits*.

101. Lewis, "Kanosh and Ute Identity in Territorial Utah," 341.

102. "From Moan Coppy," *Deseret Evening News*, August 4, 1876, 3.

103. Cannon, *My First Mission*, 66.

104. Cannon, *My First Mission*, 52.

105. Brown, *Journal of the Southern Indian Mission*, 129.

106. George Reynolds, "The Work of the Lord in the Sandwich Islands in New Zealand (March 29, 1885)," JD, 52.

107. Orson Pratt, "Celestial Marriage (August 29, 1852)," JD, 54.

108. Pratt, "Celestial Marriage," 59.

109. "Idaho Pioneer Cabin Moved to Chesterfield Site," *Oregonian*, December 2008, https://www.oregonlive.com/news/2008/12/idaho_pioneer_cabin_moved_to_c.html.

110. Cannon, "To Buy Up the Lamanite Children as Fast as They Could," 1–35.

5. MAKING NATIVE KIN

1. In 2018 I found a copy of the probate files for John T. Garr's estate for sale at a Salt Lake City bookstore. I have checked them against the microfilm copies at the Family History Library and they appear to be the same. They are currently in my possession but may be donated to a depository after the

publication of this book. I refer to them as the *John T. Garr Probate Records* hereafter.

2. The probate records for John T. Garr's estate only mention Johnny, but family records suggest that Garr fathered two children. See Jaggi, "The Garr Family Saga."

3. "In re: Garr's Estate," *Pacific Reporter* 86 (August 20–October 22, 1906): 757.

4. "In re: Garr's Estate," 757.

5. Jaggi, "The Garr Family Saga," 17.

6. Jaggi, "The Garr Family Saga," 17.

7. "More Lamanites Baptized," *Deseret News*, May 6, 1875, 3.

8. Turner, *Brigham Young*, 210.

9. Bennion, "Captivity, Adoption, Marriage and Identity," 156.

10. "Mary Mountain Biography, ca. 1950," Harold B. Lee Library, BYU.

11. Stapley, "Adoptive Sealing Ritual in Mormonism," 74–77.

12. Rich Jr., "The True Policy for Utah."

13. "Alpharetta 'Alfretta' Boice," Find a Grave, https://www.findagrave.com /memorial/72278162/alpharetta-boice.

14. Hodes, *White Women, Black Men*, 116.

15. Ferris, *Life in the Rocky Mountains*, 123.

16. Ferris, *Life in the Rocky Mountains*, 123.

17. Merkley, "Cultural Contrast and Material Change."

18. Bagley, *South Pass*, 169.

19. Blood, *Diary of Jane Wilkie Hooper Blood*, 14.

20. Bagley, *South Pass*, 169; Ricks, *The Beginnings of Settlement in Cache Valley*, 8.

21. Ricks, *The Beginnings of Settlement in Cache Valley*, 8.

22. Stansbury, *An Expedition to the Valley of the Great Salt Lake of Utah*, 95.

23. "Utah, Latter-Day Saint Biographical Encyclopedia," *FamilySearch*, https:// familysearch.org/ark:/61903/3:1:3qs7-89pc-77zv?cc=2243396, image 1 of 1; Jenson, *Latter-day Saint Biographical Encyclopedia*.

24. Bryant Stringham to Brigham Young, April 19, 1856, Brigham Young office files: General Letters, 1840–1877, St-To, 1856, CHL.

25. Ricks, *The Beginnings of Settlement in Cache Valley*, 8.

26. Cache Valley Quorum of High Priests, "Minute Book, November 1859–September 9, 1883," Samuel Roskelley Family Collection, Family History Library, Salt Lake City.

27. Hansen, *An Environmental History of the Bear River Range*, 24–25.

28. Hansen, *An Environmental History of the Bear River Range*, 25–26.

29. Brown, *Journal of the Southern Indian Mission*, 45.

30. Huis, et al, *Edible Insects*, 39.

31. Peterson, "Black Hawk War."

32. Joel Ricks, ed. "Memories of Early Days in Cache County," 4, Merrill-Crazier Library, Utah State University, Logan.

33. Ricks, *The Beginnings of Settlement in Cache Valley*, 14.

34. Peterson, "Black Hawk War."

35. Winkler, "The Circle Massacre: A Brutal Incident in Utah's Black Hawk War," 9–10.

36. The detail about Frank Timbimboo Warner holding a bowl of pine-nut gravy is frequently retold. See, for example, Edmo, *History and Culture of the Boise Shoshone and Bannock Indians*, 181; Christensen, *Sagwitch*, 54; and Hart, *The Bear River Massacre*, 227. All three books use the same phrase.

37. Snyder, *Great Crossings*, 182.

38. Madsen, *Chief Pocatello*, 72.

39. "Celebrations," *Deseret Evening News*, August 13, 1856, 8.

40. "Celebrations," 8.

41. "Celebrations," 8.

42. "Memories of Early Days in Cache County," 8, 43.

43. "Memories of Early Days in Cache County," 6.

44. "Memories of Early Days in Cache County," 38.

45. "Memories of Early Days in Cache County," 38.

46. Jensen, "Forgotten Relief Societies, 1844–1867," 109.

47. Vernon, *Hunger*, 40.

48. Blackhawk, *Violence over the Land*.

49. Peterson, *Indians in the Family*.

50. See, for example, Cannon, "To Buy Up the Lamanite Children as Fast as They Could," 1–35. The Church of Jesus Christ of Latter-day Saints has written about this history in its official publications. See "Indian Slavery and Indentured Servitude," Church of Jesus Christ of Latter-day Saints, https://www.churchofjesuschrist.org/study/history/topics/indian-slavery-and-indentured-servitude?lang=eng.

51. 1860 U.S. Census, Great Salt Lake, Utah, population schedule, 297, dwelling 2198, family 491, Ephraim and Harriet Hanks, digital images, accessed May 15, 2017, http://ancestry.com.

52. 1860 U.S. Census, Great Salt Lake, Utah, population schedule, 227, dwelling 1633, family 56, Feramorz and Fanny M. Little, digital images, accessed May 15, 2017, http://ancestry.com.

53. Muhlestein, "Utah Indians and the Indian Slave Trade," 103.

54. "Story of Alpharetta Boice—Adopted Indian Baby," *Pioneer Stories* (blog), March 22, 2012, http://pioneerstories-asay.blogspot.com/2012/03/story-of -alpharetta-boice-indian-baby.html.

55. I would like to thank Jana Riess for pointing out that the boy's name may be significant here. Lamoni may have also represented his hopes for Native American redemption. In the Book of Mormon, the Nephite converts the Lamanite king Lamoni, who preaches to his people. As Riess pointed out to me in a private conversation, it is possible that Barber hoped that his adopted child would become the redeemer of his people as his namesake had been.

56. George Barber Journal, 13–14, folder 14, Joel E. Ricks Cache Valley History Collection, Merrill-Cazier Library, Utah State University, Logan.

57. Peterson, *Indians in the Family*, 2, 37.

58. Oliver B. Huntington to Hannah Mendenhall Huntington, July 16, 1855, folder 3, box 1, Letters to Hannah Mendenhall Huntington, 1855–1899, CHL.

59. Hurtado, *Intimate Frontiers*, 1–20.

60. Reeve, *Religion of a Different Color*, 82.

61. Turner, *Brigham Young*, 210.

62. Warner, "Grandpa's New Heritage," 16.

63. Maria Yellow Horse Brave Heart discusses this phenomenon regarding Native Americans. See Yellow Horse Brave Heart, "The Return to the Sacred Path," 291.

64. Pratt, *The History of Louisa Barnes Pratt*, 215.

65. Pratt, *The History of Louisa Barnes Pratt*, 227.

66. "Frank Grouard," *Encyclopedia of North American Indian Wars*, 351.

67. Weeks, *How Desolate Our Home Bereft of Thee*, 156.

68. "Indian Dave Monson," *Saratoga (WY) Sun*, February 19, 1925. This is a widely cited source, but I have been unable yet to locate the original. Will Bagley cites it in Bagley, *The Whites Want Everything*, 505.

69. Yellow Horse Brave Heart, "Historical Trauma among Indigenous People of the Americas," 285.

70. Brian Cannon also discusses David Monson in Cannon, "To Buy Up the Lamanite Children as Fast as They Could," 8–9.

71. Bennion, "Captivity, Adoption, Marriage, and Identity," 174.

72. Bennion, "Captivity, Adoption, Marriage, and Identity," 174.

73. Mary Jane McCleve Meeks, *Personal Recollections of Mary Jane McCleve Meeks of Her Life, 1840–1913*, http://familysearch.org/photos/artifacts/4244181.

74. Bennion, "Captivity, Adoption, Marriage, and Identity," 170.

75. "Memories of Early Days in Cache County," 53.

76. "Memories of Early Days in Cache County," 59.

77. *John T. Garr Probate Records*, 105.

78. "Susan Hio "Susie" Wigegee," Find a Grave, accessed August 19, 2019, https://www.findagrave.com/memorial/184179793. I have been unable to verify these claims.

79. *John T. Garr Probate Records*, 8.

80. For homosocial relationships in the American West, see Johnson, *Roaring Camp*.

81. *John T. Garr Probate Records*, 7.

82. I have been unable to locate any information on Johnny Jones, nor do the court records provide any additional clues as to who Johnny Jones might have been.

83. *John T. Garr Probate Records*, 172.

84. *John T. Garr Probate Records*, 333.

85. *John T. Garr Probate Records*, 48.

86. Hodes, *White Women, Black Men*.

87. *John T. Garr Probate Records*, 74.

88. *John T. Garr Probate Records*, 30, 143.

89. "Death of Johnny Garr," 1.

90. *John T. Garr Probate Records*, 141.

91. "Logan Lines," *Salt Lake Herald*, October 28, 1887, 3.

92. Susan Hio "'Susie' Wigegee," Find a Grave, accessed August 19, 2019, https://www.findagrave.com/memorial/184179793.

93. Jaggi, "The Garr Family Saga," 38.

94. Jaggi, "The Garr Family Saga," 38.

95. "Dean of North Utah Attorneys Taken by Death," *Salt Lake Tribune*, July 18, 1935, 3.

96. "Heart Tells a Story," *Salt Lake Tribune*, April 18, 1902, 1.

97. "Nebeker Appointed to Government Post," *Salt Lake Tribune*, June 24, 1919, 8; "Abe Majors' Defense," *Salt Lake Herald*, July 12, 1899, 8; and "Majors Trial Concluded," *Deseret Evening News*, October 3, 1901, 7.

98. *Cornell Alumni News*, vol. 21 (Ithaca: Cornell University Press, 1918–19), 82.

99. *John T. Garr Probate Records*, 194.

100. *John T. Garr Probate Records*, 20.

101. "In re: Garr's Estate," 757.

102. "Review of Opinion in Garr Case," *Salt Lake Tribune*, August 26, 1906, 4.

103. "In re: Garr's Estate," 763.

104. For information on Chief Kanosh, see Lyman, "Chief Kanosh: Champion of Peace and Forbearance," 157–207.
105. Ardis E. Parshall, "Frank Warner: More Samples of Mormon Native Writing."
106. Lyman, *San Bernardino*, 154.
107. "Grandchildren are Legal Heirs," *Salt Lake Herald-Republican*, August 26, 1906, 15.
108. "Terwilliger Tragedy," *Vernal (ut) Express*, February 16, 1893, 3.
109. Jaggi, "The Garr Family Saga," 48.
110. Jaggi, "The Garr Family Saga," 10.
111. Jaggi, "The Garr Family Saga."
112. Jaggi, "The Garr Family Saga," 49.
113. Jaggi, "The Garr Family Saga," 62.
114. Christensen, *Sagwitch*, 84.
115. Christensen, *Sagwitch*, 84.
116. Smoak, *Ghost Dances and Identity*, 126.

6. NATIVE ZIONS

1. Orson Pratt, "Nephite America," February 11, 1872, JD.
2. Orson Pratt, "Nephite America," February 11, 1872, JD.
3. Cannon, *My First Mission*, 67.
4. Aikau, *A Chosen People, A Promised Land*, 57–60; Trask, *From a Native Daughter*, 140–42, 65–86, 113–22; Silva, *Aloha Betrayed*, 39–44.
5. Isaiah 28: 10; King James Version; 2 Nephi 28: 30 in 1841 edition of the Book of Mormon.
6. Cuch, *History of Utah's American Indians*, 53–82; Kreitzer, *The Washakie Letters of Willie Ottogary*, 1–19.
7. Larsen, "Washakie Township: Mormon Alternative to Fort Hall."
8. Larsen, "Washakie Township."
9. Smith, "The Bare Facts of Ritual," 112–27.
10. Interview, Frank Timbimboo (Shoshoni), 1967, https://collections.lib.utah .edu/details?id=348755.
11. "Mormon Indians," *Courier-Journal* (Louisville KY), March 23, 1911, 5.
12. Lee Neaman Oral Interview, cited in *Washakie of Letters of Willie Ottogary*, 4.
13. Kreitzer, "Introduction," in *The Washakie Letters of Willie Ottogary*, 4.
14. The language of Lamanites being a "chosen people" is common within the Latter-day Saint tradition. For a full exploration of this topic, see Aikau, *A Chosen People, A Promised Land*. For Cannon's revelation, see Cannon, *My First Mission*.

15. Cannon, *My First Mission*, 23, cited in Bruno, "Faith Like of the Ancients," 40.

16. "William H. Uaua," *The Journal of George Q. Cannon*, https://www .churchhistorianspress.org/george-q-cannon/people/william-h-uaua?letter= U&lang=yue.

17. February 8, 1853, *The Journal of George Q. Cannon*, https://www .churchhistorianspress.org/george-q-cannon/1850s/1853/02-1853?lang=eng.

18. Kester, *Remembering Iosepa*, 63.

19. Adler and Kamins, *The Fantastic Life of Walter Murray Gibson*, 67.

20. Marlowe and Kongaika, "Joseph F. Smith's 1864 Mission to Hawaii," 52–72.

21. Marlowe and Kongaika, "Joseph F. Smith's 1864 Mission to Hawaii."

22. Marlowe and Kongaika, "Joseph F. Smith's 1864 Mission to Hawaii."

23. Berge, "Laie Plantation Sugar Mill (1868–1900)," 44.

24. Adoniram Judson quoted in Conroy-Krutz, *Christian Imperialism*, xiii–xiv.

25. Schulz, *Hawaiian by Birth*, 38.

26. Hicks, *Mormonism and Music*, 14.

27. Pratt, *Key to the Science of Theology*.

28. Walker, "Abraham Kaleimahoe Fernandez, Hawaiian Saint and Royalist, 1857–1915."

29. Maffly-Kipp, "Assembling Bodies and Souls," 72–73.

30. Homespun [Susa Young Gates], "What the Sandwich Islands Children are Doing," *Juvenile Instructor* 23, no. 19 (October 1, 1888): 301.

31. Chase, "The Hawaiian Mission Crisis of 1874," 91.

32. Chase, "The Hawaiian Mission Crisis of 1874," 95.

33. January 5, 1888 Entry, Laie Journal, vol. 1, folder 2, box 105, Susa Young Gates Papers, 1870–1930, CHL.

34. July 23, 1887 Entry, vol. 2, folder 2, box 1, Journals of Mary Ann King, Harold B. Lee Library, BYU.

35. Letter, Susa Young Gates to Joseph F. Smith, April 1, 1887, Joseph F. Smith Family Papers, CHL.

36. Entries for January 2–24, 1886, folder 2, box 1, Julina Lambson Smith Papers, CHL.

37. January 2, 1886 Entry, Julina Lambson Smith Diary, folder 3, box 1, Julina Lambson Smith Papers, CHL.

38. Robbins, *The Servant's Hand*, 123; Kent, "Ubiquitous but Invisible," 111–28; Steedman, *Labours Lost*; Light, *Mrs. Woolf and the Servants*.

39. There has been extensive work on colonial governments' fears of the effects that tropical environments would have on white bodies. See Kupperman,

"Fear of Hot Climates in the Anglo-American Colonial Experience," 213–40; Stepan, *Picturing Tropical Nature*, 85–119.

40. Sen, *A Distant Sovereignty*, 102–5.
41. Kester, *Remembering Iosepa*, 85.
42. Kester, *Remembering Iosepa*, 85.
43. Defa, "Goshute Indians."
44. Defa, "Goshute Indians." See also Aikau, "Indigeneity in the Diaspora," 477–500.
45. "Hawaiians Observe Holiday in Utah," *Honolulu Star-Advertiser*, September 15, 1904, 3.
46. "Hawaiians in Utah," *Hawaii Herald*, February 4, 1904, 1.
47. George Frederic Stratton, "From Salt Lake to the South Sea Islands in Four Hours," *Salt Lake Herald-Republican*, September 5, 1915, 2.
48. "In Memoriam," *Woman's Exponent*, February 15, 1898, 254.
49. Wolfe, "Settler Colonialism and the Elimination of the Native," 387–409.
50. Sarah Miley, "Remembering Iosepa."
51. "Letter from Iosepa, 1913," *Nupepa Kuokoa*, January 29, 2015.
52. "Party Will Visit Hawaiian Colony," *Salt Lake Tribune*, August 27, 1915, 3.
53. "Hawaiians in Utah," *Hawaii Herald*, February 4, 1904, 1.
54. Stratton, "From Salt Lake to the South Sea Islands in Four Hours," 2.
55. Stratton, "From Salt Lake to the South Sea Islands in Four Hours," 2.
56. "Town of Iosepa is Cleanliness Model," *Salt Lake Tribune*, October 26, 1915, 3.
57. "Mrs. George Lowe, Failing Since Death of Queen, Passes On," newspaper clipping, n.d., in Lowe, Ohana Family Book, Family History Library, Salt Lake City.
58. Brigham Young College, "Joseph Fielding Smith," *Logan Republican*, December 7, 1918, 9.
59. Pioneer History of Amy Davis Phillips, The Works Progress Administration (Utah Section) Biographical Sketches, University of Utah Marriott Library, Salt Lake City.
60. Parry, "The Northwestern Shoshone," 25–72.
61. Patty Timbimboo-Madsen, "Shoshone Bear River Oral Tradition."
62. Christina Rose, "Native History: Bear River Massacre Devastates Northwestern Shoshone."
63. Cited in Madsen, *The Northern Shoshoni*, 90. "Beeves" was used in this period as a plural form of "beef."
64. Christensen, *Sagwitch*, 67.
65. Christensen, *Sagwitch*, 84.

66. Crawford, "The People of Bear River Speak," 32.

67. *Washakie Ward Record of Members, 1885–1886; 1938*, CHL.

68. *Washakie Ward Record of Members, 1885–1886; 1938*, CHL.

69. Interview with George M. Ward, August 1, 1945, Marriott Library.

70. Kristen Moulton, "At Bear River Massacre site, the names of the dead ring out," *Salt Lake Tribune*, January 30, 2013, https://archive.sltrib.com/article .php?id=55727028&itype=cmsid.

71. Brigham Young to George Washington Hill, May 5, 1875, folder 17, box 35, Brigham Young Office Files, CHL.

72. Brigham Young to George Washington Hill, July 16, 1875, folder 17, box 35, Brigham Young Office Files, CHL.

73. "From Utah," *New York Times*, July 17, 1860.

74. "Brigham Young and the Indians," *Salt Lake Tribune*, October 29, 1872, 2; "Complicity of the Mormons in the Late Emigrant Massacre," *Tennessean* (Nashville), December 9, 1857, 2.

75. "Threatened Indian War," *New York Daily Herald*, September 8, 1875, 7.

76. "The Territory of Nevada-Utah-The Mormons and the Indians," *Washington Union* (Washington DC), May 26, 1858; "Mormons Incite Indians," *Western Kansas Ensign* (Dodge City), November 21, 1890, 2; and "Mountain Meadows," *Detroit Free Press*, March 24, 1877, 4.

77. The definitive work on the Mountain Meadows Massacre is Walker, Turley, and Leonard, *Massacre at Mountain Meadows*.

78. Smoak, *Ghost Dances and Identity*, 133.

79. "XLVIIth Congress," *Jackson County Banner* (Brownstown IN), February 9, 1882, 2.

80. Parry, "The Northwestern Shoshone."

81. Mae Parry, "The Northwestern Shoshone."

82. Lemuel is a figure from the Book of Mormon who turns from God and is cursed with dark skin.

83. "Report of Labors Y.M.M.I.A.," February 9, 1883, Journal History of the Church, 163 (February 1883): 3, accessible through the CHL.

84. "Washakie," *Utah Journal*, December 1, 1883, found in Journal History of the Church 172 (November 1883): 6.

85. J. J. C., "From the Indian Farm: Sickness Among the Children, Appearance of Crickets," *Ogden Daily Herald*, June 27, 1882, 3.

86. Madsen, *The Northern Shoshoni*, 99.

87. Quoted in Madsen, *The Northern Shoshoni*, 100.

88. Charles Dibble, Interview with Phoebe Zundell Ward, July 1945, 11–12, Marriott Library.

89. Martin Seneca, Interview with Fullmer Allred, August 4, 1967, 12, Marriott Library.

90. Dibble, Interview with Phoebe Zundell Ward, 10.

91. I am grateful to Casey Pallister, who first alerted me to the existence of the Crow Fair.

92. Leona Peyope, "Washakie Indian News," *Ogden Standard-Examiner*, June 12, 1938, 2.

93. "City Erecting Fair Banner: Tremonton Busy Place as Annual County Show about to Begin," *Ogden Standard-Examiner*, September 15, 1935, 7.

94. Steve Garr had a blog about his family's history. The blog is no longer extant, but some of the biographies he obtained of family members are still available on Family Search. He provides a different version of "Susie the Indian" than his sister Margaret Garr used for her thesis. The quotes here come from his version of "Susie the Indian." See "Susan Hio 'Susie' Wigegee," Find A Grave, accessed July 21, 2021, https://www.findagrave.com/memorial/184179793/susan-hio-wigegee.

95. Parry, "The Northwestern Shoshone," 58.

96. Oral History, quoted in Parry, "The Northwestern Shoshone," 59.

97. Oral History, quoted in Parry, "The Northwestern Shoshone," 60.

98. Martin Seneca, An Interview with Moroni and Mrs. Timbimboo, July 25, 1967, 20, Marriott Library.

99. Seneca, An Interview with Moroni and Mrs. Timbimboo, 20.

100. Markosian, "Iosepa: Why Hawaiian Mormon Pioneers Were Evicted."

101. Susan Hio "'Susie' Wigegee," Find A Grave, accessed July 21, 2021, https://www.findagrave.com/memorial/184179793/susan-hio-wigegee.

EPILOGUE

1. Alma Walter Compton, untitled photographs, *Shoshone Latter-day Saint Photographs*, CHL.

2. "Mt. Pleasant to Have Big Parade," *Inter-Mountain Republican*, June 21, 1909, 3. The Mt. Pleasant Relic Home has preserved several photographs. See https://mtpleasantpioneer.blogspot.com/2022/03/dedication-of-mt-pleasant-pioneer.html.

3. "Celebrations," *Deseret Evening News*, August 13, 1856, 8.

4. I draw on Frederick E. Hoxie's analysis of the idea of parading in Hoxie, *Parading Through History*, 6.

5. "Native Hawaiian & Pacific Islander Health," *Utah Department of Health*. "Iosepa fest begins in Skull Valley," *Deseret News*, https://www.deseret .com/1999/5/28/19447961/iosepa-fest-begins-in-skull-valley.

6. Dowse, "Joseph F. Smith and the Hawaiian Temple."

7. Alexander, *Mormonism in Transition*.

8. Reeve, *Religion of a Different Color*.

9. Quoted in Alexander, *Mormonism in Transition*, 64.

10. "AIM wants Mormon money," *Billings Gazette*, April 1973, 20.

11. "AIM wants Mormon money," 20.

12. Hangen, "A Place to Call Home," 54–55.

13. Hangen, "A Place to Call Home," 60.

14. Hangen, "A Place to Call Home," 61.

15. Morgan, "Educating the Lamanites," 209.

16. Wood, "Mormons and the Indian Adoption Racket," 51. I initially learned about this article from Morgan, "Educating the Lamanites."

17. "Press Coverage of Lee's Excommunication Ambivalent," 47–49.

18. "The Lee Letters," *Sunstone* 13, no. 4 (November 1989): 54, quoted in Grua, "Elder George P. Lee and the New Jerusalem: A Reception History of 3 Nephi 21: 22–23."

19. Hangen, "A Place to Call Home," 67.

20. Interview cited in Aikau, *A Chosen People, A Promised Land*, 123.

21. Aikau, *A Chosen People, A Promised Land*, 148.

22. Hendrix-Komoto, "Mahana, You Naked!," 173–97.

23. I am drawing here on Jane C. Desmond's arguments about how white Americans think about Hawai'i. See Desmond, *Staging Tourism*, 68.

24. Sekona, "Tonga."

25. Sekopa, "Tonga."

26. Bradley, *Pedestals and Podiums*, 294.

27. Quinn, *The Mormon Hierarchy*, 403–4.

28. Reeve, *Religion of a Different Color*.

29. Desmond, *Staging Tourism*, 7, 122–30.

30. Walker, *Waves of Resistance*, 72–77.

31. Susan Hio "'Susie' Wigegee," Find a Grave, accessed August 19, 2019, https://www.findagrave.com/memorial/184179793.

BIBLIOGRAPHY

ARCHIVAL SOURCES

British Library, London, UK
    East India Office Papers
Cadbury Research Library, University of Birmingham, Birmingham UK
    Letters Additional Collection
Family History Library, Salt Lake City UT
    John T. Garr Probate Records
    Ohana Family Book
    Samuel Roskelley Family Collection
Harold B. Lee Library, Brigham Young University, Provo UT
    Journals of Mary Ann King
    Mary Mountain Biography, ca. 1950
    Richards Family Collection
Joseph Smith Papers Project (JSPP)
    Council of Fifty, Minutes, March 1844–January 1846
    Don Carlos and William Smith to Hyrum and Joseph Smith, March 6, 1839
    History, 1838–56
    John Whitmer, History 1831–circa 1847
    Journal, December 1842–June 1844, Book 2, March 10, 1843–July 14, 1843
    Letterbook 2
    Letter from Oliver Cowdery, November 12, 1830

Letter to Emma Smith, June 4, 1843
Nauvoo Relief Society Minute Book
William Clayton, Journals, 1842–45
Vision, 16 February 1832
Latter-day Saints Church History Library (CHL), Salt Lake City UT
Addison Pratt Family Collection
Benjamin F. Grouard Journal, June 1843–September 1846
Brigham Young Office Files
Brigham Young Papers
Catherine Philips Affidavit
Family Histories, ca. 2000
Florence Dean Ridges Journal
Journal History of the Church of Jesus Christ of Latter-day Saints
Julina Lambson Smith Papers
Letters to Hannah Mendenhall Huntington
Mary Fielding Smith Collection
Mehaho–Marriages, Records of the Church . . . at Toobooai [*sic*]
Mercy F. Thompson Autobiographical Sketch, 1880
Mosiah L. Hancock Autobiography
Nauvoo Records: Judicial Proceedings
Phoebe [Phebe] Whittemore Carter Woodruff, Autograph Book, 1838–44
Shoshone Latter-day Saint Photographs
Washakie Ward Record of Members, 1885–86, 1938
Wilford Woodruff Collection
Marriott Library, University of Utah, Salt Lake City
Charles Dibble interview with Phoebe Zundell Ward, July 1945
Frank Timbimboo (Shoshoni) interview, 1967
George M. Ward interview
Martin Seneca interview with Fullmer Allred, August 4, 1967
Works Progress Administration (Utah Section) Biographical Sketches
Merrill-Crazier Library, Utah State University, Logan
Joel E. Ricks Cache Valley History Collection
"Memories of Early Days in Cache County"
School for Oriental and African Studies (SOAS), London, UK
Council for World Missions/London Missionary Society
Utah State Historical Society, Salt Lake City
Susa Young Gates Papers

PUBLISHED WORKS

Adler, Jacob, and Robert M. Kamins. *The Fantastic Life of Walter Murray Gibson: Hawaii's Minister of Everything*. Honolulu: University of Hawai'i Press, 1986.

Aikau, Hokulani. *A Chosen People, A Promised Land: Mormonism and Race in Hawai'i*. Minneapolis: University of Minnesota Press, 2012.

———"Indigeneity in the Diaspora: The Case of Native Hawaiians at Iosepa, Utah." *American Quarterly* 62, no. 3 (September 2010): 477–500.

Alexander, Thomas. *Mormonism in Transition: A History of the Latter-Day Saints, 1890–1930*. Urbana: University of Illinois Press, 1986.

Allen, James, and Glen Leonard. *The Story of the Latter-day Saints*. 2nd ed. Salt Lake City: Deseret, 1992.

Alley, John R., Jr. "Prelude to Dispossession: The Fur Trade's Significance for the Northern Utes and Southern Paiutes." *Utah Historical Quarterly* 50, no. 2 (Spring 1982): 104–23.

Allgor, Catherine. *Parlor Politics: In Which the Ladies of Washington Help Build a City and a Government*. Charlottesville: University of Virginia Press, 2000.

Anderson, Lavina Fielding. "Mary Fielding Smith: Her Ox Goes Marching On." *Dialogue: A Journal of Mormon Thought* 14 (Winter 1981): 91–100.

Arrington, Leonard. *Great Basin Kingdom: An Economic History of the Latter-day Saints, 1830–1900*. Urbana: University of Illinois Press, 1958.

Bagley, Will. *South Pass: Gateway to a Continent*. Norman: University of Oklahoma Press, 2014.

———. *The Whites Want Everything: Indian-Mormon Relations, 1847–1877*. Norman: University of Oklahoma Press, 2019.

Ballantyne, Tony. *Entanglements of Empire: Missionaries, Maori, and the Question of the Body*. Durham NC: Duke University Press, 2014.

Baugh, Alexander L. *A Call to Arms: The 1838 Mormon Defense of Northern Missouri*. Salt Lake City: BYU Studies, 2000.

Berge, Dale. "Laie Plantation Sugar Mill (1868–1900): Archaeology and History." *Mormon Pacific Historical Society* 7, no. 1 (1986): 41–52.

Binney, Judith. *The Legacy of Guilt: A Life of Thomas Kendall*. Auckland, NZ: Auckland University Press, 1968.

———. "Whatever Happened to Poor Mr. Yate? An Exercise in Voyeurism." *New Zealand Journal of History* 38 (2004): 154–68.

Beecher, Maureen Ursenbach. "Women at Winter Quarters." *Sunstone* 8, no. 4 (July–August 1983): 11–19.

Belnap, Daniel. "'Those Who Receive You Not:' The Rite of Wiping Dust Off the Feet." *International Journal of Mormon Studies* 5 (2012): 81–127.

Bennett, J. C. *The History of the Saints.* Boston: Leland & Whiting, 1842.

Bennett, Richard E. *Mormons at the Missouri: Winter Quarters, 1846–1852.* Norman: University of Oklahoma Press, 1987.

Bennion, Michael Kay. "Captivity, Adoption, Marriage and Identity: Native American Children in Mormon Homes, 1847–1900." Master's thesis, University of Nevada Las Vegas, 2012.

Bergera, Gary James. "Identify the Earliest Mormon Polygamists, 1841–1844." *Dialogue: A Journal of Mormon Thought* 38, no. 3 (Fall 2005): 1–74.

Bicknell, James. *America 1844: Religious Fervor, Westward Expansion, and the Presidential Election that Transformed the Nation.* Chicago: Chicago Review, 2015.

Blackhawk, Ned. *Violence over the Land: Indians and Empires in the Early American West.* Cambridge MA: Harvard University Press, 2006.

Blood, Jane Wilkie Hooper. *Diary of Jane Wilkie Hooper Blood.* Edited by Ivy Hooper Blood. Logan UT: J. P. Smith, 1966.

Bowes, John P. *Land Too Good for Indians: Northern Indian Removal.* Norman: University of Oklahoma Press, 2016.

Bowman, Matthew. *The Mormon People: The Making of An American Faith.* New York: Random House, 2012.

Bradley, Martha Sontag. *Pedestals and Podiums: Utah Women, Religious Authority, and Equal Rights.* Salt Lake City UT: Signature, 2005.

Bradley, Martha Sontag, and Mary Brown Firmage Woodard. *Four Zinas: A Story of Mothers and Daughters on the Mormon Frontier.* Salt Lake City UT: Signature, 2000.

Britsch, R. Lanier. "The Establishment of the Church in French Polynesia, 1844–1895." *Mormon Pacific Historical Society* 1, no. 1 (1980): 27–32.

———. *Unto the Islands of the Sea: A History of Latter-day Saints in the Pacific.* Salt Lake City UT: Deseret, 1986.

Brooks, Juanita. "The Cotton Mission." *Utah Historical Quarterly* 29, no. 3 (July 1961): 201–21.

Brown, James S. *Giant of the Lord: Life of a Pioneer.* Salt Lake City UT: Bookcraft, 1960.

Brown, Richard S., and William C. Mackay. "Fall and Winter Movements of and Habitat Use by Cutthroat in the Ram River, Alberta." *Transactions of the American Fisheries Society* 124, no. 6 (1995): 873–85.

Brown, Thomas D. *Journal of the Southern Indian Mission: Diary of Thomas D. Brown.* Edited by Juanita Brooks. Logan: Utah State University Press, 1972.

Bruno, Frank Alan. "Faith Like of the Ancients: The LDS Church in Pulehu and on Maui." *Mormon Pacific Historical Society* 10, no. 1 (1989): 37–56.

Bushman, Richard. *Joseph Smith: Rough Stone Rolling*. New York: Vintage, 2005.

Butler, John Lowe. *My Best for the Kingdom: History and Autobiography of John Lowe Butler, a Mormon Frontiersman*. Edited by William G. Hartley. Salt Lake City UT: Aspen, 1993.

Butler, Jon. *Awash in a Sea of Faith: Christianizing the American People*. Cambridge MA: Harvard University Press, 1990.

Campbell, Ian C. "Gone Native." In *Polynesia: Captivity Narratives and Experiences from the South Pacific*. Westport CT: Greenwood, 1998.

Campbell, Mary. *Charles Ellis and the Erotic Mormon Image*. Chicago: University of Chicago Press, 2016.

Cannon, Brian Q. "'To Buy Up the Lamanite Children as Fast as They Could': Indentured Servitude and Its Legacy in Mormon Society." *Journal of Mormon History* 44, no. 2 (2018): 1–35.

Cannon, George Q. *The Journal of George Q. Cannon*. Salt Lake City UT: Church Historian's Press, 2018. https://www.churchhistorianspress.org/george-q -cannon?lang=yue.

———. *My First Mission*. Salt Lake City UT: Juvenile Instructor, 1882.

Crosby, Caroline Barnes. *No Places to Call Home: The 1807–1857 Life Writings of Caroline Barnes Crosby, Chronicler of Outlying Mormon Communities*. Edited by Edward Leo Lyman, Susan Ward Payne, S. George Ellsworth. Logan: Utah State University Press, 2005.

Cuch, Forrest S. *History of Utah's American Indians*. Logan: Utah State University Press, 2000.

Curtis, Sarah A. *Civilizing Habits: Women Missionaries and the Revival of French Empire*. New York: Oxford University Press, 2010.

Custer, Milo. "Kannekuk or Keeanakuk: The Kickapoo Prophet." *Journal of the Illinois State Historical Society (1908–1984)* 11, no. 1 (1918): 48–56.

Dalton, Luella Adams. *History of the Iron County Mission and Parowan, The Mother Town*. n.p, 1962.

Davidoff, Leonore. *Thicker than Water: Siblings and Their Relations, 1780–1920*. New York: Oxford University Press, 2012.

Daynes, Kathryn M. *More Wives Than One: Transformation of the Mormon Marriage System, 1840–1910*. Urbana: University of Illinois Press, 2001.

Defa, Dennis. "Goshute Indians." *Utah History Encyclopedia*. https://historytogo .utah.gov/goshute-indians.

Deloria, Ella. *Speaking of Indians*. Lincoln NE: Bison Books, 1998.

Desmond, Jane C. *Staging Tourism: Bodies on Display from Waikiki to Sea World.*
Chicago: University of Chicago Press, 1999.

Dixon, William Hepworth. *White Conquest,* vol. 1. London: Chatto and Windus,
1876.

Dowse, Richard J. "Joseph F. Smith and the Hawaiian Temple." In *Joseph F. Smith:
Reflections on the Man and His Times,* edited by Craig K. Mascill, Brian D. Reeves,
Guy L. Dorius, and J. B. Haws. Provo UT: Religious Studies Center, 2013.

Doxey, Cynthia. "The Church in Britain and the 1851 Religious Census." *Mormon
Historical Studies* 4, no. 1 (2003): 107–38.

Doyle, Arthur Conan. *A Study in Scarlet.* 1887; repr. Oxford: Oxford University
Press, 1994.

Dunbar, Erica. "Writing for True Womanhood: African-American Women's
Writings and the Antislavery Struggle." In *Women's Rights and Transatlantic
Antislavery in the Era of Emancipation,* edited by Kathryn Kish Sklar and James
B. Stewart, 299–318. New Haven CT: Yale University Press, 2007.

Edmo, William D. *History and Culture of the Boise Shoshone and Bannock Indians.*
Pittsburgh PA: Dorrance, 2010.

Elbourne, Elizabeth. *Blood Ground: Colonialism, Missions, and the Contest for Christianity in the Cape Colony and Britain, 1799–1853.* Montreal: McGill-Queen's
University Press, 2002.

Ellsworth, George, ed. *Dear Ellen: Two Mormon Women and their Letters.* Salt Lake
City UT: Signature, 1974.

*Encyclopedia of North American Indian Wars, 1607–1890: A Political, Social, and Mili-
tary History.* Edited by Spencer C. Tucker. Santa Barbara CA: ABC-Clio, 2011.

Esplin, Ronald K. "Joseph, Brigham and the Twelve: A Succession of Continuity."
byu Studies 21, no. 3 (1981): 301–41.

———. "Joseph Smith and the Kirtland Crisis." In *Joseph Smith, the Prophet and
Seer,* edited by Richard Neitzel Holzapfel and Kent P. Jackson, 261–90. Provo
UT: Religious Studies Center, Brigham Young University, 2010.

Flanders, Robert Bruce. *Nauvoo: Kingdom on the Mississippi.* Urbana: University of
Illinois, 1965.

Ferris, Warren Angus. *Life in the Rocky Mountains, 1830–1835.* Edited by Leroy R.
Hafen. Denver: Old West, 1983.

The First Fifty Years of Relief Society: Key Documents in Latter-day Saint Women's History
(web version). Salt Lake City UT: Church Historian's Press, 2016. https://
www.churchhistorianspress.org/the-first-fifty-years-of-relief-society/part-1/1
-14?lang=eng.

Fleisher, Kass. *The Bear River Massacre and the Making of History.* Albany NY: SUNY Press, 2004.

Foster, Lawrence. *Religion and Sexuality: The Shakers, the Mormons, and the Oneida Community.* New York: Oxford University Press, 1981.

———. *Women, Family, and Utopia: Communal Experiments of the Shakers, the Oneida Community, and the Mormons.* Syracuse NY: Syracuse University Press, 1991.

Fraser, Nancy. "Rethinking the Public Sphere: A Contribution to the Critique of Actually Existing Democracy." *Social Text,* no. 25–26 (1990): 56–80.

French, Kara. "The Politics of Sexual Restraint: Debates Over Chastity in America, 1780–1860." PhD diss., University of Michigan, 2013.

Garrett, John. *Footsteps in the Sea: Christianity in Oceania to World War II.* Suva, Fiji: World Council of Churches/Institute of Pacific Studies, 1992.

Gates, Susa Young. *History of the Young Ladies' Mutual Improvement Association of the Church of Jesus Christ of Latter-day Saints.* Salt Lake City UT: Deseret, 1911.

Gentry, Leland Homer, and Todd Compton. *Fire and Saved: A History of the Latter-day Saints in Northern Missouri, 1836–1839.* Draper UT: Greg Kofford, 2010.

Givens, Terryl. *By the Hand of Mormon: The American Scripture that Launched a New World Religion.* New York: Oxford University Press, 2002.

———. *The Viper on the Hearth: Mormons, Myths, and the Construction of Heresy.* New York: Oxford University Press, 1997.

———. *Wrestling the Angel: The Foundations of Mormon Thought: Cosmos, God, Humanity.* New York: Oxford University Press, 2015.

Givens, Terryl, and Matthew Grow. *Parley P. Pratt: The Apostle Paul of Mormonism.* New York: Oxford University Press, 2001.

Godbeer, Richard. *Sexual Revolution in Early America.* Baltimore: Johns Hopkins University Press, 2002.

Godfrey, Kenneth. "The Zelph Story." *byu Studies* 29, no. 2 (1989): 32–56.

Gordon, Sarah Barringer. *The Mormon Question: Polygamy and Constitutional Conflict in Nineteenth-Century America.* Chapel Hill: University of North Carolina Press, 2002.

Grua, David. "Elder George P. Lee and the New Jerusalem: A Reception History of 3 Nephi 21: 22–23." *Juvenile Instructor* (blog), August 27, 2013. http://www.juvenileinstructor.org/elder-george-p-lee-and-the-reception-history-of-3-nephi-2122–23/.

Gunson, Niel. "An Account of the Mamaia or Visionary Heresy of Tahiti, 1826–1841." *The Journal of the Polynesian Society* 71, no. 2 (1962): 209–43.

———. "The Deviations of a Missionary Family: The Henrys of Tahiti." In *Pacific Island Portraits*, edited by J. W. Davidson and Deryck Scarr, 31–54. Canberra: Australian National University Press, 1970.

———. *Messengers of Grace: Evangelical Missionaries in the South Seas, 1797–1860*. London: Oxford University Press, 1978.

Hales, Brian C. "Emma Smith, Eliza R. Snow, and the Reported Incident on the Stairs." *Mormon Historical Studies* 10, no. 2 (Fall 2009): 63–75.

Hall, Catherine, and Leonore Davidoff. *Family Fortunes: Men and Women of the English Middle Class, 1780–1850*. Chicago: University of Chicago Press, 1987.

Hangen, Tona Yonce. "A Place to Call Home: Studying the Indian Placement Program." *Dialogue: A Journal of Mormon Thought* 30, no. 1 (Spring 1997): 54–55.

Hansen, Bradley Paul. *An Environmental History of the Bear River Range, 1860–1910*. Logan: Utah State University, 2013.

Hart, Newell. *The Bear River Massacre*. Preston ID: Cache Valley Newsletter, 1982.

Hatch, Nathan. *The Democratization of American Christianity*. New Haven CT: Yale University Press, 1989.

Hemphill, C. Dallett. *Siblings: Brothers and Sisters in American History*. New York: Oxford University Press, 2011.

Hendrix-Komoto, Amanda, and Joseph R. "Mahana, You Naked!: Modesty, Sexuality, and Race in the Mormon Pacific." In *Out of Obscurity: Mormonism after 1945*, edited by Patrick Mason and John Turner, 173–97. New York: Oxford University Press, 2016.

Hendrix-Komoto, Amanda, and Joseph Stuart. "Race and Gender in Mormonism, 1830–1978." In *Routledge Handbook on Mormonism and Gender*, edited by Taylor Petrey and Amy Hoyt, 26–37. New York: Routledge, 2020.

Heitzenrater, Richard. *Wesley and the People Called Methodists*. Nashville TN: Abingdon, 1995.

Hicks, Michael. *Mormonism and Music: A History*. Urbana: University of Illinois Press, 1989.

Hill, George Washington. "An Indian Vision." *Juvenile Instructor* 12, No. 1 (January 1877): 11.

Hoberman, Michael. *New Israel/New England: Jews and Puritans in Early America*. Amherst: University of Massachusetts Press, 2011.

Hodes, Martha. *White Women, Black Men: Illicit Sex in the Nineteenth-Century South*. New Haven CT: Yale University Press, 2014.

Howe, Eber D. *Mormonism Unvailed or, A Faithful Account of that Singular Imposition*. Painesville OH: self-published, 1834.

Hoxie, Frederick. *Parading Through History: The Making of the Crow Nation in America, 1805–1935*. New York: Cambridge University Press, 1995.

Huis, Arnold Van, et al. *Edible Insects: Future Prospects for Food and Feed Security.* Rome: Food and Agriculture Organization of the United Nations, 2013. http://www.fao.org/3/i3253e/i3253e.pdf.

Hurtado, Albert. *Intimate Frontiers: Sex, Gender, and Culture in Old California.* Albuquerque: University of New Mexico Press, 1999.

Irving, Gordon. "The Law of Adoption: One Phase of the Development of the Mormon Conception of Salvation, 1830–1900." *byu Studies Quarterly* 14, no. 3 (1974): 291–314.

Isaac, Rhys. *The Transformation of Virginia, 1740–1790.* Chapel Hill: University of North Carolina Press, 1982.

Iversen, Joan Smyth. *The Antipolygamy Controversy in U.S. Women's Movements, 1880–1925: A Debate on the American Home.* New York: Garland, 1997.

Jaggi, Margaret Garr. "The Garr Family Saga: The Connection Power of Oral Narrative." Master's thesis, University of Utah, 2003.

Jarman, William. *U.S.A., Uncle Sam's Abscess, or Hell upon Earth.* Exeter UK: H. Leduc, 1884.

Jensen, Richard L. "Forgotten Relief Societies, 1844–1867." *Dialogue: A Journal of Mormon Thought* 16, no. 1 (Spring 1983): 105–25.

Jenson, Andrew. *Latter-day Saint Biographical Encyclopedia.* 4 vols. Salt Lake City: Andrew Jenson, 1901.

Jeter, Edje. "Cephalopods 4 of 4: The Nineteenth Century Octopus." *Juvenile Instructor* (blog), July 14, 2013. http://juvenileinstructor.org/cephalopods-4 -of-4-the-nineteenth-century-octopus.

Johnson, Janiece. "Becoming a People of the Books: Toward an Understanding of Early Mormon Converts and the New Word of the Lord." *Journal of Book of Mormon Studies* 27 (2018): 1–43.

———."Give Up All and Follow Your Lord: Testimony and Exhortation in Early Mormon Women's Letters, 1831–1839." *byu Studies* 41, no. 1 (2002): 77–107.

Johnson, Paul, and Sean Wilentz. *The Kingdom of Matthias: A Story of Sex and Salvation in Nineteenth-Century America.* 2nd ed. New York: Oxford University Press, 2012.

Johnson, Susan Lee. *Roaring Camp: The Social World of the California Gold Rush.* New York: W. W. Norton, 2000.

Johnstun, Joseph. "A Victim of the 1838 Mormon-Missouri War: The Tragedy of Hannah Kinney Johnstun." Mormon History Association Conference, Independence MO, May 2010. *Journal of Discourses by Brigham Young, His*

Two Counsellors, the Twelve Apostles and Others. Vols. 1–16. Liverpool: various publishers, 1854–56.

Juster, Susan. "Mystical Pregnancy and Holy Bleeding: Visionary Experience in Early Modern Britain and America." *William and Mary Quarterly* 57, no. 2 (April 2000): 249–88.

Kane, Elizabeth. *A Gentile Account of Life in Utah's Dixie, 1872–73: Elizabeth Kane's St. George Journal.* Edited by Norman R. Bowen. Salt Lake City: University of Utah Press, 1995.

Kaplan, Amy. *The Anarchy of Empire in the Making of U.S. Culture.* Cambridge MA: Harvard University Press, 2005.

Karras, Christy. *More than Petticoats: Remarkable Utah Women.* Guilford CT: Morris, 2010.

Keitzer, Matthew. *The Washakie Letters of Willie Ottogary, Northwestern Shoshone Journalist and Leader, 1906–1929.* Logan: Utah State University Press, 2000.

Kelley, Mary. *Learning to Stand and Speak: Women, Education, and Public Life in America's Republic.* Chapel Hill: University of North Carolina Press, 2006.

Kenney, Scott G. "Before the Beard: The Trials of Young Joseph Smith." *Sunstone* 120 (2001): 20–43.

Kent, D. A. "Ubiquitous but Invisible: Female Domestic Servants in Mid-Eighteenth-Century London." *History Workshop Journal* 28 (1989): 111–28.

Kern, Louis. *An Ordered Love: Sex Roles and Sexuality in Victorian Utopias—The Shakers, the Mormons, and the Oneida Community.* Chapel Hill: University of North Carolina Press, 1981.

Kester, Matthew. *Remembering Iosepa: History, Place, and Religion in the American West.* New York: Oxford University Press, 2013.

"The King Follett Sermon." *Ensign,* April 1971. https://www.lds.org/ensign/1971/04/the-king-follett-sermon?lang=eng.

Koven, Seth. *Slumming: Sexual and Social Politics in Victorian London.* Princeton NJ: Princeton University Press, 2004.

Koziak, Barbara. *Retrieving Political Emotion: Thumos, Aristotle, and Gender.* University Park: Penn State University Press, 2000.

Kupperman, Karen. "Fear of Hot Climates in the Anglo-American Colonial Experience." *William and Mary Quarterly* 41, no. 2 (April 1984): 213–40.

Lansdown, Robert. *Strangers in the South Seas: The Idea of the Pacific in Western Thought.* Honolulu: University of Hawai'i Press, 2006.

Larsen, Natalie. "Washakie Township: Mormon Alternative to Fort Hall." *Intermountain Histories,* June 7, 2018. https://www.intermountainhistories.org/items/show/206.

Lawrence, Anna. *One Family Under God: Love, Belonging, and Authority in Early Transatlantic Methodism.* Philadelphia: University of Pennsylvania Press, 2011.

LeSueur, Stephen. *The 1838 Mormon War in Missouri.* Columbia: University of Missouri Press, 1987.

Lewis, Hyrum S. "Kanosh and Ute Identity in Territorial Utah." *Utah Historical Quarterly* 71, no. 4 (Fall 2003): 332–47.

[Lieber, Francis]. "The Mormons: Shall Utah Be Admitted to the Union?" *Putnam's Monthly* 5, no. 27 (March 1855): 225–36.

Light, Alison. *Mrs. Woolf and the Servants.* New York: Bloomsbury, 2008.

Loether, Christopher. "Shoshones." In *Encyclopedia of the Great Plains*, edited by David Wishart, 181–82. Lincoln: University of Nebraska Press, 2007.

Lowe, Howard. "Walter Murray Gibson: Shepherd L.D.S. Leader of Lanai." *Mormon Pacific Historical Society* 3. no. 147 (1982): 41–50.

Lyman, Edward Leo. "Chief Kanosh: Champion of Peace and Forbearance." *Journal of Mormon History* 35, no. 1 (2009): 157–207.

———. *San Bernardino: The Rise and Fall of a California Community.* Salt Lake City UT: Signature, 1996.

Lyons, Clare. *Sex Among the Rabble: An Intimate History of Gender & Power in the Age of Revolution, Philadelphia.* Chapel Hill: University of North Carolina, 2012.

Lystra, Karen. *Searching the Heart: Women, Men, and Romantic Love in the Nineteenth Century.* New York: Oxford University Press, 1989.

Madsen, Brigham. *Chief Pocatello, the "White Plume."* Salt Lake City: University of Utah Press, 1998.

———. *The Northern Shoshoni.* Caldwell ID: Caxton, 1980.

Madsen, Carol Cornwell, ed. *In Their Own Words: Women and the Story of Nauvoo.* Salt Lake City UT: Deseret, 1994.

Maffly-Kipp, Laurie. "Assembling Bodies and Souls: Missionary Practices on the Pacific Frontier." In *Practicing Protestants: Histories of Christian Life in America, 1630–1965*, edited by Laurie F. Maffly-Kipp, Leigh E. Schmidt, and Mark Valeri, 51–76. Baltimore: Johns Hopkins University Press, 2006.

———. *Religion and Society in Frontier California.* New Haven CT: Yale University Press, 1994.

Manktelow, Emily. "Missionary Families and the Formation of the Missionary Enterprise: The London Missionary Society and the Family, 1795–1875." PhD diss., King's College, London, 2010.

———. "Rev. Simpson's Improper Liberties: Moral Scrutiny and Missionary Children in the South Seas Mission." *Journal of Imperial and Commonwealth History* 40, no. 2 (2012): 159–81.

Marcus, Sharon. *Between Women: Friendship, Desire, and Marriage in Victorian England.* Princeton NJ: Princeton University Press, 2007.

Markosian, Richard. "Iosepa: Why Hawaiian Mormon Pioneers Were Evicted." *Utah Stories*, August 10, 2011. https://utahstories.com/2011/08/iosepa -mystery-utahs-hawaiian-pioneer-town.

Marlowe, Eric, and Isileli Kongaika. "Joseph F. Smith's 1864 Mission to Hawaii: Leading a Reformation." In *Joseph F. Smith: Reflections on the Man and His Times*, edited by Craig K. Manscill, Brian D. Reeves, Guy L. Dorius, and J. B. Haws, 52–72. Provo UT: Religious Studies Center, 2013.

Maude, H. E. "Beachcombers and Castaways." *Journal of the Polynesian Society* 73, no. 3 (1964): 254–93.

Mauss, Armand. *All Abraham's Children: Changing Mormon Conceptions of Race and Lineage.* Urbana: University of Illinois Press, 2003.

McGrath, Ann. *Illicit Love: Interracial Sex and Marriage in the United States and Australia.* Lincoln: University of Nebraska Press, 2015.

McKenzie, Bettie. "Mormon Women on the 1846 Iowa Trail." *Nauvoo Journal* 8 (Fall 1996): 48–61.

Mercado, Kiya. "Reexamining the Bear River Massacre." *Intermountain Histories.* Accessed June 11, 2021. https://www.intermountainhistories.org/items/show/23.

Merkley, Anne. "Cultural Contrast and Material Change: The Wrensted-Garvey Photographs of Northern Shoshone and Bannock Indians." Master's thesis, Idaho State University, 1994.

Miley, Sarah. "Remembering Iosepa." *Honolulu Magazine*, October 21, 2008. https://www.honolulumagazine.com/remembering-iosepa/.

Mims, Bob. "Bear River Massacre Stirs Tears." *Los Angeles Times*, October 1, 1995. https://www.latimes.com/archives/la-xpm-1995-10-01-mn-51950-story.html.

Morgan, Brandon. "Educating the Lamanites: A Brief History of the LDS Indian Student Placement Program." *Journal of Mormon History* 35, no. 4 (Fall 2009): 191–217.

Morgan, Jennifer. "'Some Could Suckle Over Their Shoulder': Male Travelers, Female Bodies, and the Gendering of Racial Ideology, 1500–1770." *William and Mary Quarterly* 54, no. 1 (January 1997): 167–92.

Mueller, Max. *Race and the Making of the Mormon People.* Chapel Hill: University of North Carolina Press, 2017.

Muhlestein, Robert M. "Utah Indians and the Indian Slave Trade: The Mormon Adoption Program and its Effect on the Indian Slaves." Master's thesis, Brigham Young University, 1991. https://scholarsarchive.byu.edu/etd/4968.

The Nauvoo City Council and High Council Minutes. Edited by John S. Dinger. Salt Lake City UT: Signature, 2011.

Newbury, Colin. *Tahiti Nui: Change and Survival in French Polynesia.* Honolulu: University Press of Hawaii, 1980.

Newell, Linda King, and Valeen Tippetts Avery. *Mormon Enigma: Emma Hale Smith.* Urbana: University of Illinois Press, 1984.

Nicol, James. *Introductory Book of the Sciences.* Edinburgh UK: Oliver & Boyd, 1853.

Obermeyer, Brice. *Delaware Tribe in a Cherokee Nation.* Lincoln: University of Nebraska Press, 2009.

O'Reilly, Patrick, and Raoul Teissier, *Tahitiens: Répertoire biographique de la Polynésie Française.* 2nd ed. Illustrated by J. Bouilaire, Ch. Dessirier, J. Lebedeff, J. L. Saquet. Paris: Publications de la Société des Océanistes, Musée de l'Homme, 1975.

Park, Benjamin. "Salvation through a Tabernacle: Joseph Smith, Parley P. Pratt, and Early Mormon Theologies of Embodiment." *Dialogue: A Journal of Mormon Thought* 43, no. 2 (Summer 2010): 1–44.

Park, Benjamin, and Robin Scott Jensen. "Debating Succession, March 1846: John E. Page, Orson Hyde, and the Trajectories of Joseph Smith's Legacy." *Journal of Mormon History* 39 (Winter 2013): 181–205.

Park, Benjamin, and Jordan T. Watkins. "The Riches of Mormon Materialism: Parley P. Pratt's 'Materiality' and Early Mormon Theology." *Mormon Historic Sites* 11, no. 2 (September 2010): 159–72.

Parkin, Max H. "Lamanite Mission of 1830–1831." In *Encyclopedia of Mormonism,* edited by Daniel H. Ludlow, 802–4. New York: Macmillan, 1992.

Parry, Darren. *The Bear River Massacre: A Shoshone History.* Salt Lake City UT: By Common Consent, 2019.

———. "Mae Timbimboo Parry, Historian and Matriarch of the Northwestern Band of the Shoshone, 1919–2007." *Better Days 2020.* Accessed February 7, 2019. https://www.utahwomenshistory.org/bios/mae-timbimboo-parry.

Parry, Mae. "The Northwestern Shoshone." In *A History of Utah's American Indians,* edited by Forrest S. Cuch, 26–70. Logan: Utah State University, 2000.

Parshall, Ardis E. "Frank Warner: More Samples of Mormon Native Writing." *Keepapitchinin* (blog), November 14, 2014. http://www.keepapitchinin.org/2014/11/14/frank-w-warner-more-samples-of-mormon-native-writing/.

Perry, Adele. *On the Edge of Empire: Gender, Race, and the Making of British Columbia, 1849–1871.* Toronto: University of Toronto Press, 2001.

Pierpaoli, Paul. "Frank Grouard." *Encyclopedia of North American Indian Wars, 1607–1890: A Political, Social, and Military History,* edited by Spencer C. Tucker, 351–352. Santa Barbara CA: ABC-Clio, 2011.

Peterson, John A. "Black Hawk War." *Utah History to Go.* Accessed August 3, 2018. https://historytogo.utah.gov/black-hawk-war.

Peterson, Dawn. *Indians in the Family: Adoption and the Politics of Antebellum Expansion.* Cambridge MA: Harvard University Press, 2017.

Plamper, Jan. "The History of Emotions: An Interview with William Reddy, Barbara Rosenwein, and Peter Stearns." *History and Theory* 49, no. 2 (May 2010): 237–65.

Pratt, Addison. *The Journals of Addison Pratt: Being a Narrative of Yankee Whaling.* Edited by S. George Ellsworth. Salt Lake City: University of Utah Press, 1990.

Pratt, Louisa Barnes. *The History of Louisa Barnes Pratt.* Edited by S. George Ellsworth. Logan: Utah State University Press, 1998.

Pratt, Parley P. *Autobiography of Parley Parker Pratt.* New York: Russell Brothers, 1874.

———. *Key to the Science of Theology.* Liverpool: F. D. Richards, 1855.

"Press Coverage of Lee's Excommunication Ambivalent." *Sunstone* 13 (August 1989): 47–49.

Quinn, D. Michael. *The Mormon Hierarchy: Extensions of Power.* Salt Lake City UT: Signature, 1997.

———. "The Succession Crisis of 1844," *byu Studies* 16, no. 2 (1976).

Radke, Andrea [Andrea Radke-Moss]. "We Also Marched: The Women and Children of Zion's Camp." *byu Studies Quarterly* 39, no. 1 (2000): 147–65.

Radke-Moss, Andrea. "'I Hid [the Prophet] in a Corn Patch': Mormon Women as Healers, Concealers, and Protectors in the 1838 Mormon-Missouri War." *Mormon Historical Studies* 15, no. 1 (Spring 2014): 25–40.

———. "Silent Memories of Missouri: Mormon Women and Men and Sexual Assault in Group Memory and Identity." In *Mormon Women's History: Beyond Biography,* edited by Rachel Cope, Amy Easton-Flake, Keith A. Erekson, and Lisa Olsen Tait, 49–82. Lanham MD: Farleigh Dickinson Press, 2017.

Reeve, W. Paul. *Religion of a Different Color: Race and the Mormon Struggle for Whiteness.* New York: Oxford University Press, 2005.

Rich, Christopher, Jr. "The True Policy for Utah: Servitude, Slavery, and 'An Act in Relation to Service." *Utah Historical Quarterly* 80, no. 1 (2012): 54–75.

Ricks, Joel E. *The Beginnings of Settlement in Cache Valley.* Logan: Utah State University, 1953.

Robbins, Bruce. *The Servant's Hand: English Fiction from Below.* New York: Columbia University Press, 1986.

Romig, Ronald. "The Lamanite Mission." *John Whitmer Historical Association* 14 (1994): 25–33.

Rose, Christina. "Native History: Bear River Massacre Devastates Northwestern Shoshone." *Indian Country Today,* January 29, 2014. https://indiancountrytoday.com/archive/native-history-bear-river-massacre-devastates-northwestern-shoshone.

Rubin, Julius H. *Tears of Repentance: Christian Identity and Community in Colonial Southern New England.* Lincoln: University of Nebraska Press, 2013.

Ryan, Bill. "A Huntington's Mohegan Mission." *New York Times,* October 6, 1995. https://www.nytimes.com/1996/10/06/nyregion/a-huntington-s-mohegan-mission.html.

Ryan, Mary P. *Cradle of the Middle Class: The Family in Oneida County, New York, 1790–1865.* New York: Cambridge University Press, 1981.

Schulz, Joy. *Hawaiian By Birth: Missionary Children, Bicultural Identity, and U.S. Colonialism in the Pacific.* Lincoln: University of Nebraska Press, 2017.

Sekona, Harvalene K. "Tonga: A Land Dedicated to God" *Ensign,* August 2014. https://www.lds.org/liahona/2014/08/tonga-a-land-dedicated-to-god?lang=eng&query=Tonga.

Sen, Sudipta. *A Distant Sovereignty: National Imperialism and the Origins of British India.* New York: Routledge, 2002.

Sessions, Patty Bartlett. *Mormon Midwife: The 1846–1888 Diaries of Patty Bartlett Sessions.* Edited by Donna Toland Smart. Logan: Utah State University Press, 1999.

Seton, Rosemary. *Western Daughters in Eastern Lands: British Missionary Women in Asia.* Santa Barbara: ABC-CLIO, 2013.

Shipps, Jan. *Mormonism: The Story of a New Religious Tradition.* Urbana: University of Illinois Press, 1987.

———. *Sojourner in the Promised Land: Forty Years among the Mormons.* Urbana: University of Illinois Press, 2000.

Shirts, Kathryn H., and Morris A. *A Trial Furnace: Southern Utah's Iron Mission.* Provo UT: Brigham Young University Press, 2001.

Silva, Noenoe K. *Aloha Betrayed: Native Hawaiian Resistance to American Colonialism.* Durham NC: Duke University Press, 2004.

Smith, Jonathan Z. "The Bare Facts of Ritual." *History of Religions* 20, nos. 1/2 (1980): 112–27.

Smith, Joseph, Jr. "Extracts from the History of Joseph Smith, the Prophet." The Church of Jesus Christ of Latter-day Saints. Accessed November 2, 2014. https://www.lds.org/scriptures/pgp/js-h/1.18?lang=eng.

Smith, Merina. *Revelation, Resistance, and Mormon Polygamy: The Introduction and Implementation of the Principle, 1830–1853.* Boulder: University Press of Colorado, 2013.

Smith-Rosenberg, Carroll. "The Female World of Love and Ritual: Relations between Women in Nineteenth-century America." *Signs* 1, no. 1 (Autumn 1975): 1–29.

Snyder, Christina. *Great Crossings: Indians, Settlers and Slaves in the Age of Jackson.* New York: Oxford University Press, 2017.

Spencer, Thomas. "'Was This Really Missouri Civilization?' The Haun's Mill Massacre in Missouri and Mormon History." In *The Missouri Mormon Experience,* edited by Thomas Spencer, 100–118. Columbia: University of Missouri, 2010.

Stanley, Brian ed., *Christian Missions and the Enlightenment.* Grand Rapids MI: William B. Eerdmans, 2001.

Stansbury, Howard. *An Expedition to the Valley of the Great Salt Lake of Utah.* Philadelphia: Lippincott, Grambo, 1852.

Stapley, Jonathan. "Adoptive Sealing Ritual in Mormonism." *Journal of Mormon History* 37, no. 3 (Summer 2011): 53–118.

Steedman, Carolyn. *Labours Lost: Domestic Service and the Making of Modern England.* London: Cambridge University Press, 2009.

Stegner, Wallace. *The Gathering of Zion: The Story of the Mormon Trail.* Lincoln: University of Nebraska Press, 1964.

Stepan, Nancy Leys. *Picturing Tropical Nature.* Ithaca NY: Cornell University Press, 2001.

"Story of Alpharetta Boice—Adopted Indian Baby." *Pioneer Stories* (blog), March 22, 2012. http://pioneerstories-asay.blogspot.com/2012/03/story-of-alpharetta-boice-indian-baby.html.

Tagupa, William H. "Missionary Lamentations: Early Educational Strategies in Tahiti, 1800–1840." *Journal de la Société des océanistes* 36, no. 68 (1980): 165–72.

Taves, Ann. *Fits, Trances, and Visions: Experiencing Religion and Explaining Experience from Wesley to James.* Princeton NJ: Princeton University Press, 1999.

Taylor, Lori Elaine. "Elder Nigeajasha and Other Mormon Indians Moving Westward." *John Whitmer Historical Association Journal* 24 (2004): 111–24.

Taylor, Samuel. *Nightfall at Nauvoo.* New York: Macmillan, 1971.

Thayne, Stan. "Indian Removal, Zion, and the Westward Orientation of Early Mormonism." *Juvenile Instructor* (blog), November 23, 2013. http://www

.juvenileinstructor.org/indian-removal-zion-and-the-westward-orientation-of
-early-mormonism.

Thomas, Nicholas. *Islanders: The Pacific in the Age of Empire.* New Haven: Yale University Press, 2010.

Thompson, E. P. *Customs in Common: Studies in Traditional Popular Culture.* New York: New Press, 1993.

Timbimboo-Madsen, Patty. "Shoshone Bear River Oral Tradition." Presentation given at the Annual Meeting of the Utah State History Conference, 2012. https://www.youtube.com/watch?v=eucjVvd7wQs.

———. Interview #2. Northwestern Band of the Shoshone Nation, Cultural Resource Director. *We Shall Remain,* KUED. Accessed February 10, 2019. https://www.kued.org/sites/default/files/pattytimbimboo2.pdf.

Tinker, George E. *Missionary Conquest: The Gospel and Native American Cultural Genocide.* Minneapolis: Fortress, 1993.

Trask, Haunani-Kay. *From a Native Daughter: Colonialism and Sovereignty in Hawai'i.* 1993; rev. ed., Honolulu: University of Hawaii Press, 1999.

Tullidge, Edward. *History of Salt Lake City and Its Founders.* Salt Lake City UT: Edward W. Tullidge, 1850.

Turner, John. *Brigham Young: Pioneer Prophets.* Cambridge MA: Harvard University Press, 2012.

Twain, Mark. *Roughing It.* Hartford CT: American, 1872.

Twells, Alison. *The Civilising Mission and the English Middle Class, 1792–1850: The 'Heathen' at Home and Overseas.* London: Palgrave MacMillan, 2009.

Ulrich, Laurel Thatcher. "The Early Diaries of Wilford Woodruff, 1835–1839." In *Foundational Texts of Mormonism: Examining Major Early Sources,* edited by Mark Ashurst-McGee, Robin Scott Jensen, and Sharalyn D. Howcroft, 268–97. New York: Oxford University Press, 2018.

———. *A House Full of Females: Plural Marriage and Women's Rights in Early Mormonism, 1835–1870.* New York: Vintage, 2017.

Underwood, Grant. *The Millenarian World of Early Mormonism.* Urbana: University of Illinois Press, 1999.

Utah Department of Health. "Native Hawaiian & Pacific Islander Health." Accessed October 10, 2021. https://health.utah.gov/disparities/utah-minority-communities/native-hawaiian-pacific-islander.html.

Van Kirk, Sylvia. *Many Tender Ties: Women in Fur-Trade Society, 1670–1870.* Norman: University of Oklahoma Press, 1983.

Van Noord, Roger. *King of Beaver Island: The Life and Assassination of James Jesse Strang.* Urbana: University of Illinois Press, 1988.

Van Wagoner, Richard S. "Sarah M. Pratt: The Shaping of an Apostate." *Dialogue* 19, no. 2 (Summer 1986): 69–99.

———. *Sidney Rigdon: A Portrait of Religious Excess.* Salt Lake City: Signature Books, 1994.

Vernon, James. *Hunger: A Modern History.* Cambridge MA: Harvard University Press, 2007.

Vickery, Amanda. "Golden Age to Separate Spheres? A Review of the Categories and Chronology of English Women's History." *Historical Journal* 36, no. 2 (1993): 383–414.

Vicinus, Martha. *Independent Women: Work and Community for Single Women, 1850–1920.* Chicago: University of Chicago Press, 1985.

Walker, Isaiah Helekunihi. "Abraham Kaleimahoe Fernandez, Hawaiian Saint and Royalist, 1857–1915." *Mormon Pacific Historical Proceedings.* Laie, Hawaii, March 17, 2007.

———. *Waves of Resistance: Surfing and History in Twentieth-Century Hawaii.* Honolulu: University of Hawai'i Press, 2011.

Walker, Pamela. *Pulling the Devil's Kingdom Down: The Salvation Army in Great Britain.* Berkeley: University of California Press, 2001.

Walker, Ronald. "Seeking the 'Remnant:' The Native American during the Joseph Smith Period." *Journal of Mormon History* 19, no. 1 (Spring 1993): 1–33.

Walker, Ronald W., Richard Turley, and Glen Leonard. *Massacre at Mountain Meadows.* New York: Oxford University Press, 2008.

Warner, Aaron. *A remarkable dream, or vision, which was experienced on the night of the 20th of May, 1799.* Hartford CT: John Babcock, 1801.

Warner, Ernest Wayne. *A Record of the Ancestry, Life, and Descendants of Amos Warner: Member of a Pioneering L.D.S. Family.* Ogden UT: Glen F. Harding, 1972.

Watkins, Jordan, and Steven C. Harper. "'It Seems That All Nature Mourns': Sally Randall's Response to the Murder of Joseph and Hyrum Smith." *byu Studies* 46, no. 1 (2007): 95–100.

Webb, Stephen H. *Jesus Christ, Eternal God: Heavenly Flesh and the Metaphysics of Matter.* Oxford: Oxford University Press, 2012.

Weber, Curtis G. "Skulls and Crossed Bones? A Forensic Study of the Remnants of the Remains of Hyrum and Joseph Smith." *Mormon Historical Studies* (April 2013): 1–29.

Weeks, Susan Jensen. *How Desolate Our Home Bereft of Thee.* Melbourne AU: Clouds of Magellan, 2014.

Weslager, C. A. *The Delaware Indians: A History.* New Brunswick NJ: Rutgers University Press, 2003.

Whittaker, David J. "The Bone in the Throat: Orson Pratt and the Public Announcement of Plural Marriage." *Western Historical Quarterly* 18, no. 3 (1987): 293–314.

Wigger, John. *Taking Heaven by Storm: Methodism and the Rise of Popular Christianity in America.* New York: Oxford University Press, 1998.

Winkler, Albert. "The Circle Massacre: A Brutal Incident in Utah's Black Hawk War." *Utah Historical Quarterly* 55 (1987): 4–21.

Wolfe, Patrick. "Settler Colonialism and the Elimination of the Native." *Journal of Genocide Research* 8, no. 4 (2006): 387–409.

Wood, Beth. "Mormons and the Indian Adoption Racket: The Case of Tiffany Butts," *fps: Magazine of Youth Liberation* (April 1979): 51.

Woods, Fred E. "Latter-day Saint Missionaries Encounter the London Missionary Society in South Pacific, 1844–1852." *byu Studies* 52, no. 3 (2013): 102–25.

Woodward, Jed. "Mercy Thompson and the Revelation on Marriage." In *Revelations in Context: The Stories Behind the Sections of Doctrine and Covenants,* edited by Matthew MacBride and James Goldberg. Salt Lake City UT: Church of Jesus Christ of Latter-day Saints, 2016. https://www.churchofjesuschrist.org/study/manual/revelations-in-context/title-page?lang=eng.

Yellow Horse Brave Heart, Maria. "The Return to the Sacred Path: Healing the Historical Trauma and Historical Unresolved Grief Response among the Lakota through a Psychoeducational Group Intervention." *Smith College Studies in Social Work* 68, no. 3 (February 2010): 288–305.

Yeo, Eileen Janes. "Virgin Mothers: Single Women Negotiate the Doctrine of Motherhood in Victorian and Edwardian Britain." In *Women on Their Own: Interdisciplinary Perspectives on Being Single,* edited by Rudolph M. Bell and Virginia Yans, 40–57. New Brunswick NJ: Rutgers University Press, 2008.

INDEX

To order or obtain more information on these or other University
of Nebraska Press titles, visit nebraskapress.unl.edu.

CPSIA information can be obtained
at www.ICGtesting.com
Printed in the USA
LVHW041657190922
728750LV00003B/270

9 781496 233462